The

EVERYTHING

Writing Poetry Book

Dear Reader:

Every day you have experiences that affect your outlook on life. Over the years you may have lived with interesting family members, watched your hometown grow and change, traveled across the globe, suffered through losses, and fallen in love. As people, we have had similar experiences, and as poets, we have tried to capture these feelings and events in poems.

Since we also happen to be teachers and editors, we have read several poems about these topics as well. In the classroom, we have tried to pass along the skills our students need to express themselves through poetry. Now, we are passing along our knowledge of this craft to you. We hope that with our help, you will continue to find pleasure in reading and writing poems, and we wish you the best of luck in your future poetic pursuits!

Tina D. Eliopulos

Todd Moffett

The EVERYTHING® Series

Editorial

Publishing Director	Gary M. Krebs
Managing Editor	Kate McBride
Copy Chief	Laura M. Daly
Acquisitions Editor	Gina Chaimanis
Development Editor	Katie McDonough
Production Editors	Jamie Wielgus
	Bridget Brace

Production

Production Director	Susan Beale
Production Manager	Michelle Roy Kelly
Series Designers	Daria Perreault
	Colleen Cunningham
	John Paulhus
Cover Design	Paul Beatrice
	Matt LeBlanc
Layout and Graphics	Colleen Cunningham
	John Paulhus
	Daria Perreault
	Monica Rhines
	Erin Ring
Series Cover Artist	Barry Littmann

Visit the entire Everything® Series at *www.everything.com*

THE
EVERYTHING®
WRITING POETRY
BOOK

A practical guide to style,
structure, form, and expression

Tina D. Eliopulos and Todd Scott Moffett

Adams Media
Avon, Massachusetts

We dedicate this book to our own perfect poem,
Madelynne Crisi Moffett.

An Everything® Series Book.
Everything® and everything.com® are registered trademarks of F+W Publications, Inc.

Published by Adams Media, an F+W Publications Company
57 Littlefield Street, Avon, MA 02322 U.S.A.
www.adamsmedia.com

ISBN: 1-59337-322-8
Printed in the United States of America.

J I H G F E D C B A

Library of Congress Cataloging-in-Publication Data
Eliopulos, Tina D.
The everything writing poetry book / Tina D. Eliopulos and Todd Scott Moffett.
p.   cm.
(An everything series book)
ISBN 1-59337-322-8
1. Poetry--Authorship. I. Moffett, Todd Scott II. Title. III. Series: Everything series

PN1059.A9E44 2005
808.1--dc22

2005007437

This book is available at quantity discounts for bulk purchases.
For information, please call 1-800-872-5627.

Contents

Acknowledgments

We owe a debt of gratitude to the following individuals: for their expertise, professionalism, and collegiality, Barb Doyen of Doyen Literary Services, Gina Chaimanis, Lynn Best, Mary Dalton-Hoffman, and Jeredith Merrin; for their wisdom, humor, and friendship, Robert Sherfield and Richard Logsdon; and for their presence in our lives, the divine Yiayia of Las Vegas and the Moffetts of Laguna Beach.

Top Ten
Poetic Inspirations

1. **Falling in love:** Expressing the feelings of first love, fleeting romance, or a lasting relationship.

2. **Falling out of love:** Treasuring love, even when it leaves.

3. **Becoming a parent:** The softness of baby skin and the sound of first words.

4. **Observing nature:** From towering trees to trickling streams.

5. **Traveling to faraway places:** Foreign languages, exotic foods, and enchanting people.

6. **Discovering something new about yourself or someone else:** Something as small as a smile or as big as a career change.

7. **Moving:** To the next town or to a new nation.

8. **Facing mortality:** Coping with loss and confronting your own fate.

9. **Finding humor:** From laughing through troubling times to laughing with friends.

10. **Uncovering your spirituality:** Discovering your place in the world.

Introduction

▶ The ancient Greeks used the term *furor poeticus* to describe poetry as a frenzy sent by the gods. Through the centuries poetry has continued to amaze humankind. Ideas come to the poet unbidden, and then she must work them into polished pieces of art.

Many people first experience literary art in the form of poetry; take Mother Goose, for example. Many students fashion poems for school projects and others do so to nurse their broken hearts. Usually these creations get stuffed into scrapbooks only to be forgotten. For some reason, people often ignore the desire to express themselves, and they leave poetry writing to pop stars and academics. But to create true poetry you must not be afraid to identify your inner voice, indulge it, and set it free.

This book will help you find your poetic voice. We'll give you some poetic tools and teach you to use them. First, you'll learn how to tap sources of inspiration, choose a writing instrument, and pick the perfect place to do your work. Next, we will cover the writing process itself: creating and selecting significant details, using sound and language, and working with meter. The remainder of the book will acquaint you with the poetic forms (such as the sonnet and the ode), discuss ideas for subject matter, cover revision strategies, and guide you through the publishing process.

Once you have read this book, writing poems should be easier for you—not easy, but easier. No matter how many books you read or how many ideas you are blessed with, writing poetry is rarely easy. You won't create poetry by thinking about it, reading about it, wishing you could write it, or talking about it with friends—though these activities may provide motivation. Instead, the poetry will come from deep within you, flow through you, and even surprise you.

Practiced poets will tell you that they rarely, if ever, write a polished poem in a single draft. They make thousands of mistakes and deletions and have drawers full of early drafts, dead-end inspirations, and desperate scribbles. These same poets will tell you that such writing is never futile, but rather an inevitable and valuable part of the process.

The goal of this book is to inspire you to write and to keep writing. Several examples of professional poems and many writing exercises included here will give you plenty of guidance. But you will also need to try new methods to create more inspiration. You'll write lists, descriptions, and journal entries to get you on the right track. Always remember that every poet works differently, and that all talent takes time to develop. Be patient with yourself, enjoy the process, and don't be afraid to share your poetry with the world. Good luck!

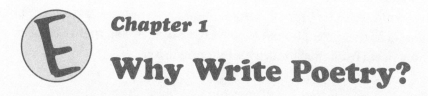

Chapter 1

Why Write Poetry?

There are endless reasons to write poetry. Perhaps you want to express an overwhelming emotion—joy, love, or anger. Or maybe you wish to reshape a childhood memory. If something terrible has happened to you, writing may offer a way to cope with or understand the tragic event. Whatever your reasons, you might feel creating poetry is a compulsion—something you just need to do to relieve your feelings. In this chapter, you'll discover why poetry provides an artistic outlet unlike any other.

Self-Expression

One of the many reasons why people write is to tell others what is happening to them. This is a natural human impulse. Any caregiver knows that an infant will cry when she needs her diaper changed, her bottle refilled, or her blankets wrapped more snugly around her. Likewise, though adults cannot scream every time they need something, everyone encounters moments in their lives that prompt them to self-expression. These moments often come in the form of changes, discoveries, or decisions.

Change

Life is a continual process of change, so just about any moment can inspire you to write.

Throughout your life you will experience overwhelming changes, like marriages, births, and deaths, and seemingly insignificant ones, like new tastes in food and variations in your appearance. Each of these events affects how you perceive and interact with the world.

Create a timeline of major events in your life to get an idea of when great changes have taken place. Write brief descriptions next to each event, including the date and the location in which it happened. Then choose one or two of these and use them as starting points for poems. Consider your emotions during these times as well.

Changes, in turn, lead you to make discoveries and decisions. If a close friend moves away, you may discover how much you value having her in your life. If a family member becomes ill, you may make the decision to visit him in his time of need. A person's reactions to changes in life are often reflected in his poetry. If you lose your job, you may feel the need to express feelings of anger or disappointment in written form. Change is inevitable, but writing can help you cope. And if a decision must be made, organizing your thoughts on paper can help you take the correct action.

Discovery

Moments of discovery occur every day; sometimes these discoveries are life changing, and other times they are much more subtle. For example, in Walt Whitman's brief poem "A Noiseless Patient Spider," the speaker is watching a spider spinning a web:

A noiseless patient spider,
I mark'd where on a little promontory it stood isolated,
Mark'd how to explore the vacant vast surrounding,
It launch'd forth filament, filament, filament, out of itself,
Ever unreeling them, ever tirelessly speeding them.

And you O my soul where you stand,
Surrounded, detached, in measureless oceans of space,
Ceaselessly musing, venturing, throwing, seeking the spheres to
        connect them,
Till the bridge you will need be form'd, till the ductile anchor hold,
Till the gossamer thread you fling catch somewhere, O my soul.

Though this does not seem to be a momentous event, the speaker discovers several things while watching the spider. He notices that the spider is creating a web where none existed before, and he also identifies with the spider on a personal level, likening the activity of his soul to the spinning of a web.

FACT

One of the most famous discoveries in literature is that made by Oedipus at the end of the play *Oedipus Rex*. He learns that he has murdered his father and married his mother, fulfilling a lifelong prophecy. In his agony, he pokes out his eyes! Instead of doing this when you make your own discoveries, try writing a poem.

Of course, not all discoveries are as simple or harmless as a spider's activity. Learning that a spouse has been unfaithful, for example, can cause a great deal of sadness, discomfort, and heartbreak. However, finding the courage to cope with such a situation may lead you to make yet another discovery or to make a very important decision. By exploring the feelings surrounding a discovery, whether in writing or through using another form of expression, you can make informed and appropriate decisions.

Decision

You have to make decisions every day of your life. For example, you may decide to delay a shopping trip to make needed repairs on your car. You might choose to accept an attractive job offer and therefore move your family to a new city. But the most common choices you make are small ones: what to eat for lunch, which television programs to watch, and how to style your hair.

Whether a decision is important or trivial, you will likely feel the need to express your reasons for making this decision to others, as well as gain their approval. While you will sometimes need the guidance of friends and family to make important decisions, working out your thoughts in poetry can help you become your own advisor. By assessing your own feelings and releasing them in poetic language, you may come closer to a solution or decision. And even if you don't find the right choice this way, you will at least have created a piece of personal art.

FACT

Shakespeare is well known for having his characters make important decisions in his plays. In *Othello*, the title character must decide whether to believe his junior officer Iago's claims about his wife's infidelity or trust his wife's virtue. His decision eventually leads to many deaths, including his own.

Whatever the situation—a change, a discovery, or a decision—you might feel that the moment is an intensely personal one. Truthfully, it is the intensity of that moment, not the moment itself, that inspires you to write. As a beginning writer, you should become aware of that intensity, whether it occurs in the midst of an experience or some time afterward. That intense feeling is a signal that you're ready to express yourself. Grab a blank sheet of paper and begin.

Using Feelings

Singers and songwriters use feelings as a basis of their craft. Painters and sculptors try to depict their emotions on canvas and in clay. Television shows, movies, and books generally revolve around the conflict of human feelings. But what do feelings mean to a poet? Everything. A poet draws from her feelings in a less direct way—using raw emotion as fuel to produce poems.

Interestingly, the literary form that students least like to study is poetry. Beginning students of poetry usually have trouble understanding these creations of deep thought and feeling. In part, this reaction is due to the fact that poetry is a highly personal genre. Just as students are reluctant to study it, they're also afraid to reveal the pages of scribbled verse they may have stashed in their drawers or beneath their mattresses. Their feelings are safe in these private places, and protected from critical eyes. It is true that a portion of your work is meant to stay hidden. However, some of these emotionally charged drafts are the seeds of brilliant poetry, and they should be read by others.

Displacement

The act of writing poetry is an example of displacement, meaning that you express the emotions you have in your life through your writing when you create poetry. By displacing these emotions in poetry, you can channel anger, sadness, joy, and other strong feelings in a productive manner.

ALERT!

Not all emotions should simply be displaced in poetry. If you have an argument with a friend, it is important that you work it out with her, in addition to releasing your angst on paper. Displacement may help your poetry, but relying too heavily upon this method could hurt your personal relationships.

Recently, Tina, one of the authors of this book, was invited to read one of her student's poems. The student had been hurt when her boyfriend broke up with her using their high school's public address system. He didn't shout "It's over!" for all to hear, but instead dedicated "Three Times a Lady" to another girl, who happened to be the student's best friend. The student was so upset by the dual betrayal that she decided to write a poem. She used the opportunity to displace her strong emotions and titled the poem "Three Times a Jerk."

Displacement happens all the time in everyday life. If you have a fight with your wife one night and then overreact to the broken water cooler at work the next day, you have displaced your personal frustration onto an inanimate object. The key is to focus these emotions on your writing and not on other people who happen to be in the wrong place at the wrong time. Gaining control of your feelings, and effectively displacing them, can help improve your poetry and your mental state. Don't be discouraged if this method doesn't work for you the first time. The more you practice this, the easier and more natural it will be for you.

Perhaps the easiest technique for displacing emotions is finding a symbol to represent the feelings you have. Any object, person, or place can function as a symbol. For example, if you have a heated argument with someone, try using the symbol of fire in your poetry to represent your anger or frustration.

Indulgence

Almost any experience you have can translate into strong poetry. Even if it's something as minor as stepping in a puddle, if an experience resonates with you and causes you to feel intense emotion, it can be great inspiration for poetry. No one has to know that stepping into a puddle on a rainy day made you feel as though you were drowning, and you never have to reveal the other circumstances in your life that led you to have that feeling. The important thing is that you channel these thoughts and emotions into your art. You can embellish to your heart's content—that's the beauty of poetry!

After some practice, you'll be able to identify your emotional triggers with relative ease. You may notice that rain clouds make you feel lonely or ice cream trucks cause you to long for your childhood. Make lists of these occurrences and think of them as your trigger symbols. Whenever you want to write about (and displace) your loneliness, think of dark, brooding rain clouds. And whenever you want to create a poem about your childhood, begin with memories involving the ice cream truck. Indulge yourself—that's what poetry is all about.

Drawing from Memory

Many poets, young and old alike, use their memories to create their poetry. Memory is a deep well from which to draw inspiration. However, it is also an area of creativity that beginning writers require time to adjust to. Memory can provide you with endless ideas for poetry, but you should not let it restrict you in any way.

Shaping Reality

As teachers, one of our favorite writing exercises that calls upon memory requires students to bring a photo album to class. We ask the students to randomly turn to any page in the album and pick a photo to write about. After fifteen to twenty minutes of nonstop writing, most students set down between 500 and 700 words. Most of this writing is disjointed, and if not disjointed, it is more than likely a narrative surrounding the taking of the photo.

We then ask students to prune their words into single lines of description: one line each for the location, people, weather conditions, etc. After some initial shaping, the student writers find they've created the first draft of a poem. But as they continue the revision process, they tend to impede their own progress for fear that their creativity is replacing the truth of the moment.

Many writers wrongly assume that the contents of poems must be true to life, and thus, they work to make their poetry replicate moments in time. But poetry is not nonfiction; it does not claim to be memoir. In a way similar to the method of a fiction writer, the poet should free up her memories and embellish them. You will still be drawing upon your own life experiences and observations, but you should feel free to enjoy the flexibility of the genre. Shape reality to make it fit your feelings.

Many readers believe that the "I" pronoun in a poem always represents the poet. This person may seem to be speaking from the poet's point of view, but as readers, we should understand that this speaker is simply a persona adopted by the poet to give a voice to the poem. This is also an example of displacement.

Our literary canon contains abundant examples of reshaped reality. For example, Tennessee Williams's play *The Glass Menagerie* was loosely based on his own family. Williams coupled his own memories with his talent as a writer and depicted the pained lives of the Wingfield family. The events in the play do not match those of his own life, but the primary reality of the story gives it more strength.

Using Memory

As you look through your photo albums and search the recesses of your mind for forgotten memories, you'll realize that your memories have been affected, if not enriched, by distance and time. Use this to your advantage. Find ways to recall those memories and make them feel new again.

One of the best ways to invoke a memory is to allow your senses to reawaken the past. As you breathe in the aroma of your morning coffee, think back on a scene of your mother preparing breakfast for your family. Or, as you peel an onion, recall the vision of your father's eyes tearing as he chopped onions for Thanksgiving stuffing. You can also use this method to recollect negative memories. Poetry doesn't always have to be pleasant.

Music, film, and other forms of stimulation might also help your memories resurface. If you want to remember times spent with your grandmother, rent and watch her favorite movie or play her favorite song, and try to imagine the way she would react to the sights and sounds. If you used to go fishing with your grandfather when you were a young boy, try going out in his old rowboat to reawaken those feelings. Once you have captured enough images and emotions, put them on paper and begin your poem.

A Fly on the Wall

The contemporary poet Dorianne Laux describes the act of writing poetry as "private, mysterious, and criminal." She names the writer a thief: "As you might steal a heart or a flower from someone's garden, writing is often a theft of some sort, stealing an image, an idea, a scrap of conversation from an unsuspecting passerby." Like thieves, writers are perceptive listeners and spectators and are acutely aware of their external environment. In this regard, as a poet, you can think of yourself as a fly on the wall.

The Fly's Collection

As you observe the scenes around you, keep in mind that you will eventually have to break down these experiences. You will gather a wealth of information and then decide what essence of the observation you will bring to your poem. Remember, you do not want to retell the moment in its entirety. Instead, try to pluck from the scene a sentence, a giggle, a scent, or a posture.

ESSENTIAL

As a fly on the wall, the best moments for you to steal are the candid ones, when the people you are observing are not aware of your presence. At these moments, they will behave without reservations, and you might see gestures or hear words that you would not be exposed to otherwise.

This sensation of observation is present in the poem "The Last Man to Know Adam" by Todd Scott Moffett. The speaker of the poem, an older man, remembers what it was like to live in the company of the biblical Adam. In the last several stanzas of the poem that follow, the speaker describes his childhood memory from one night when he followed Adam and spied upon him:

We feared him, father of us all,
this man who had seen in his second son's
death-marbled eyes the fate he'd wished,
who despite his gray-maned hair stood

a full head taller, a full shoulder wider
than his offspring. His back and torso
still held muscle firm and rippled
from his clay molding. His eyes, wild

as a squid's, stared at his grown
children as if they were the whale's teeth,
we kids snares to his path-weary feet.
He glared when family gathered, joked

through stories, ate wheat bread, drank
honey beer, slaughtered the ritual lamb
and drained its blood into stained pots
while raising hands to our unnamed God.

One night, from our ring of tents and sleeping
cookfires I followed him into a rocky
darkness climbing to a moon-swaddled cave.
At the mouth he lit a lamp, uncloaked

brushes and a small stone pot. Inside,
a smoke-yellowed wall, stone smelling
older than the earth's nine hundred
years, face rising two man-heights.

And look! What we learned later to call pictures—
deer, elk, lion, bear, rooster, cow:
some creatures familiar and some
fantastic, unrecognizable.

At the top, thin lines smooth and rounded,
the animals gamboled in twos
through oaks, beeches, figs, apricots,
broad-leafed maples.

Then below, sharp, hard-lined,
each animal charged alone through a barren plain
to the last low empty corner
where he squatted and set the lamp.

His thick strokes stabbed the wall, knifed
into being a creature with mane,
wings, claws. Then readied a stick man,
arm cocked with spear.

And whizz! whizz! his brush gored
the creature, the lions, bears, deer, elk, eagles,
slew all he could reach, a great final hunting,
calling their names back to him.

Because the speaker acts as a fly on the wall, the object of his attention (Adam) has laid bare a side of his personality that brings the speaker into Adam's world. To craft the poem, the poet begins with a description of Adam himself and of how he related to his offspring. Each person and item, including the speaker, is linked to Adam. Yet the speaker—if recognized at all—is nothing more than a cause for suspicion, in Adam's eyes.

Places to Be a Fly

In order to successfully make observations as a fly on the wall, you first need to find good locations. In general, these should be places where you can blend into a crowd, observe people from afar, or huddle in the corner of a room, unnoticed. Here are some places you might try:

- Shopping plaza or mall
- Workplace lunchroom

- Coffee shop
- Public transportation
- Waiting room

Even if the people you are observing are not talking or moving, you can still take note of the clothes they're wearing, the books or magazines they're reading, their facial expressions, their jewelry, or of what they're buying, eating, or waiting in line for. Record these details and let your imagination wander. Take special notice of unusual things and then ask yourself questions. Why is the gray-haired man on the city bus wearing a wool sweater in midsummer? What could the fashionably attired young businesswoman be shopping for in a thrift store? This kind of interesting information can make a great starting point for a poem.

The Writer's Ego

Brainchild is a term often used to describe a creative idea or invention. The ancient Greeks depicted this concept in a myth in which Zeus, the king of the gods, once had a fierce headache that threatened to split open his head. He asked his son Hephaestus to cleave his skull with an ax, and from the breach sprang Athena, goddess of wisdom and warfare, fully grown and ready for battle.

QUESTION?

Why should you nurture ideas and observations before putting them into poetic form?
The initial observations you make about people or places using the "fly on the wall" or other techniques will only leave you with snippets of larger ideas. By giving your imagination time to develop small details, you will end up with stronger images and concepts.

Similar to one's flesh-and-blood child, a brainchild is something that must be nurtured and cared for. You watch an idea progress and grow and even feel proud that you have brought it to life. And on the day that you present your idea to someone else, you feel the greatest pride of all, similar to what you may feel when your real child graduates from college or gets married.

This cycle of generating, nurturing, and presenting ideas is what maintains a writer's ego. It's natural that the state of your ego may change throughout this cycle: During the primary stages of an idea's existence you may feel worried or protective over it, and by the time you present an idea to others, you may have full confidence in its value. The positive feedback you receive from others reinforces your self-image and gives your ego the support it needs to move on to a new project.

The Freudian Ego

Another way to look at this idea of the ego is to study Sigmund Freud's model of the mind. Freud theorized that the human mind is split into three zones—the id, the ego, and the superego—and that one's mental energies are a balance between these three zones. The id represents one's most basic desires: food, sleep, sex, etc. The superego symbolizes the customs, rules, morals, and laws imposed upon a person by parents, cultures, and societies. The ego is the facilitator—finding a way that the id's desires can be met, in a manner that is acceptable to the superego.

FACT

Sigmund Freud (1856–1939) is considered the founder of modern psychoanalysis. His theories of the id, ego, and superego, the competing drives of *Eros* and *Thanatos*, and the Oedipus complex still get considerable attention and cause much debate in literary and medical circles.

It's interesting to think of a writer's process in terms of Freud's theories. Most writers truly do need to find a balance between the id and the superego in Freud's model of the mind. In part, you are probably writing to earn money or to fulfill a career goal. Simultaneously, you are also trying to express yourself and communicate with others through your writing. In Freud's opinion, your ego finds a balance between these desires.

The Jungian Ego

Carl Jung, a younger contemporary of Freud, set forth an equally useful theory of the ego. He argued that the ego, a smaller unit within the self, forms the center of the conscious mind and the seat of the free will. The ego's boundary is determined in large part by the unconscious aspects of one's personality. The unconscious, in turn, is formed by uniquely personal factors—those that individuals acquire in their own lives—and by collective factors—those that are common to all of humanity. The ego forms and develops as conscious and unconscious and external and internal factors collide.

FACT

At one time, Carl Jung (1875–1961) worked closely with Freud, but he later developed his own school of psychoanalysis. Among his many theories is that of *archetypes*—modes of thought and behavior that are common to all of humankind throughout the ages.

Against this backdrop, the desire to write may be seen as an outcome of the clashes between the will of the ego and the known and unknown forces surrounding you. Personal motives, both conscious and unconscious, will enter your writing, the experiences of your own life providing color and content. However, your writing may also give voice to ideas that are inherent in all humans—drives, desires, symbols, and images that everyone experiences and relates to.

Chapter 2

Beginning the Journey

Preparing yourself to write can be just as important as finding the inspiration that moves you to write. You must find a place that makes you feel creative and comfortable, choose a pen or keyboard that works smoothly, and learn how to overcome the notorious writer's block. Most importantly, you must read as many poems as possible to put yourself in the right frame of mind to create your own verses.

Read, Read, Read!

Before you write, you need to read. Pick up several books of poetry and read them again and again. Also, remember to read poetry slowly. It can be a complicated genre, and you won't be able to fully grasp most poems with only a single read. Also, the more poetry you read, the more familiar you will become with different styles, forms, and subjects of poetry.

The most important reason for reading poems again and again is that this will train you to compose your own poems. When discussing fiction, John Gardner once said that you can write only the stories that you have read. The same statement can be made about poetry. You can't write a poem if you don't know what one looks like. So, reading several kinds of poems—sonnets, odes, blank verses, free verses, epics—will expose you to the available forms you can use when you begin to express yourself.

ALERT!

You will lose your motivation to read if your books remain on shelves. To make sure that you pick up a book at least once a day, put them in different places all over your house. Place a book on your breakfast table, one on your windowsill, and even one in a kitchen cupboard. This simple reminder will reawaken your desire to read and to write.

Read Poems for Pleasure

You probably won't write poetry if you don't enjoy reading it. So, your first task is to find poems you like to read. Also, don't simply stick with one style or subject in poetry; find uplifting poems you like, as well as mournful ones. Read poems about nature and poems about family. Gather a wide variety of poems you like and read them often.

In addition to filling your shelves with books of poetry, hang single poems on your walls or slip them into the pockets of your coat. Surrounding yourself with poetry will get you in the mood to create your own.

You might also consider using outside resources to help you enjoy poetry. For example, go to your local library and ask if they offer or host classes, clubs, or meetings pertaining to poetry. Do the same at a local university or bookstore. Another place to search for poetry and talk with poets and readers like you is on the Internet. Do a general search for a poet or a specific poem and you will likely find a variety of chat rooms, merchandise sites, and anthologies related to your search.

Read Poems for Reflection

Once you have found a number of poems you enjoy, you should reread them and begin to contemplate them more deeply. Ask yourself why you like each poem. Is the poem funny? Is it thoughtful? Does it remind you of someone you love? With practice you will begin to notice which lines have specific effects on you. Remember these when you write your own poems.

You should also consult a dictionary each time you come across an unfamiliar word. And always consider all of the possible meanings listed. Even if you think you know the meaning of a word, look it up anyway. Common or familiar words may have additional meanings you're not aware of, and the writer may have chosen the word for its duality or to create a play on words.

It is a good idea to reflect on what you have read for five or ten minutes immediately after setting down your book. Studies show that this can increase your retention rate up to 40 percent. In addition to making time for personal reflection, try to engage in conversation with someone about the information you read.

Another way to reflect on poetry is to memorize poems. You may have memorized and recited lines at several points in your education, but the pressure of performance for a grade is long gone. You can now memorize poems to recite to friends and loved ones or just to remember in your own mind. The exercise of memorization will sharpen your attention to future poems and familiarize you with certain forms and styles.

Read Poems for Study

As you read, you should create a dialogue with the poems. By writing your responses and questions in the margins, you can become more engaged in the study of poetry. If you cringe at the idea of writing in a book, then buy a second copy, or have lots of Post-its or notepaper handy to keep track of your thoughts.

There are several things you can take note of when reading poetry. You can write out your impressions, the definitions of words you look up, questions about passages that puzzle you, and any observations you make about the poet's use of language. These last observations are particularly important because they will aid you in the next step of your poem study: line-by-line analysis.

You will read more about such analyses later in the book, but for now, you should try to jot down a few key observations about the lines you read. How many words and syllables does each line contain? What sorts of words come at the end of each line? Do you detect any rhymes? Do the sentences in the poem end when the lines end, or do they go beyond the line breaks? Are the sentences short or long? Do you see places where the poet chose not to use complete sentences?

If you can answer each of these questions about a single poem, you will gain much insight into the writing of poetry itself. Finding similarities and differences between your poems and those of published writers will reveal your own strengths and weaknesses. You can then take this information and apply it to your own writing, while composing or editing.

Writing Tools

Because the writing process will likely keep you at a desk for hours at a time, you must find a tool that helps you write comfortably. You may choose a specific brand of pen for its smooth ink flow. Perhaps you'll choose an especially thick pencil or one that makes strong, dark marks on the paper. If you choose to write using a computer, you must be comfortable with your keyboard and mouse, the brightness of your screen, and other various details.

Accessories

There are many products and accessories available to help you write more comfortably. Many pens and pencils come with special grips to protect your fingers and secure your grasp, and all have point sizes or hardness levels that will affect the writing quality. If you prefer a typewriter, look for one that won't distract you with its noises, that will offer your fingers the right amount of striking space, and that won't give you difficulties when you change the ribbon. If you prefer a computer, make certain that all the keys of your keyboard depress fully, your computer screen is adequately bright and clear, and your mouse glides smoothly over your desk surface. You may also want to purchase wrist rests for your keyboard and mouse, and a mouse pad with a smooth, flat surface.

QUESTION?

Where can I buy writing tools and accessories?
Most office supply stores will carry a wide selection of writing utensils, papers, ink cartridges, binders, and even computers and typewriters. Usually, it is better to buy a computer at a computer store, although you may be able to find one online. The same goes for typewriters. Do some research before making one of these large purchases.

When it comes to choosing paper, you have a wealth of possibilities. Paper is available in all colors, sizes, and weights, some best suited for handwriting and others for typing and computer printing. Some writers prefer to set down their inspirations in notebooks or diaries before typing out a draft. These products can range from a basic three-ring binder filled with lined paper to an elegant hardcover book with a sewn binding and pressed parchment pages. This decision is up to you, as long as your writing materials are easily accessible at all times.

Ease and Comfort

When you write poetry, you should not expect to create a perfect poem on your first attempt. You will inevitably need to whiteout, erase, delete, or cross out words multiple times before you're happy with a poem. Therefore, it is wise to have erasers, bottles of whiteout, and extra paper with you as you write.

Both pencils and pens have the advantage of mobility and ease of use, and they are very inexpensive. But these tools also make writing a somewhat lengthy process. Writing by hand can cause your fingers, hand, and arm to become sore after a significant period of time. However, if you are just beginning as a poet, you might still consider the pencil or pen your primary tool for early drafts. More experienced writers would probably appreciate the efficiency and versatility of a computer. Just keep in mind that typing on a computer can give you sore fingers, wrists, and arms as well.

ALERT!

Typewriters and computers are very expensive to buy new. A typewriter can cost up to a few hundred dollars, and a computer, with all its accompanying software and parts, can cost up to a few thousand. Furthermore, having a computer also requires you to purchase a printer, ink, paper, and other various supplies.

Many writers still prefer to use typewriters, even though computers have largely replaced them in the marketplace. A modern typewriter can be a great tool, especially if it comes with correction ribbons. These ribbons will allow you to correct mistakes quickly. However, a typewriter is not as mobile as a pad of paper or even a laptop computer. Typewriters are generally heavy and cumbersome, so you may have trouble moving one around the house or taking it outside. Also, even if you only need to make one revision to a completed page, you will always have to retype the whole page when using a typewriter.

One major benefit to using a computer is that it allows you to save your work and return to it as many times as you like. However, like a typewriter, a computer is useless unless you know how to use a keyboard. A computer is not very mobile, either, unless you've purchased a laptop. Computers also force you to learn word-processing programs, operating software, and troubleshooting techniques for recovering lost files, stopping viruses, or managing system crashes.

Finding Your Place

A common image of a writer is a lonely, angst-filled idealist sitting alone in a dimly lit room struggling to create art. Conversely, many people envision a writer as a person with a glamorous career of traveling to beautiful places, sampling exquisite foods, and getting paid to write about it. The truth is that writers throughout history have fit countless different descriptions, from heartbroken recluse to inspired celebrity.

Hollywood has significantly glamorized the world's perceptions of the writer. In films like *Something's Gotta Give* and *As Good as It Gets*, the main characters maintain somewhat stereotypical writing lifestyles. Other films, like *Shakespeare in Love* and *The Hours*, re-create the lives of real writers as strings of dramatic or romantic events. However, it's important to remember that each writer is different, and while some may fit the stereotypes, others stray far from them. Disregard what you've seen in movies and read in books and find your own perfect writing space and style.

Writing Spaces

Some poets seek solitude; others seek Starbucks. If you prefer a quiet environment, make sure you choose a place where you will not be interrupted by people, sounds, or time constraints. If you prefer to be in a populated area, select a café, library, or bookstore as your writing space. And if you don't find your perfect space the first, second, or third time around, keep looking. You'll discover it eventually.

If you choose a writing space that is outside of your home, it's important that it is nearby. If you pick a place too far from home, you'll start to find reasons not to go. Your writing space should be convenient, inexpensive to use, and comfortable enough to stay in for long periods of time. However, you shouldn't feel that you have to be writing the entire time you're there. If you plan to stay at your favorite café and write for three hours, you will likely get an arm cramp or a backache from sitting in the same position for the entire duration. To keep yourself fresh and motivated, take small breaks intermittently throughout your writing time. Go for a walk, have a conversation with someone else in the café, or read a magazine. Taking your eyes off your computer screen or notebook page for a while will refresh you for a second round.

Regardless of location, most writers find success through established routine. Practice, repetition, and consistency must become part of your writing technique. Writing is much like playing an instrument—if you practice every day, you'll make progress. If you work on one poem every day for fifteen days, you'll produce two poems a month. At this rate, you'll be halfway to a collection in one year.

What to Do When You're Away

If you take a weekend trip or travel to visit family, you may find yourself far away from your normal writing space. In this case, make sure to have a notepad or tape recorder with you so you can capture as many of your ideas as possible. Some of your greatest inspirations may come while traveling, so it is especially important to be prepared while you're away.

In addition to being far from your writing space, you may also have to deal with several distractions while you're away from home. If you are visiting friends or family, you will probably have little, if any, time to yourself. But this doesn't mean that you should break your writing routine. If you normally write for thirty minutes a day, wake up a half an hour earlier when you're visiting others. If you do your writing first thing in the morning, chances are everyone else will still be asleep and you'll have some time to yourself.

Do you brush your teeth before going to bed at night? Do you take a shower every day? Writing should be as much a part of your daily routine as these simple tasks. If you stick to a routine, even when you're traveling, you will be much happier with your writing output.

Your Muse

Your muse is the guiding spirit or source of inspiration that drives you to write. Sometimes you will be able to call upon your muse, and other times she will come to you unbidden. No matter what the case, you should give your muse an identity and always be ready to entertain her. However, don't make the mistake of hastily trying to call your muse; she will visit only if you welcome her and provide her with genuine hospitality. Likewise, if she arrives unexpectedly, never turn her away. Have your writing materials handy at all times.

Visits from Your Muse

To guarantee a meaningful relationship with your muse, you must embrace her every day. Don't stand her up, and don't let her learn that you're swapping her time for hours spent cleaning, studying, watching television, or chitchatting. If you do, she may not return for a good long while.

ALERT!

When your muse calls, you'll need to have your writing tools ready. Nothing is more frustrating than losing an idea because you didn't have a pen or a piece of paper handy. To prevent this, place a notebook and pen on your bedside table, in your office, and even in your car. Driving inspires a lot of ideas, and you might just need to pull over and record one.

Your muse will come to you during moments of clarity. For some, these moments may occur early in the morning, and for others, very late at night. Perhaps the sunlight on your face will awaken you, and you'll feel the need to express a few thoughts or feelings. Or maybe you'll feel a sudden burst of inspiration after watching a late-night television show. Your muse could even visit you midday at the coffee shop, the library, or your office at work. No matter what the circumstances, your thoughts must be recorded before you sleep or continue the rest of your day.

Your Muse in the Moment

There are poetic stories in everyday moments. The trick is learning how to use the material you're given. If you witness a heartfelt hug between two friends, an argument between two young brothers, or even the dance of a bee around a flower blossom, think about the relationship you've seen. Even a leaking carton of milk in the grocery store can provide inspiration; it all depends upon how you look at it. However, if you don't record experiences and feelings immediately after they happen, you might lose them. What's worse, though, is that you'll lose a potential poem.

When your muse comes to call, be prepared. Even if she catches you off guard, in a public place, or in the middle of a conversation, don't ignore her. Excuse yourself from the gathering and jot a quick note to remind yourself later. The best ideas may come at inconvenient times, but you don't want to miss them!

How to Beat Writer's Block

At some point in your writing journey you will come to a screeching halt. Perhaps you will be writing late at night and lose your energy. Maybe you will come to a pause at the end of a stanza and your inspiration will suddenly vanish. Perhaps an idea will move you to your typewriter, but the sight of the blank page will shut down your thoughts. Whatever you do, don't despair! There are ways to unlock writer's block.

If a blank sheet of paper intimidates you or the glare of your empty computer screen immediately freezes your thoughts, consider using another material for a first draft. If you find your greatest inspiration comes when you're sitting in a bar or restaurant, gather up some cardboard coasters or paper napkins for scrawling notes and ideas. An informal approach may relieve some of the pressure.

The first thing you should always do when you hit a mental roadblock is silence your internal naysayer. This is the voice in your head that constantly scolds you as you write, saying, *That's not the right word!* or *Those words don't rhyme!* A first draft belongs to the creative, free-spirited impulse that brought you to your writing place, and you must allow that impulse free rein, no matter how many mistakes you are making. Once you have a draft or two of your poem completed, you can switch on your internal editor again.

Free-Writing

Part of the difficulty with writer's block is that it often freezes you both mentally and physically. Not only will your brain shut down, but you might also find it hard to tear your eyes from the blank page or get up from your chair. Free-writing is a good remedy for writer's block because it forces you into the physical act of writing. It gets your hands moving again and jogs your brain back into action.

To free-write, you need your writing tool of choice, some paper, and ten uninterrupted minutes. Free-writing is a sort of rant on paper—a stream-of-consciousness exercise. You might find it useful to begin with a prompt. Write out the prompt, and then finish it with ten minutes of steady writing. Here is a list of prompts you can try:

- _____ makes me angry because . . .
- I like to eat _____ because . . .
- I'm going to talk to _____ tomorrow and say . . .
- The last time I saw _____ was . . .

You should not stop writing at any time during these ten minutes. Don't answer the door, get a snack, or pet the dog. The purpose of the exercise is to get your ideas flowing again. If you feel yourself getting stuck, write the last word you set down over and over again until you get back on track. And above all, don't stop to correct mistakes. Keep at your task for the entire time, and stop only when your clock or timer reaches the ten-minute mark.

Keeping a Journal

A journal is a private collection of writing that you add to every day. You should approach the task at the same time each day, too, and create a habit that will become more and more natural. Your mind will come to see that time as writing time, and hopefully, this will prepare your brain for creative thought.

FACT

The word *journal* comes from a French word meaning "daily." The word *diary* comes from a Latin word meaning "day." A related word with Latin roots, *diurnal*, also means "daily" and was an archaic word for *diary* or *journal*.

A journal is not exactly the same thing as a diary. A diary is a companion with whom you share your thoughts, feelings, hopes, and fears. Certainly, you can write about these things in your journal as well, but the journal is also a place for you to try out exercises, experiment with ideas, or, if you wish, expand on the free-writes you have done at other times. But, in general, a journal should not be filled with free-writing exercises. It is a place for more thoughtful, careful writing that you can undertake without distraction.

The exercises that you attempt in your journal can come from this book, from teachers and friends, or from your own invention. If you have trouble starting a journal, make a list of your dreams, fears, dislikes, loves, and so on, as you would in a diary. Or you can treat your journal as a camera. Walk around your house, your workplace, or a favorite park and simply record your reactions as you go—people, places, sights, sounds, or whatever else impresses you.

Using Keywords

Another source of inspiration is a list of keywords. The keywords themselves aren't special; you can find them by opening a book, newspaper, or magazine to a random page. Go through that source and jot down every fifth or sixth word that you see, including nouns, verbs, and adjectives (avoid prepositions, articles, and conjunctions), until you have a list of about fifteen words. Then begin writing, and as you write, drop in your keywords when they seem appropriate. You don't have to use all of the words on your list—you don't have to use any words on the list—but creating the list will physically engage you in the task of writing.

Another way to create a list of keywords is to start with word categories such as colors, sounds, foods, etc. Next, jot down four or five words under each category. Once you have created your list, you can begin writing, using whichever words you please. Again, you don't have to use all the words on the list, but creating the list will get you going.

Knowing When to Quit

As a poet, your primary goal is to produce poetry. You may write poetry for publication, for sharing with friends and family, or just for venting personal frustration, but finished poems will still be your objective. While building a routine, keeping a journal, and finding a writing space are all good ways to become a more productive poet, you should also know when to simply set your writing down and walk away.

If you are not working under a strict deadline, it is important that you take adequate breaks from your writing. If you stare at a piece of paper or keep your hands on your keyboard for too long, you will likely begin to suffer from aches and pains, not to mention writer's block. Instead of forcing yourself to create something, go work on another project, fold some laundry, or take a walk until you feel refreshed. You might also want to pick up a book and read during your break. Though you'll still be focusing on a page filled with words, the words are not your own—this will help your mind relax. When you return to your writing you will have a clear perspective and perhaps some new ideas to work with.

Of course, taking too many breaks or repeatedly finding excuses not to write will not leave you with much finished poetry. So, try your best to abide by your routine and take breaks only when you really need them. Sometimes you will just know it's time to quit, but there will also be circumstances in which, if you just press on a little longer, an epiphany might be right around the corner.

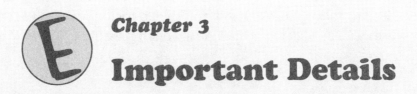

Chapter 3

Important Details

Perhaps the most vital part of writing poetry is the use of significant details. Your poems will describe your mother's callused hands, your dog's warm, soft face, the smell of your grandmother's apple pie, or the colors of a sunset through your window—any topic that inspires you to write. But to share your work with a circle of readers, you must describe each of these central images in a way that makes them come alive. Your readers should be able to see, hear, taste, feel, or smell exactly what your words describe.

The Five Senses

From the moment you are born, you learn about the world using your five senses. As a child, you make a lot of discoveries, but even as you grow older, you continue to delight in objects that appeal to your senses: the smell of fresh-brewed coffee, the feel of a warm sweater, the melody of a favorite song. Keeping these things in mind, you should try to appeal to your reader's senses with the details you include in your poetry.

Sight

You use your eyes to examine the physical environment around you. You learn how close or how far away people and objects are. You learn how small or large those objects are, what colors they are, and what shapes they take. Your first impressions of people, places, and things often depend upon your first sight of them. Sight also dictates a lot of the decisions you make. In part, you might choose a car because of how it looks, an outfit for the way it complements your figure, or a mate based on physical attraction.

QUESTION?

How do you appeal to a reader's sense of sight in a poem?
Don't simply write "He is tall." Use size, shape, color, and any other visual cues. Instead, write, "He ducked his head, covered with a blue ball-cap, and twisted his shoulders to the left, just barely fitting through the dwarfed doorframe."

Likewise, your sense of sight also determines the way you decorate your home. The art you choose, the carpet you select, and the colors you paint your walls are all efforts to make yourself feel more comfortable in your living space. Additionally, you may be trying to attract and impress guests with the decorations you choose. Think of the poems you write in a similar way. You are trying to create an environment for your reader. By describing visible details, such as the color of a coffee cup or the stillness of a lake, your reader will be prompted to use his own sense of sight as he imagines the scene of your poem in his mind.

Sound

Though visual description is very important when creating a poem, sound details can further heighten a reader's experience. Not only do sounds help a reader experience the scene of a poem in her mind, but they are also important when a poem is being read or recited aloud. In addition to the vision of a red car going by, the reader should also hear the *whizzing* or *roaring* sound it makes as it passes. Just as size, color, and shape create vision, so do pitch, tone, and volume create sound, giving the reader the information she needs to learn about a poem's environment. For example, you may mention a woman's voice, but is the sound high-pitched and harsh or deep and delicate?

To create convincing sounds in your poetry, you need to be aware of the sounds that fill the air around you. Does your keyboard *clack-clack* or *tick-tick* when you type on it? Does the water leaking from a pipe in your house *trickle* down the wall or *splatter* on the floor? Does the wind *whoosh* through the oak tree in your front yard or does it gently *hiss*? These seemingly small distinctions will help your reader imagine the scene you're constructing.

Smell

Your sense of smell directly connects the outer world to the most primitive portions of your brain. As a result, your strongest memories are often associated with smells, and frequently triggered by them. By using strong scent description, you can make a poem an even more personal experience for your reader.

To practice identifying and describing smells, do some cooking. As you stir cookie dough or sauté potatoes, choose three words to describe the aromas of the food you're preparing. You can do a similar exercise anywhere. If you're walking through a park in autumn, try to describe the smell of fallen leaves or the smoke rising from a chimney. Keep a list of these words, and refer to them as you write your poetry.

If you walk into a friend's home and smell pumpkin pie, you might remember with perfect clarity a bright November morning in your mother's kitchen as she prepared a Thanksgiving feast. If you pass a construction site and smell sawdust, it could trigger a memory of your father's workshop. You'll immediately envision the floor covered in wood shavings and an oak rocking chair in midcreation. If you identify these essential details of the moments you are trying to re-create, then your poems will be that much more believable.

Touch

Unlike sight, sound, and smell, the sense of touch requires your body to be in physical contact with the things you perceive. Your sense of touch perceives temperature, pressure, and pain, but it also alerts you to more intimate feelings, like love. A pat on the back from a parent, a kiss from a spouse—these are physical acts that reveal a level of contact between two people. Describing these sensations can make a poem more real to your reader. For example, show your reader the warm, smooth stroke of a parent's palm on your back or the cushioned softness of a pair of lips reaching out for a kiss.

ALERT!

Be careful not to force all five senses into every poem you write. Poetry does not have to follow a recipe or a mathematical formula. Only include details that will help your reader experience the subject matter. Too many details can negate one another. The imagery you select must be natural to the poem's purpose.

One way to come up with touch descriptions is to use your fingertips. Your fingertips are very sensitive and will give you the most acute sensations when touching objects. So, if you're trying to describe the skin of a peach, touch it with your fingertips instead of the palm of your hand. The descriptions you choose through this method will probably be more intense and realistic than those you would use otherwise.

Taste

The sense of taste is highly connected to the sense of smell. When you smell a pie baking in the oven, your taste buds and salivary glands are aroused. These reactions set in motion an entire chain of reactions in the digestive tract—upon smelling food, your body is already preparing itself to digest it. Once you actually taste the food, you experience one of the most intense sensations possible. Eating delicious foods is pleasurable, and you want to provide your readers with the same pleasure when reading your poem.

Because the sense of taste works inside the mouth, it has to be used thoughtfully. In other words, don't go out of your way to include taste sensations within a poem simply to broaden the reach of your sensory details. However, certain emotional and physical states, like fear or sickness, can bring a taste to the mouth. Describing these states might be a more effective way of capturing them than simply writing "She felt sick." Instead, write something like "The taste of sickness filled her mouth, like a thousand dirty pennies, as she watched the giant worm moving inside the sink."

Abstract Versus Concrete

Imagine you are walking through a fine-art gallery. Perhaps you will see a painting comprised of distorted shapes and colors and it will remind you of the anger you recently felt during an argument with a friend. Or a painting of a woman in a boat may resonate with you because you enjoy boating in your spare time. Neither painting is better than the other, but each stimulates a different part of your psyche; one is abstract and the other concrete. You can use these two concepts in your poetry, depending on what kind of emotion you want to express or what response you want to generate in your reader.

FACT

Renowned Chinese-American poet Stephen S. N. Liu says that in China, poets have a guaranteed way to test if a poem is too abstract. The poem is given to a child. If the child can't read the poem, then the poem isn't quite right. When the child can read it, it's then considered poetry.

For example, consider Christine Boyka Kluge's poem "Dancing on Ice." Throughout the poem, Kluge uses concrete language to bring her reader to the place she describes. In stanzas two and three of the poem, which follow, the speaker is entranced by the sounds of the winter night:

This is music beyond hearing,
a sweet tickle in my ear.
This is the whistle of warming wind
lifting snowy branches—
branches lined with buds
that pulse like thawing hearts.

The sound makes me dance
on the lake in my nightgown,
makes me pound my white heels
on the booming, cracking ice.
I press my palms flat
on the cold smooth glass of it,
willing upward the sleeping fish.

From Teaching Bones to Fly, *Bitter Oleander Press, 2003. Reprinted with the permission of the author.*

Even if you've never danced on a pond of ice beneath a winter sky, you can certainly get a sense of the moment through the poet's use of concrete language. You hear the "whistle" of the "warming wind"; you feel the "cold smooth glass" of the ice. While most of the imagery is concrete, the poem still concludes with an abstract thought: In "willing upward the sleeping fish" the speaker reveals a longing for the spring.

Using Concrete Nouns and Verbs

Nouns and verbs are the most important parts of speech because you must use them to create complete sentences. If you use nouns and verbs that do not work as hard as they should, you will have listless images in your poems. For example, the words *double-axle personnel transport vehicle* can mean almost anything with two axles: a car, a truck, a tank, a plane, a bicycle, or a skateboard.

The word *car* is more concrete but still may lead to confusion. Mention the word *car* to twenty adults, and one will think of a Corvette, one will think of an SUV, one will think of a Toyota Camry. If you want your readers to envision one car specifically, then you must include much more detail, starting with a concrete noun: "Frank drove a blue Lexus ES with gold rally stripes, gold rims, a white leather interior, a ten-speaker Bose 200-watt tuner, tinted windows, and a six-speed manual V-8 engine." Now each reader can visualize the car the same way. An important effect to note is that once the car has been described, the readers can begin to form ideas about Frank. One can tentatively speculate what Frank does for a living, how much money he earns, where he might live, and so on, all from this simple description of the car.

Another example highlights the need for strong verbs. In the sentence "She made her way across the room," the reader gains a sense that the character is moving through a crowd of people, but the verb is too vague to really show her movement. If a more concrete verb were used, the sentence would be more engaging. For example: "She slithered through a sea of people to the other side of the room."

Active and Passive Voice Verbs

Verbs can be used in active or passive voice, and the voice of the verb tells you the relationship between the verb and its subject. The subject of an active voice verb performs the action of the verb. The subject of a passive voice verb receives the action of the verb.

QUESTION?

Why is the word *voice* used to describe a subject-verb relationship?
Since *voice* in the verb sense has nothing to do with speaking, it isn't necessarily the best word to use. Some grammarians have tried different terms, but without success. Interestingly, verbs also have mood, tense, and other qualities.

For example, if you write "Elliot hits the ball," *hits* is the verb, and *Elliot* is the subject. The subject is doing the action stated by the verb, so it is in *active voice*. If you write "The ball is hit by Elliot," the phrase *is hit* is the verb and *ball* is the subject, but the subject now receives the action stated by the verb, making it *passive voice*. A passive voice verb will always take a form of *be* as a helping verb. But notice also that the true actor, *Elliot*, is now set forth in the prepositional phrase *by Elliot*. Grammatically, you do not need to include *by Elliot* to have a complete sentence in the passive voice.

Similarly, in the sentence "He is a police officer," the verb *is* shows a state of being rather than an action. Linking verbs such as *to be* force the writer to tell the readers about people, objects, and places rather than use details to reveal those subjects. By using active verbs, you can rewrite the previous sentence in lines of poetry:

> *Badge flashing in the dim light,*
> *holster creaking as he draws his gun,*
> *the man drops to a crouch.*
> *"Freeze!" he shouts.*

Now the details of the badge and the holster reveal that the subject is a police officer, and his actions provide a sense of expectation—what will happen next? Passive constructions will not help your poetry. Avoid them, and instead use active verbs to create tension and excitement in your writing.

Avoiding Modifiers

Adjectives tell you *how many*, *which one*, and *what kind* and describe nouns. Adverbs tell you *when, where, how, how often, why, to what degree,* and *in what condition* and describe verbs, other adverbs, and adjectives. Adjectives and adverbs—and the phrases and clauses that operate the same way—will add extra detail to your nouns and verbs, just like garnishes add extra color to your dinner entrées. Don't use too many sprigs of mint or parsley in your poetry. The main course—the nouns and verbs in the poem—must be the thing that stands out to your reader.

For example, in the phrase "walk slowly," the verb *walk* is accompanied by an adverb, *slowly*, that may be unnecessary. A careful writer should find a stronger verb that means the same as *walk slowly* to eliminate the adverb and bring more strength to the verb. For example, the verbs *creep*, *dawdle*, and *trudge* all indicate a slow walk, but they also show with more detail the intent behind the walk—without the use of an adverb.

ALERT!

Beginning poets should avoid the adjective *beautiful* when describing a person, landscape, or other noun. The word offers an opinion but no detail to show the beauty. Instead, tell the reader about the color of her eyes, the shape of his lips, the grandeur of the mountains—anything that includes concrete nouns and verbs.

Some adjectives and adverbs imply judgment rather than add detail. For example, in the sentence "David clumsily lifted the chair," the adverb *clumsily* reveals the speaker's assessment of how David lifted the chair. Similarly, the sentences "She is beautiful" and "The ugly man entered the room" contain vague, judgmental adjectives *(beautiful, ugly)*. They offer little help to the weak verb *(is)*, the pronoun *(she)*, and the abstract noun *(man)* forming the sentences.

Grammar Tricks

You may be surprised to learn that grammar can help you with your use of details. However, the better you understand grammar, the more ways you can intensify the description in your poetry. For example, adjectives, appositives, participles, and absolutes are just four of the grammatical structures that can help you build poetic details.

Adjectives

If you insist on finding a home for your adjectives, try this trick first. Adjectives commonly appear in two places: immediately before the nouns they modify, as in the phrase "the *dirty* car"; or after a linking verb, as in "The car is *dirty*." If you are placing your adjectives only in these two spots, try putting them in another place. Much like rearranging the furniture in your living room gives your house a new look, moving your adjectives will give your sentences, and your writing, a fresh appearance.

Here's how to do it. Let's take the previous phrase: "The dirty car." Take the adjective *dirty* and put it behind the noun *car*, and set it off with a comma: "The car, dirty." Now you probably sense that the adjective is out of place. For instance, you would not say: "The car, dirty, sat in the driveway." But in its new position, the adjective can take on an added detail—a comparison, for example, beginning with the word *as*:

> *The car, dirty*
> *as a pig in slop,*
> *sat in the driveway.*

You can also add more detail using the word *with*:

> *The car, dirty*
> *with muck and sand*
> *from a foray through the riverbed,*
> *sat in the driveway.*

Appositives

Appositives are structures that repeat something using different terms. For example, consider the phrase "the dirty car, an old Mustang." The word *Mustang* is another way of referring to the noun *car* that comes before it. A noun that repeats another noun is the most common form of appositive. In the previous example, the second noun, *Mustang*, is more concrete than the first noun, *car*. This shows the power of good appositives. They don't just rename; they also make more specific the object, person, or place being described.

You can make appositives out of other grammatical structures, too. For example, take the sentence used earlier, "The dirty car sat in the driveway," and tag more verbs onto it:

The dirty car sat in the driveway,
settled into the deepening snow,
hunkered beneath a layer of ice.

The verbs *settled* and *hunkered* add more detail about the way the car sits in the driveway. First, they are more concrete than the original verb, *sit*, and second, they allow for the addition of more concrete nouns—*deepening snow* and *layer of ice*—to describe the state of the car. Here are some more examples of appositives:

- Noun phrase: She found the court jester *a rascal, a buffoon, a loud-mouthed braggart.*
- Prepositional phrase: *At dawn, at the moment the rooster crowed,* the farm came alive.
- Subordinate clause: *Before he left that day, before he took that suitcase filled with his manuscripts, old love letters, and underwear,* he left me the goodbye note on the mantel.

Participles

Participles are words that look like verbs but don't work like verbs. They have the *-ing* or the *-ed* (or *-en, -t, -d*) endings that belong to verbs, but they behave differently. For example, look at these two sentences:

- I am eating a pie.
- Eating a pie, I watched cartoons on TV.

The word *eating* has the *-ing* ending. In the first sentence, the word *am* appears before it. That little word in front of an *-ing* word tells you that the phrase "am eating" is working as a verb. Other words such as *is, are, was, were, has been,* and *had been* will also tell you that an *-ing* word is working as a verb. Without those little words to signal the verb function of the *-ing* word, the *-ing* word is working as a participle.

But what exactly does that mean? In the sentence "Eating a pie, I watched cartoons on TV," the word *eating* still names an action—the action of eating the pie—and someone is still doing the action—the *I* in the sentence.

However, the verb in the sentence is *watched*. The words *I watched* form the subject-verb pair necessary to create that sentence. The words *eating a pie* add an extra detail about the subject of the sentence—a secondary action—that gives us more information to work with.

Here are more examples of the participle in use:

- *Shuddering*, the dirty car sat in the driveway.
- The dirty car, *sputtering* and *spinning its wheels*, sat in the driveway.
- The dirty car sat in the driveway, *dented in the hood by the falling branches*.

In all of these examples, no matter what form the participles take, and no matter what position the participles are in, they add extra details about the subject of the sentences, the word *car*.

Absolutes

The absolute in its most basic form appears as a noun plus a participle. Like the other structures, the absolute adds a specific detail about something that already appears in a sentence. For example, if you return to the sentence about the dirty car, you can add different absolutes to give new information about the car:

- *Wipers swishing*, the dirty car sat in the driveway.
- *Windshield covered with ice*, the dirty car sat in the driveway.
- The dirty car, *driver's seat spattered with mud*, sat in the driveway.

The first example has the basic form of the absolute, noun plus participle. The second example shows the participle *covered* with a modifier of its own, *with ice*. The third example shows that the absolute, like the participle, can appear in different places in the sentence. In each of the previous examples, the absolute focuses on a specific part of the car—the wipers, the windshield, the driver's seat—and attaches a detail to that part. This gives the reader a fuller impression of the car itself.

The absolute can come in different forms—noun plus prepositional phrase, noun plus adjective, noun plus noun—but all work in the same manner as the basic form. Here are examples of the other forms:

- Noun plus prepositional phrase: The dirty car, *open door at attention*, sat in the driveway.
- Noun plus adjective: The dirty car, *headlights bright* and *door open*, sat in the driveway.
- Noun plus noun: The dirty car, *its open door a gateway to freedom*, sat in the driveway.

As with the earlier examples, the absolutes focus the reader's attention on a specific detail about the car—in this case, the open door and the bright headlights.

One way to practice using different grammar structures is to do exercises while you're driving or taking a walk. Try to describe the things you see around you in detail using adjectives, appositives, participles, or absolutes. For example, describe a house you pass by using an appositive: "I see a blue house, a ranch-style home."

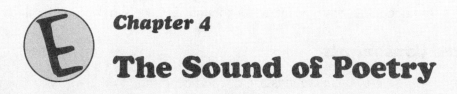

Chapter 4

The Sound of Poetry

The sound of poetry is different from that of a short story, essay, or novel. Prose forms can be poised and polished, but they do not sustain the musical quality that poetry does. Poetry is derived from a time before writing was used—a time when religious rites, family histories, and stories were spoken, sung, or chanted. As you write, keep in mind the history of verse and pay close attention to the sounds of the language you use.

Consonants

Since languages generally begin in spoken rather than written form, the smallest units of English are its sounds. The English language divides sounds into two well-known categories: consonants and vowels. Within these categories there are hard and soft consonants and short and long vowels. There are about four times as many consonants as vowels in the English alphabet.

Hard Consonants

The consonant sounds are divided according to the way you use your lips, tongue, nasal passages, and vocal cords. For example, there is one pair of consonants whose sounds are created by stopping the air at your lips. Say the letters *b* and *p* to yourself. Notice how you close your lips to start each sound. Notice also that you voice the *b* and keep the *p* silent. These are both hard sounds because of the small burst of air and sound you release when you open your mouth again.

When writing poetry you want to keep in mind the sounds of the letters and words you use. For example, if you are trying to describe the slow, relaxed movement of a woman, you may choose the word *saunter* over the word *walk*. *Saunter* begins and ends with soft consonants and has a smoother sound (and more description) than *walk*, which ends with a hard *k* sound.

Now say the letters *d* and *t*. Notice this time that you stop the air by pressing the tip of your tongue against the ridge behind your upper teeth. You should also notice that you voice the *d* and keep the *t* silent. Like *b* and *p*, these sounds are hard because of the burst of air and sound that comes when you pull your tongue away again.

Now say the letters *g* ("hard" *g*) and *k*. With these two you stop the air by pressing the back of your tongue against the back of your mouth. The *g* sound is voiced, and the *k* sound is voiceless. Again, the hard sound is produced by the burst of air that occurs when the breathing passage is opened again.

Soft Consonants

Now, try saying the letters *v* and *f* to yourself. You should immediately notice three differences between these two letters and the six that you sounded out earlier. First of all, you do not completely stop the air as it passes through your mouth when saying these two letters. Secondly, you can maintain the sound of the *v* or the *f* for several seconds, but you can't do this with *b, p, d, t,* (hard) *g,* or *k.* Finally, the sounds of the *v* and the *f* are softer; you do not produce a burst of sound and air but rather a steady stream. For these reasons, *v* and *f* are considered soft consonants.

There are several other pairs of voiced and voiceless soft consonants, but there are also a few single voiced soft consonants. One of the latter is *l,* heard at the beginning of words like *licorice, laughter,* and *love.* The *r* sound appears in words such as *rug, real,* and *royal.* The *w* sound, made by blowing the air stream through puckered lips, appears in *window* and *windy.* The *y* sound (*yellow, yes*) is made by pushing the middle of the tongue toward the roof of the mouth.

Vowels

Though you learn that the vowels in English are *a, e, i, o, u,* and sometimes *y,* there are actually several vowel sounds, sometimes classified roughly as long or short. However, these classes are not steadfast, as vowels are affected by the consonants in the syllables around them. For example, the *u* sound in the word *pup* is considered a short sound. But if you say the word *pub,* that short *u* suddenly sounds longer. The difference is that in the word *pup,* the short *u* sound is followed by the voiceless sound of *p,* while in *pub,* it is followed by the voiced *b.*

F A C T

The majority of syllables in English have a vowel sound, which is considered the loudest part of the syllable. Some syllables, however, have two vowel sounds. These sounds are called *diphthongs,* and you can hear them in the words *bright, snout,* and *toy.* For practice, try to think of other words that contain diphthongs.

A better way of classifying vowel sounds is by the tongue's position when each is spoken. The words *front*, *central*, and *back* are used to describe which part of the tongue is raised highest toward the roof of the mouth, and the words *high*, *mid*, and *low* describe how high the tongue is raised. A mid-central vowel is one that causes the middle of your tongue to rise halfway to the roof of your mouth.

Rhyme: Part I

Probably the one sound tool that is most closely associated with poetry is rhyme. If two lines end with words having the same terminal sounds, you might automatically assume that you have found a song, nursery rhyme, jingle, or poem. Rhyme creates a melody or rhythm that may correspond well with the subject matter you choose for a particular poem.

The essential feature of a rhyme is two or more words that end in the same vowel-consonant sound combination, regardless of spelling. For example, the words *bored*, *board*, and *toward* rhyme. The words *father* and *bother* also rhyme. Certain types of poems can be identified by the pattern of rhymed words they contain. But before you learn how to identify poems by their rhymes, you need to identify the different types of rhymes themselves.

Places to Rhyme

The most common place to put rhyming words in poetry is at the ends of lines. This kind of rhyme is called *end rhyme*. Here is an example of some end rhyming taken from Sonnet 73 by William Shakespeare:

That time of year thou may'st in me behold
When yellow leaves, or none, or few, do hang
Upon those boughs which shake against the cold,
Bare ruined choirs where late the sweet birds sang.

The words that rhyme here are *behold/cold* and *hang/sang*, placed at the ends of alternating lines. Note, however, that although Shakespeare ends each line with a rhyming word, he does not end a sentence with each line. He weaves all four lines into a single sentence. If the poem is read as though it has no line breaks, the rhymes almost vanish among the other words.

Another form of rhyme is called *internal rhyme*. With this technique, the rhyming words can be tucked anywhere within a line or in consecutive lines. Sometimes, a word within a line can rhyme with a word at the end of the line. An example of such an internal rhyme appears in the second stanza of Samuel Taylor Coleridge's "Rime of the Ancient Mariner":

> *The Bridegroom's doors are opened wide,*
> *And I am next of kin;*
> *The guests are met, the feast is set:*
> *May'st hear the merry din.*

The internal rhyme appears in the third line with the words *met/set*. Note also that Coleridge uses the end rhymes *kin/din*. The strong rhyme pattern, reinforced by the phrases that end when the lines end, gives the poem a songlike quality.

Types of Rhyme

The English language, despite its huge treasury of words, does not make rhyming easy. Several rhyming dictionaries—all slender volumes—offer lists of rhyming combinations. To make up for the language's lack of rhyming options, poets have resorted to rhyming variations. As a result, there are three broad categories of rhymes.

The first category is *true rhyme*. In this variation, the vowel/consonant combination at the end of two or more words sounds exactly the same. The words *true, clue, blew, through, new, flu, zoo*, though spelled differently, all have the same vowel sound (the high back vowel) at the end.

The next category is *slant rhyme*, also called *near rhyme* or *off rhyme*. In this type, one of the sounds in the combination, either the consonant or the vowel, is changed. The result is that instead of having words that ring in your ear (*baby/maybe*), you have words that ring and clatter alternately (*baby/barber*). Other examples of slant rhymes are *creak/croak, wish/wash, play/plough*, and *heaven/even*. The advantage of the slant rhyme is that it gives you more opportunity to delight your readers with original rhyme combinations.

The last category is *eye rhyme.* Unlike the other variations, this form of rhyme depends upon words that have the same spelling but different sounds when spoken. For example, consider this group of words ending with *-ough: through, though, tough, cough.* Also, look at these words that end with *-ove: love, prove, dove* (past of *dive*). These words look as if they should be spoken the same way but strangely are not. Still, like slant rhymes, eye rhymes allow you to expand your rhyme combinations.

To see how limited the English language is when it comes to rhyme, create a list of true rhymes based on a common vowel/consonant ending—for example, the *-at* ending in *cat.* Then expand the possibilities by adding slant and eye rhymes to your list. Consider these options when you write your poetry.

Rhyme: Part II

Consider the difference between these two pairs of words: *believe/relieve* and *matter/batter.* If you say them out loud to yourself, you should be able to hear a distinction. In the first pair, the second syllables of the words are stressed, and in the second pair, you stress the first syllables.

Rhyme Stress

This difference in stress, or beat, is another way to categorize rhymes. The first pair of words, *believe/relieve,* is called a *masculine* or *rising rhyme* because your voice rises as you say the rhyming syllable. The second pair, *matter/batter,* is called a *feminine* or *falling rhyme* because your voice falls when you say the rhyming syllable. If you go back to the lines quoted earlier from Shakespeare and Coleridge, you will note that both poets used masculine (rising) rhymes. Note also that most of the rhyming words in the poems are monosyllabic—a common feature of masculine rhyme.

When to Use Rhyme

Since rhymes are so often present in songs, nursery rhymes, and poems, many people believe that poems cannot be written without them. You may therefore be surprised to learn that a great number of modern poems do not depend on rhymes. In fact, with the exception of oral poetry, poets have generally avoided using strict rhymes since the early 1900s.

If you do choose to use rhymes in your poems, you should take the following advice to heart. First of all, if you are not writing in a form that demands a rhyme pattern, you should make every effort not to overpower your reader with rhymes. The occasional use of rhyme will provide an interesting sound and rhythm in a poem. Secondly, if you are writing in a form that demands a rhyme pattern, you should try to create interesting, surprising rhymes, without deviating from the theme of the poem. Your rhymes should not distract your readers from the rest of the poem; they should only augment the sound structure that already exists.

FACT

There are only two commonly used words in the English language that end in *-gry: angry* and *hungry.* There are several other words with this ending, but they are either ancient or rarely used. For example, according to the *Oxford English Dictionary,* the word *aggry* refers to a type of colored glass bead found in Africa, and *begry* is a fifteenth-century spelling of the word *beggary.*

Alliteration

Another nice pattern to use in poetry is alliteration. If you delighted in tongue twisters when you were younger—such as "She sells seashells by the seashore"—you will recognize this pattern immediately. Alliteration is the repetition of sounds (usually consonants) at the beginnings of words. As with rhyme, you can vary the pattern of alliteration by embedding the repeated sounds within words. This embedding is known as *consonance.* You can also repeat vowel sounds initially and internally. The repetition of vowel sounds is called *assonance.*

For example, consider the phrase "big, bad Bob." This phrase displays simple alliteration. Now, add a few words to this phrase to make it a full sentence: "Bumps abound aboard the barge, big, bad Bob." The added words *bumps* and *barge* add to the existing alliteration, but in the words *abound* and *aboard*, the *b* sound is embedded within the words. However, the *b* sound in both words appears at the front of stressed syllables, so the repetition still strikes your ears. Also, the two words *abound* and *aboard* repeat the initial *a* sound (the mid-central vowel), so these words show assonance as well.

FACT

In the English language, alliteration actually has an older presence than rhyme in poetry. Alliterative verse, based on patterns of alliteration and stressed syllables, dates back to Old English times and was the basis of poems such as *Beowulf* and *Sir Gawain and the Green Knight*.

Oral Poetry

It's clear that plays are written for the purpose of performance, but what about poems? You may intend some of your poetry to be read silently, but other poems are meant to be heard. Poetry, in general, is a performance art. It employs so many tools of sound that it often won't reach its potential until it is read for an audience.

The Value of Reading Aloud

The ancients committed to memory such works as *Beowulf* and *The Epic of Gilgamesh,* passing them down from generation to generation. Today, poets continue to display the beauty of the spoken word. But whether or not you want to read your works to an audience, you must be brave enough to read them aloud to yourself. You must listen to your own words.

Primarily, reading your work aloud is a method of editing that will allow you to find the poem's natural pauses and cadences. The manner in which you pronounce a word or pause at a punctuation mark may assist you in determining the poem's line breaks. Secondly, the more you read the poem aloud, the more you will absorb the poem's nuances. The sounds may spark ideas for development.

To get a better sense of your own voice and style as you read aloud, you should use a tape recorder. Listening to your own voice may seem strange, but this might help you be more objective about the language of the poem and about your own performance. Record yourself reading a first draft and then a revised one. Identify the improvements and learn from them.

Listening to Other Poets

There is an interesting dynamic that occurs as a result of listening to a poet read her or his work. For one, an individual with a gifted speaking voice can make even a bad poem sound adequate. Think of the voices of James Earl Jones or Patrick Stewart. Even the commercials these actors narrate seem captivating. Likewise, a great poem can be obliterated by a shaky or monotone voice. The best form of practice is observation. Listen to other poets read their work and learn from their delivery techniques.

FACT

If you want to hear some well-known poems performed for you, try visiting a Web site with streaming capabilities. The Academy of American Poets, for example, has a listening-booth link at their site, ✐ *www.poets. org,* so you can hear the poetry you are reading spoken out loud.

The poet Olga Broumas will often recite a piece, committed to memory, like a song. The musical quality of her poems draws in audience members and captivates them through to the end of her performance. Another contemporary poet, David Lee, reads many of his poems as though he were speaking to you over a beer at your favorite bar. His folksy charm is appealing, but it never undermines the poem. His conversational style allows the poem's narrative to take center stage. And Charles Harper Webb, who has edited an entire anthology on poetry as standup entertainment, reads many of his poems like comic monologues. His delivery guides the audience to the punch line. Through the ease of these poets' deliveries, an intimacy is created between the poem and the audience.

Performance Poetry

A great way to enhance your poetry technique is to try performance or slam poetry. Slam poetry blends poetry and performance, and it involves competition. Typically, a poet must perform an original work in a set time period, typically three minutes. But the poet must perform without the assistance of costumes, props, or musical accompaniment.

If you're interested in slam poetry, there are several different ways to try it out. Most likely there are competitions in your city that you can attend for free or at a low cost. Many colleges, libraries, and poetry groups host slam competitions. If you've done slam poetry a few times and are looking for a challenge, keep in mind that competition ascends to very high levels. For example, the National Poetry Slam is the annual championship tournament for slam. A different city hosts it each year, and four-person teams from North America and Europe gather to compete for the national title.

If you are interested in performing your poetry but don't enjoy competition, you could try reading your work at local bookstores, colleges, libraries, or clubs. And if even those options intimidate you, start out small. Gather a group of close friends to be your first audience. As you get more comfortable with poetry performance, you might consider trying some other options. Whatever method you choose, performing your poetry for others will increase your confidence and provide you with useful feedback.

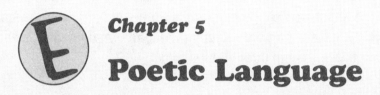

Chapter 5

Poetic Language

Words, like families and nations, have rich histories that can be traced through written records. Words have meanings that you encounter every day and others that lurk only in dictionaries. Many of these meanings can be used to create figures of speech that add texture to your poetry. You can also shift these words around to create special effects and leave a lasting impression on your readers.

Definitions

While chatting with a friend about the weather, you might mention that the sky is blue. However, you will probably not acknowledge that the word *blue* may have more than one meaning. In fact, the word *blue*—and many other words, for that matter—has two sets of meanings. One set, called *denotative*, refers to the literal, original meaning of a word—its "dictionary" meaning. The other set, called *connotative,* refers to the informal or slang meanings that a word has picked up throughout its life.

Denotation

In a good dictionary, such as *Merriam-Webster's* or *American Heritage*, you will probably see *blue* listed as a noun, its primary definition related to a particular color of a certain electromagnetic wavelength. This definition would be considered the denotative meaning. This meaning may seem ordinary, but it plays an important role in your language, as do the denotative meanings of all English words.

FACT

The most comprehensive dictionary of the English language is the *Oxford English Dictionary*, or *OED*. This vast multivolume record took decades to compile and contains a definition for every word used since A.D. 1000. If you love words, the *OED* is your dream! There's only one catch—it costs hundreds of dollars.

In addition to giving you the denotative definitions of words, a good dictionary will also tell you the history of a word. For example, the word *tawdry* arose from the name of St. Audrey. The word originally described a fine lace necktie, but because the quality of the lace declined over the years, eventually the word came to mean any cheap or shameful object. That's quite a change for a word originally associated with a saint!

Connotation

The dictionary will also list a series of meanings that a word has acquired since its inception. These meanings are the word's connotations. When words have several connotations, a person must rely upon its context to derive its meaning.

Take a look at some of the connotations that the word *blue* has gathered. First, *blue* refers to the color. There are also dress *blues*, a term referring to a military uniform. *Blue* can also mean depressed or melancholy, and from that connotation comes the *blues*, the musical genre. It also appears in the common expressions "blue in the face" and "out of the blue."

As you can see, this one small word has quite a lot of meaning packed into it. Many other words carry a list of connotative meanings just as long. As a poet, you should do your best to learn as many connotative meanings as possible. Using words with several meanings in your poetry can broaden the scope of your work and can also help you reach a more diverse population of readers.

Category and Function Shift

An idea related to the denotative and connotative meanings of words is *category and function shift*. This shift occurs when words develop uses that they did not previously have. For example, the word *paper* began as a noun naming the sheet of pressed plant fibers you write upon. Then it acquired verb capabilities for use in a sentence like "He will paper her mirror with love notes." *Paper* can also be used as an adjective, such as in the phrase "paper plate."

The word *paper* changed categories from noun to verb to adjective without changing spelling. It changed functions, too, since nouns, verbs, and adjectives play different roles in sentences. Shakespeare was a master of creating new meanings for words through category and function shift. For example, he turned the nouns *tongue*, *boy*, and *peace* into verbs to accommodate his writing purpose.

You might practice this idea of category and function shift by taking a word—perhaps start with the word *yellow*—and using it in a sentence first as a noun, then as a verb, then as an adjective or adverb, all without changing the spelling of the word. Try the exercise again on another word.

This is a great way to stretch your language skills and find a fresh use for a familiar word.

Word Choice

When you're searching for a synonym, what book do you pick up? Chances are, you reach for a thesaurus. A thesaurus offers synonyms and antonyms for every word you can find in the dictionary. In fact, the English language includes numerous words that mean virtually the same thing. Isn't that a bit repetitive? Not for a poet! Each and every word has a slightly different pattern of sound and shade of meaning that will create a certain individual effect on your reader. As a result, you have the power of word choice at your disposal.

The sound of a word can be very important to the mood you are establishing in a poem. For example, compare these two separate stanzas:

The old man wrenched
his sack of guts
and hacked a cough

The senior detected
a murmur
in his intestines

You should be able to hear how the hard sounds of the first stanza contrast with the softer sounds of the second. The sounds also affect the meaning and the melody of each line. The old man of the first stanza seems to be in a much worse state than the senior of the second example. The words *hacked* and *cough* echo the hard sounds of the man's coughing, while the words *murmur* and *intestines* in the second example reduce the senior's illness to minor discomfort.

Choosing words for a poem is usually a case of trial and error. You may try anywhere from three to thirty words for one particular spot. The trick is not to give up until you've found the perfect word for the poem. Consult your dictionary, your thesaurus, and even your friends if you're having trouble coming up with the right word to complete a rhyme or end a stanza.

Word Order

While choosing the words for your poems, you will also have to determine the order in which they appear. This choice may seem obvious—you simply put the words together to make sentences, right? Wrong. Organizing the words in a poem is a delicate process that requires much thought and patience.

The precise placement of words in your poems will have a great effect on their combined meaning. For example, here are two sentences that contain exactly the same words:

- I nearly lost $100.
- I lost nearly $100.

Which event would you rather experience? Most likely you would prefer the first event. Though only one word changes position, the meanings of these two sentences are quite different. The first sentence says that you did not lose any money. However, the second says you definitely lost something—maybe $87, $92, or even $99.

FACT

English speakers use approximately seven patterns to create clauses. The most common of these patterns is noun/verb/noun. Sentences such as "Sarah hits the ball" and "Sarah is a mother" follow this order. For practice, think of some other examples that fit this pattern.

More so than many other languages, English depends on word order to make meaning clear. For example, the order of the words in the sentence "The cat ate the mouse" tells us something different from the order "The mouse ate the cat." Because word order is so important in the language, English has a set series of patterns for phrase and clause construction.

Whenever the basic patterns are changed, however, you must recognize the difference and determine the meaning. For example, if you read "Sarah the ball hits" or "Sarah a mother is," you can probably figure out that Sarah is the subject in both cases, but you would wonder why *the ball* and *a mother* have been moved. In poetry, moving words in this way can improve a piece. Rearranging words in a unique way can give your poem a stronger meaning or rhythm.

Some examples of altered word order can be seen in Robert Browning's "Soliloquy of the Spanish Cloister." Three appear in the fifth stanza of the poem:

> *When he finishes refection,*
> *Knife and fork he never lays*
> *Cross-wise, to my recollection,*
> *As I do, in Jesu's praise.*
> *I the Trinity illustrate,*
> *Drinking watered orange-pulp—*
> *In three sips the Arian frustrate;*
> *While he drains his at one gulp!*

Browning alters the normal clause pattern when he writes "Knife and fork he never lays / Cross-wise," "I the Trinity illustrate," and "In three sips the Arian frustrate." In the common word order pattern, the first clause would read "He never lays knife and fork cross-wise." The second would read "I illustrate the Trinity." And the third would read "Frustrate the Arian in three sips." But what has Browning gained by altering the pattern? The first and most obvious improvement is that every other line makes a rhyme. By altering the word order, he can rhyme *lays* with *praise* and *illustrate* with *frustrate*.

As an exercise, write the following sentence on a piece of paper: "The girl found the ball in the attic." Then, without adding or dropping any words from the original, shift the words into different positions. Which arrangements sound natural to you? Which sound forced or lack meaning?

A second reason for changing the word order has to do with the meaning of the poem itself. The poem is told from the point of view of a monk who feels great indignation toward a fellow monk (the *he* of the poem). His anger, which he keeps internalized, is at odds with his pious actions—his observance of Jesus and the Trinity at the dinner table—and also opposes the calm demeanor that normally characterizes men of faith. The altered word order thus highlights the defiance of the speaker, showing how his frustration has disrupted his life.

When to Use Repetition

Throughout much of your formal education you were probably instructed to avoid repeating words in your writing. Certainly, in the sentence "He put the hat on and the hat sank down over his eyes," repeating the word *hat* makes the sentence seem choppy and unpolished. Such repetitions can be avoided with a little extra effort.

However, word repetition can work well in poetry. As with music, good repetition in writing can establish a melody that you can use to reinforce a message or strengthen an image. You've already read about rhymes, alliteration, consonance, and assonance; these are good forms of repetition to use in poetry. But there are several other forms of repetition that could be useful to you when writing poetry.

The book *Style and Statement*, written by Edward P. J. Corbett and Robert J. Connors, includes examples of what they call *schemes of repetition*. Following are some of the schemes, given in their original Greek names:

- *Anaphora:* repetition of a word or phrase at the beginning of lines or clauses
- *Epistrophe:* repetition of a word or phrase at the end of lines or clauses
- *Epanalepsis:* repetition of a word at the start and the end of a word group
- *Anadiplosis:* repetition of the last word of a group in the next group of words
- *Antimetabole:* reversal of the word order of a pair of phrases

- *Chiasmus:* reversal of the structure of a pair of phrases
- *Polyptoton:* use of words taken from the same root

Here are some examples of these schemes in action:

- *Anaphora:* I am crazy about apple pie. I am crazy about baseball. I am crazy about this great, big country of ours.
- *Epistrophe:* My friends are happy, my family is happy, and I am happy.
- *Epanalepsis:* Luck will always bring more luck; sorrow will always bring more sorrow.
- *Anadiplosis:* The drawer will go in the desk, the desk will go in the moving van, and the moving van will go to our new home.
- *Antimetabole:* One may fight to live but one should not live to fight.
- *Chiasmus:* He throws away his valuables but his garbage keeps.
- *Polyptoton:* She can dream the undreamable, and find the unfindable.

From this brief sampling, you should be able to sense the rhythm established by the repetitions. Some of that rhythm is reinforced by word order, too. Another way to think of these repetitions is to think of them as swings of a hammer tapping the nails of your sentences in place. Each blow secures the nails more firmly, and the construction of your poem takes shape with artful and solid design.

Figures of Speech

You also have at your disposal tools called *figures of speech*. Also known as *tropes* or *conceits*, these figures will add depth to the meaning of your poems and add originality to the images you summon. You are probably already familiar with the two most common figures, the *metaphor* and the *simile*, but many others can help you as well. Again, Corbett and Connors's book *Style and Statement* has a thorough list of these figures. Here is just a sample from the list:

- *Metaphor:* a comparison in which one word or phrase that normally designates one thing is used to designate another
- *Simile:* a comparison using the word "like" or "as"
- *Synecdoche:* a reference to something by naming one of its parts
- *Metonymy:* a reference to something by naming a closely related object
- *Pun:* a play on words
- *Onomatopoeia:* words that sound like what they mean
- *Paradox:* two statements that seem contradictory but may actually be true

Here are some examples of these figures:

- *Metaphor:* My mother is a saint.
- *Simile:* My mother is as giving as a saint.
- *Synecdoche:* All hands on deck!
- *Metonymy:* He always pays with plastic.
- *Pun:* The price of shingles is going through the roof.
- *Onomatopoeia:* The only sound was the twitter of a bird.
- *Paradox:* The silence was so loud it hurt my ears.

As beneficial as good figures of speech may be, you must be careful not to overuse these tools. When a writer overuses figures of speech and other methods of repetition it often takes away from the substance of the work. One common problem occurs when writers rely on clichés. Remember: They're called clichés for a reason. So, don't beat a dead horse! Use repetition wisely.

Using Contrasts

Another tool that is useful in poetry is *contrast*. When a poet uses contrasting images and moods in a poem, she is better able to underscore the poem's dominant purpose. As an exercise, read the following poem, "Neutral Tones," by Thomas Hardy, and underline any sets of contrasting words or images. Additionally, next to the stanzas in which they appear, name the conflicts between the speaker and the object of his frustration found in these contrasts.

> *We stood by a pond that winter day,*
> *And the sun was white, as though chidden of God,*
> *And a few leaves lay on the starving sod;*
> *   —They had fallen from an ash, and were gray.*
>
> *Your eyes on me were as eyes that rove*
> *Over tedious riddles of years ago;*
> *And some words played between us to and fro*
> *   On which lost the more by our love.*
>
> *The smile on your mouth was the deadest thing*
> *Alive enough to have strength to die;*
> *And a grin of bitterness swept thereby*
> *   Like an ominous bird a-wing. . . .*
>
> *Since then, keen lessons that love deceives,*
> *And wrings with wrong, have shaped to me*
> *Your face, and the God-curst sun, and a tree,*
> *   And a pond edged with grayish leaves.*

The first contrast is found in stanza one: a frozen pond and a sun so white it appears to have been chastised by God. The speaker also notes a few scattered leaves "on the starving sod." They have fallen from a dormant ash. Here the landscape mirrors the weary love between the speaker and the woman. He, like the sod, is starving for affection, but neither the woman nor the sun will nourish anything. Ironically, from this point on in the poem, the "we"—a collective, unifying pronoun—is separated.

In stanza two, the woman's eyes, rather than focusing on her love, "rove." Forget the notion "I only have eyes for you." Their dialogue is not an expression of desire or affection but a "tedious riddle" that weakens their love further. The eyes and the lips, therefore, betray a love gone wrong.

In stanzas three and four, contrast underscores the death of love. In stanza three, the smile is "the deadest thing / Alive"; the grin shows "bitterness" and foreshadows the end of their relationship. In the last stanza, love has not made the speaker happy; instead, "love deceives," and nature, which is usually a restorative force, holds all the dead-ends and wrongs that "have shaped" his memories.

Two ways to create contrast are to find opposing word pairs—like *winter* and *summer* or *hot* and *cold*—or to find one word that holds two opposing ideas, like the smile described in Hardy's poem, "Neutral Tones." After writing down a list of such opposing images or words that hold two meanings, you can then use them in a poem.

So, is there anything "neutral" about this poem? Not really. The title is the starkest use of contrast. This single moment in life ends the speaker's hope of love. But the contrasting title allows the reader to work toward a better understanding of the poem's content. Using contrast allows a poet to draw attention to her main focus, while exciting the reader's senses and challenging his preconceived notions.

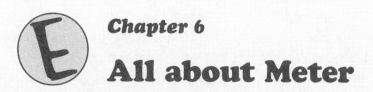

Chapter 6

All about Meter

Reading poems aloud will give you insight into a very important poetic resource: the stress, or lack of stress, given to certain words and syllables. You can arrange these syllables in such a way that you create rhythm in your poetry; this is called *meter*. Meter can give your poems a stronger musical quality—a cadence that gives shape to a line, a stanza, or indeed, a whole poem.

Dealing with Stress

When you speak, certain sounds and syllables receive stress—that is, your voice rises in pitch and volume, and you enunciate all of the letters. Certain sounds and syllables remain unstressed—your voice lowers in pitch and volume, and you blend, change, or drop the sounds of some letters. For instance, when an English speaker says the word *television*, she puts stress on the first syllable, raising her voice in pitch and volume and enunciating all of the letters. In contrast, the last syllable receives no stress—her voice drops in pitch and volume, the *s* changes to a *zh* sound, and the vowels *i* and *o* disappear between the *s* and the *n*.

The patterns of stressed and unstressed sounds and syllables in English are very difficult to follow. Pronunciation has undergone significant changes over the centuries, and regional dialects and words taken from other languages have their own pronunciation patterns. Words can change their stress patterns according to their functions in a sentence as well. For example, the first syllable of the word *reject* is stressed when it is used as a noun ("I want the rejects sent back"). But when it is used as a verb, the stress is on the last syllable ("He will reject the faulty merchandise"). The first syllable of the word *placid* (an adjective) is stressed, but if you change it into the word *placidity* (a noun), the second syllable is stressed.

Stress can also change according to the type of sentence you are making. For instance, in a normal statement such as "She is beautiful," your voice starts high on the word *she* but then descends steadily through the sentence until hitting the bottom with the syllable *-ful*. In contrast, if you ask the question "Is she beautiful?" your voice find its highest pitch on the syllable *-ful*. Finally, if you exclaim "She is beautiful!" your voice tends to emphasize the word or syllable you want to be the center of attention. For example, if you want to highlight her beauty, the stress will fall on the syllable *beaut-*.

Rules of Stress

Fortunately, there are a few general rules that can help you distinguish between stressed and unstressed sounds and syllables. Modern English still retains elements of its root language, Old English. For example, when you say the word *watchfulness*, you place the stress on the first syllable because that is the syllable that carries the most meaning. When you say the word *forgiveness*, you place the stress on the second syllable for the same reason. Words borrowed from other languages—*dependent, regrettable, insanity*—also follow the same pattern.

FACT

Compounds generally undergo a process of transformation that can last decades or even centuries. They begin as two words (*to morrow*), but their closeness in meaning or importance draws them together, first with a hyphen (*to-morrow*) and then with no separation at all (*tomorrow*).

In words and phrases known as *compounds*, Old English indicates stress on the first part of the group, especially if the compound has been present in the language for a while. Thus, when you say *bookkeeper, manhunt, busybody,* or *panhandle*, the stress falls on the first syllable. In newer compounds, however, especially those that remain two separate words, the stress tends to fall evenly: *knickknack, Mad Hatter, spring break*.

It is also important to listen for changes in vowel sounds. Remember that the majority of syllables in English have a vowel sound, which is considered the loudest part of that syllable. However, those vowel sounds will weaken or disappear if placed within an unstressed syllable. For example, when the vowel appears in an unstressed final syllable, especially a suffix, the vowel sound may be reduced to the mid-central vowel (or *schwa*), because it requires less action by the tongue. Thus in the word *able*, the initial *a* sound is the long mid-front vowel, but in the suffix -*able*, as in *available* or *believable*, the *a* sounds like the *u* in *nut*.

The vowel may be reduced in an unstressed initial syllable as well. In the word *con* (as in *con man*), the *o* is a low back vowel. But in words like *container* or *constrain*, the *o* becomes a schwa or is dropped altogether. Vowels will also disappear between consonants that are formed with similar tongue positions. Thus in words like *pistol* or *bitten*, in which the *t*, the *l*, and the *n* sounds require the tongue tip to touch the roof of the mouth, the *o* and the *e* vowels are dropped.

Another point to consider is parts of speech, which will be discussed in more detail later. For now, simply remember that the more important words, like nouns and verbs, tend to be stressed, and less important words, such as prepositions, conjunctions, and determiners (including articles), remain unstressed. Thus, in a sentence such as "A big fly landed in the milk," stress will naturally fall on *fly* (noun), the first syllable of *landed* (verb), and *milk* (noun). *Big* (adjective) is stressed because it forms a unit with the noun *fly*, but the words *A* (article), *in* (preposition), and *the* (article), and the suffix *-ed* are not stressed.

In English, prefixes and suffixes change the root in different ways. Generally speaking, a prefix will change the meaning of the word, while a suffix will change the function of the word. Thus *inflect* and *reflect* are two different verbs from the root *-flect-*, but the suffix *-ion* transforms both verbs into nouns.

The following points should help you keep these general rules straight:

- *Unstressed syllables:* articles, conjunctions, prepositions, prefixes, suffixes, linking and helping verbs
- *Stressed syllables:* nouns, roots and bases, main verbs (showing action)

These tendencies are not 100 percent accurate, but they provide a reasonable starting point. Note that certain parts of speech (adjectives, adverbs, pronouns) are not listed; they are usually stressed according to the needs and the syntax of the sentence or to the other general tendencies noted previously.

Use Your Dictionary

The easiest way to distinguish between the stressed and unstressed syllables of polysyllabic words is to look them up in a dictionary. For example, if you locate the word *modulate*, you will see a guide for pronunciation and syllabification next to it, likely using parentheses or backward slashes.

Hyphens or centered periods will set off the syllables; a high-set mark will precede the syllable with the primary stress, a low-set mark will precede syllables with secondary stress, and alternative letters and symbols will show the pronunciations of the letters. A good desk dictionary, rather than a simple spelling dictionary, will give you the information you need.

FACT

If you want to learn more about the history of stresses and sounds in English, consult the book *Essentials of English Grammar* by Otto Jespersen. It is a condensed version of a longer study he made. Much of the information about stresses in this chapter comes from this source.

Solid Footing

Partly because of the way words are pronounced and partly because of the early influence of music on poetry, certain patterns of stressed and unstressed syllables emerge in poems and create recognizable beats. A poet may use a specific pattern in a poem to give it shape and structure. This pattern of stressed and unstressed syllables is called a *foot* (plural *feet*).

Foot Patterns

Just as footfalls in an empty corridor can create a rhythm of sound to your ear, the foot patterns of some poetry create very strong rhythms. Consider the following chart:

Eight Foot Patterns Found in English Poetry

Foot Name	Adjective Form	Pattern	Scansion Marks	Example
iamb	iambic	unstressed STRESSED	˘ ´	be FORE
trochee	trochaic	STRESSED unstressed	´ ˘	AL ways
spondee	spondaic	STRESSED STRESSED	´ ´	DEAD HEAD
pyrrhic	pyrrhic	unstressed unstressed	˘ ˘	(HOT) on the (TRAIL)

Eight Foot Patterns Found in English Poetry (continued)				
Foot Name	**Adjective Form**	**Pattern**	**Scansion Marks**	**Example**
anapest	anapestic	unstressed unstressed STRESSED	˘ ˘ ´	un der STOOD
dactyl	dactylic	STRESSED unstressed unstressed	´ ˘ ˘	HICK o ry
amphibrach	amphibrachic	unstressed STRESSED unstressed	˘ ´ ˘	re DUN dant
tribrach	tribrachic	unstressed unstressed unstressed	˘ ˘ ˘	(MIS) e ra ble

In case you're wondering, the scansion marks are called *breves* (˘) and *accents* (´). You can use them when you are reading poetry and want to record the foot patterns you see. In the examples throughout this book, you may see capital letters or accents used to set off the stressed syllables. The unstressed syllables will remain in lowercase, unmarked.

Now, look at some examples of foot patterns as they appear in real verses. To start, consider Sonnet 2 by William Shakespeare:

When forty winters shall besiege thy brow,
And dig deep trenches in thy beauty's field,
Thy youth's proud livery so gazed on now,
Will be a tatter'd weed of small worth held:
Then being asked, where all thy beauty lies,
Where all the treasure of thy lusty days;
To say, within thine own deep sunken eyes,
Were an all-eating shame, and thriftless praise.
How much more praise deserv'd thy beauty's use,
If thou couldst answer "This fair child of mine
Shall sum my count, and make my old excuse,"
Proving his beauty by succession thine!
This were to be new made when thou art old,
And see thy blood warm when thou feel'st it cold.

As you read the sonnet, take note of which syllables are stressed and which are not stressed. For example, in the first line, the stresses seem to fall most naturally on the syllables as follows: "When FORTy WINTers shall beSIEGE thy BROW." The capitalized (stressed) syllables belong mostly to nouns and verbs, with one stressed syllable falling within an adjective. Three of the four stressed syllables appear in two-syllable words, so consulting a dictionary would tell you which of the syllables is stressed.

FACT

The names of the feet come from ancient Greece, and some actually have to do with hands and feet. For example, *dactyl* means *finger* and *pyrrhic* is a form of dance. However, in Greek, stresses have to do with the length of the syllable. For example, the one-syllable word *strength* is long, or "stressed," and the syllable in the word *pip* is short, or "unstressed."

Now, look at the stressed and unstressed syllables of the second line: "And DIG DEEP TRENCHes in thy BEAUTy's FIELD." The same rules seem to apply to the stressed syllables here—all but one belong to nouns and verbs, with that one (*deep*) being an adjective. The unstressed syllables in both lines seem to be the least important syllables—suffixes, prefixes, or words like conjunctions, helping verbs, and prepositions.

Finding Patterns

At this point, you should be able to detect any patterns in the stressed and unstressed syllables. For one thing, if you count the number of syllables in the first two lines of Shakespeare's sonnet, you come up with ten in each. Noticing this pattern, you find that Shakespeare deliberately chose this arrangement. Now, go back and reference the chart of all the different feet for a moment. All of the feet listed have either two or three syllables. Since two goes evenly into ten five times, you can use lines to mark the divisions as follows:

When FORT | y WINT | ers shall | beSIEGE | thy BROW,
And DIG | DEEP TRENCH | es in | thy BEAUT | y's FIELD,

You should be able to see that most of the syllable pairs (seven out of ten) contain an unstressed syllable followed by a stressed. To confirm this pattern, take a look at the next two lines:

Thy YOUTH'S | PROUD LIV | ery | so GAZED | on NOW,
Will be | a TAT| ter'd WEED | of SMALL | WORTH HELD:

In these lines, too, six out of ten syllable pairs follow the unstressed/ stressed pattern. On the chart, this pattern of unstressed/stressed syllables is called an *iamb*. The dominant foot pattern for the poem, as analyzed so far, is therefore *iambic*.

In English verse, though the language itself fights regularity, the most widely used foot pattern is the iamb. Many of the older forms still used in English poetry, such as the sonnet and the ballad, lend themselves most easily to this foot pattern. Even blank verse operates with it.

Shakespeare has used other two-syllable foot patterns here: spondees and pyrrhics. The reason is that English does not lend itself to a regular foot pattern. Forcing the entire poem to hold to a single foot pattern would make it sound unnatural. Shakespeare therefore allowed the spondees and pyrrhics to remain so the poem would approximate spoken English.

Measuring Meter

Once you have found the stressed and unstressed syllables, and once you have found the foot patterns of a poem, you can begin to look for a *meter*. *Meter* is another word for *measure*. So when you are looking for a poem's meter, you are measuring its lines by the number of feet they contain. Therefore, measuring the lines of a poem is much like measuring the walls of a room. But it will be much easier once you become familiar with the tools you are using. To do this, go back to the four lines that you have analyzed from Shakespeare's poem so far:

When FORT | y WINT | ers shall | beSIEGE | thy BROW,
And DIG | DEEP TRENCH | es in | thy BEAUT | y's FIELD,
Thy YOUTH'S | PROUD LIV | ery | so GAZED | on NOW,
Will be | a TAT| ter'd WEED | of SMALL | WORTH HELD:

Each line has been divided into five feet. This five-foot meter has a special name, which, like the names of the feet, comes from Greek. In Greek, the word *penta* means "five," so any line with five feet is written in *pentameter*. The following chart names the meters most commonly used in English poetry:

- *Monometer:* one foot in a line
- *Dimeter:* two feet in a line
- *Trimeter:* three feet in a line
- *Tetrameter:* four feet in a line
- *Pentameter:* five feet in a line
- *Hexameter:* six feet in a line
- *Heptameter:* seven feet in a line
- *Octometer:* eight feet in a line

QUESTION?

Why is iambic pentameter also known as heroic verse?
Iambic pentameter quickly established itself as a prevailing metric form in English poetry during and after the Renaissance. Many of Shakespeare's plays, for example, and John Milton's epic *Paradise Lost*, were written in that meter. For that reason, iambic pentameter is also commonly known as *heroic verse*.

To categorize the meter of a line or a poem, you must name the foot pattern and then count the number of feet in a line. In the example from

Shakespeare, the lines are written in *iambic pentameter*. Poems can also be written in iambic tetrameter, dactylic hexameter, or trochaic trimeter, and some poems may vary the meter from line to line.

Scansion

You are now almost ready to do a complete metrical analysis of any poem you read or write. This process is called *scansion*, or *scanning* a poem, and the whole task begins by finding the stressed and unstressed syllables. One more detail must be added to this process, and that detail takes you back to rhyme. As you look for the stressed and unstressed syllables, the feet, and the meter, you should also look for any rhyming patterns—called *rhyme schemes*—that may be shaping the poem.

Poem Analysis

To see what scansion looks like, examine the following complete analysis of Shakespeare's poem. The vertical lines divide the poem into feet, and the accents fall upon the stressed syllables (the unstressed syllables are left alone). The letter at the end of each line identifies the rhyme scheme. Two lines that rhyme will have a matching letter at their ends, while lines that don't rhyme with any others (none are present in this poem) are usually marked with an X.

When fórt | y wínt | ers shall | besíege | thy brów,	A
And díg | déep trénch | es in | thy béaut | y's fíeld,	B
Thy yóuth's | próud lív | ery | so gázed | on nów,	A
Will be | a tát| ter'd wéed | of smáll | wórth héld:	B
Then bé | ing ásked, | where áll | thy béaut | y líes,	C
Whére áll | the tréas | ure of | thy lús | ty dáys;	D
To sáy, | withín | thine ówn | déep sún | ken éyes,	C
Were an | áll-éat | ing sháme, | and thríft | less práise.	D
How much | móre práise | desérv'd | thy béaut | y's úse,	E
If thóu | couldst án | swer "Thís | fáir chíld | of míne	F
Shall súm | my cóunt, | and máke | my óld | excúse,"	E
Próving | his béaut | y by | succéss | ion thíne!	F

Thís were | to be | néw máde | when thóu | art óld,   G
And sée | thy blóod | wárm when | thou féel'st | it cóld.   G

First of all, take a look at the rhyme scheme. Almost all of the rhymes are true rhymes, the exception being the slant rhyme *field* and *held*, and all are masculine or rising rhymes. The letters to the right of the lines show a pattern of alternation, ABAB CDCD EFEF, until you get to the last two lines, GG, which form a *rhyming couplet.*

The poem itself is fourteen lines long, so a continuous pattern of alternation would not be possible. Hence, the final couplet gives the poem a harmonious end. Note that Shakespeare took great care to punctuate these last two lines as a separate sentence. He also gave them a meaning that shapes the ideas set forth in the previous twelve lines. Many of these characteristics make this poem a sonnet. The following chapter will include more information on poetic forms.

The meter of the poem, pentameter, is consistent from first to last. But the feet vary from line to line, with only the fifth line being iambic throughout. Three of the lines start with stressed syllables. Line twelve, beginning with the word *proving*, feels almost dactylic, until you get to the word *succession*.

One of the feet in the last line, *thou feel'st*, has been brought into the two-syllable count by a contraction, *feel'st* being a shortened form of *feelest*. This *-est* ending is one that was once used to make verbs agree with the pronoun *thou*, as the modern *-s* ending in *talks* or *sleeps* makes those verbs agree with the subjects *he*, *she*, or *it*.

FACT

Several signs of the changes that have come over English in the last several centuries appear in Shakespeare's poem. Aside from the archaic *-est* ending on *couldst* and *feel'st*, you also see the old-fashioned pronouns *thy, thou,* and *thine,* which were the second-person singular pronouns. Today, *you, your,* and *yours* are used for both the singular and the plural.

Finally, a few words were given stress though they normally would not receive it. The words *where* in line six, *more* in line nine, and *this* in line thirteen are neither nouns nor verbs. But a speaker would emphasize these words in normal speech to highlight her meaning.

The word *where* is stressed in line six because the word group in which it appears does not contain a verb. In line five, *where* receives no stress because the verb *lies* carries it. The word *more* gains extra emphasis to highlight the increase in praise that is to come with having a beautiful child. The word *this* gains extra emphasis because it is being used to sum up the argument made in the previous four lines. It gains similar emphasis in line ten because it points out a specific child.

Measurements

To give you some practice with scansion, you can reference Shakespeare's Sonnet 73, which follows. Copy out the poem on a piece of paper, preferably in longhand. Then, applying the ideas set forth in this chapter, try to determine the stressed and unstressed syllables, the foot divisions, the meter, and the rhyme scheme. Once you have finished, check your exercise against the answer following. Good luck!

That time of year thou mayst in me behold
When yellow leaves, or none, or few, do hang
Upon those boughs which shake against the cold,
Bare ruin'd choirs where late the sweet birds sang.
In me thou seest the twilight of such day
As after sunset fadeth in the west,
Which by and by black night doth take away,
Death's second self, that seals up all in rest.
In me thou seest the glowing of such fire
That on the ashes of his youth doth lie
As the death-bed whereon it must expire,
Consumed with that which it was nourish'd by.
This thou perceiv'st, which makes thy love more strong,
To love that well which thou must leave ere long.

That tíme | of yéar | thou máyst | in mé | behóld   A

When yéll | ow léaves, | or nóne, | or féw, | do háng   B

Upón | those bóughs | which sháke | agáinst | the cóld,   A

Báre rú | in'd chóirs | where láte | the swéet | bírds sáng.   B

In mé | thou séest | the twí | light of | such dáy   C

As áf | ter sún | set fád | eth in | the wést,   D

Which bý | and bý | bláck níght | doth táke | awáy,   C

Déath's séc | ond sélf, | that séals | up áll | in rést.   D

In mé | thou séest | the glów | ing of | such fíre   E

That on | the ásh | es of | his yóuth | doth líe   F

As the | déath-bed | whereón | it múst | expíre,   E

Consúmed | with thát | which it | was nóur | ish'd bý.   F

Thís thou | percéiv'st, | which mákes | thy lóve | more stróng,   G

To lóve | that wéll | which thóu | must léave | ere lóng.   G

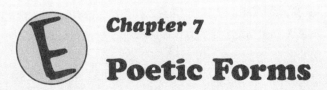

Chapter 7
Poetic Forms

Poetry can take a number of different forms. Some forms are long and some short. Some follow rules and others are free flowing. Though poems can take many shapes, there are four main categories under which all poems can be classified: *narrative, lyric, open form,* and *closed form.* Studying the forms songs take will also help you in your poetic pursuits.

Narrative Poetry I: Epic and Ballad

The narrative poem, among the oldest forms of literature, can be as long as any modern novel. But it can also be relatively short, perhaps contained on a single page. The key requirement of this form is that it must contain a narrative—a story told by a narrator. The first two forms you'll learn about are the *epic* and the *ballad*, which originated with preliterate or semiliterate people. These works were memorized and then performed at celebrations and other gatherings.

The Epic

The epic is an ancient form that is rarely used nowadays. However, it used to be a popular method of recording history and communicating within societies. Being a narrative, the epic borrows some of the techniques of storytelling, including plot, character, setting, point of view, and so on.

- *Plot:* a sequence of events taking place within the narrative
- *Character:* the person whose story is followed throughout the narrative
- *Setting:* the time and place of the narrative
- *Point of view:* the perspective through which the narrative is told

One of the few successful English epics written in the classical convention is John Milton's *Paradise Lost*. Composed about 350 years ago, the poem still inspires many to attempt the epic form or to write a response to the poem itself. One such response is Zachary Chartkoff's "Syn," part of which follows:

> *In the valley; before the factotum*
> *of God's riot with their rosy, hallowed*
> *slaughter machine; before panzered, darksome*
> *Morning Star's first barrage, she up, rambled*
> *out of battle, leaving her night-fitted*
> *father's yowling machines and the valley's*
> *kilns and grogshops burning. Which one quoted*

*poorly rendered handbooks that claim furies
do not drive their greedy mouths like we do?
Her name is Syn. This is not Patriarch's
poem; death did not come in the Hebrew
form of woman. Syn left tiny hoof marks
over the dunes; a winged pear, green as wine
held up before callowed sky's scythe sunshine.*

Printed with permission of the author.

The Ballad

The narrative ballad comes in two forms: the *folk ballad*, typically composed and sung by people with little formal education, and the *literary ballad*, composed by more educated writers in imitation of the folk ballad. Aside from the difference in education levels, the main difference between the forms is that the literary ballad is not composed to be sung. Other than that, both forms share the trait of telling a story, and both tend to focus on subjects such as unrequited love, disaster, murder, and magical or otherworldly events. Coleridge's "Rime of the Ancient Mariner," discussed in Chapter 4, is an example of a literary ballad written about a strange and supernatural ship voyage.

As an exercise, write your own ballad. Choose an event to write about, whether it is from personal experience or a world event. Try to select one of the traditional subjects of the ballad (love, death, illness, etc.), and shape it into a narrative. Even if the event is not your own experience, do your best to give it a personal spin.

The ballad, being a popular song, is organized simply. Its lines, divided into *quatrains* (four-line stanzas), follow an 8-6-8-6 syllable pattern. You also have your choice of rhyme schemes: You can rhyme the alternating lines in an ABAB pattern, or you can simply rhyme lines two and four in an XAXA pattern.

Consider the Scottish folk ballad, "Bonny Barbara Allan," which is several centuries old. The subject matter of the poem is unrequited love, and this leads to the deaths of both characters. The characters themselves are not greatly developed, and the dialogue is not always introduced with tags (he said, she said) as in a polished story. The focus is on the events themselves, and on the final twist that leads Barbara Allan to her own end.

It was in and about the Martinmas time[1],
When the green leaves were a-falling,
That Sir John Græme, in the West Country,
Fell in love with Barbara Allan.

He sent his men down through the town,
To the place where she was dwelling:
"O haste and come to my master dear,
If ye be Barbara Allan."

O slowly, slowly rose she up,
To the place where he was lying,
And when she drew the curtain by:
"Young man, I think you're dying."

"O it's I'm sick, and very, very sick,
And it's all for Barbara Allan."
"O the better for me ye's[2] never be,
Though your heart's blood were a-spilling."

"O don't you recall, young man," she said,
"When the red wine ye were a-filling,
That ye made the toasts go round and round,
And slighted Barbara Allan?"

He turned his face unto the wall,
And death was with him dealing:
"Adieu, adieu, my dear friends all,
And be kind to Barbara Allan."

And slowly, slowly, raise she up,
And slowly, slowly left him,
And sighing said she could not stay,
Since death of life had reft him.

She had not gone a mile or two,
When she heard the dead-bell ringing,
And every stroke that the dead-bell gave,
It cried, "Woe to Barbara Allan!"

"O mother, mother, make my bed!
O make it soft and narrow!
Since my love died for me today,
I'll die for him tomorrow."

[1] *November 11*
[2] *you shall*

Narrative Poetry II: Drama and Monologue

Like the epic, *drama* relies on many of the elements of storytelling, including plot, character, and setting. The characters are usually presented with a problem to be solved, or they may have a conflict among themselves that needs to be dealt with. The purpose of the drama is to see how the characters resolve the issues they face.

The Drama

Unlike the epic, which is usually performed by one singer, the drama has several actors who perform the roles of the characters. The interplay between the characters—often in the form of dialogue—can create many complexities in the verse form. For instance, in *Romeo and Juliet*, Shakespeare wrote the first dialogue exchange between Romeo and Juliet in sonnet form:

Romeo: If I profane with my unworthiest hand
This holy shrine, the gentle fine is this:

My lips, two blushing pilgrims, ready stand
To smooth that rough touch with a tender kiss.
Juliet: Good pilgrim, you do wrong your hand too much,
Which mannerly devotion shows in this;
For saints have hands that pilgrims' hands do touch,
And palm to palm is holy palmers' kiss.
Romeo: Have not saints lips, and holy palmers too?
Juliet: Ay, pilgrim, lips that they must use in prayer.
Romeo: O, then, dear saint, let lips do what hands do;
They pray—grant thou, lest faith turn to despair.
Juliet: Saints do not move, though grant for prayers' sake.
Romeo: Then move not, while my prayer's effect I take.

Dramatic Poetry

Many poets create dramatic narrative poetry by having two or more characters exchange dialogue within a poem. The characters, however, do not perform onstage, nor is the poem meant to be acted out. The ballad form relies on dialogue and drama to present its narrative.

As an exercise, write a poetic scene that includes both narration and dialogue. To keep the poetic feel, however, maintain a regular metric pattern as you go, perhaps by using iambic pentameter. You can even attempt to use rhymes or alliteration to add to the music of the language. Read the poem aloud to hear its rhythm.

An example of a dramatic poem using dialogue is Robert Frost's "Home Burial." This poem renders a brief but emotionally powerful scene between a husband and a wife who have lost a child. The tension mounts between the characters as the wife becomes disgusted and horrified by the husband's growing anger and violence. The poem actually ends in mid-speech, with the husband menacing the wife. In this way, the dialogue adds to the suspense of the poem.

The Monologue

The *monologue* is closely related to the drama. The monologue, though, has one trait that distinguishes it. While two or more actors perform the drama, and the point of view disappears behind the action on the stage, the monologue involves only one speaker.

FACT

Robert Browning (1812–1889) didn't receive much acclaim for his serious poetry until the end of his life. He was better known as the husband of Elizabeth Barrett and the author of "The Pied Piper of Hamelin."

The speaker of the monologue can be addressing an audience or can simply be speaking within his or her own mind. You have already looked at a portion of such a monologue in Chapter 5, Robert Browning's "Soliloquy of the Spanish Cloister" (page 58). Here is another portion of this poem:

> Gr-r-r—there go, my heart's abhorrence!
>   Water your damned flower-pots, do!
> If hate killed men, Brother Lawrence,
>   God's blood, would not mine kill you!
> What? your myrtle-bush wants trimming?
>   Oh, that rose has prior claims—
> Needs its leaden vase filled brimming?
>   Hell dry you up with its flames!
>
> At the meal we sit together;
>   Salve tibi![1] I must hear
> Wise talk of the kind of weather,
>   Sort of season, time of year:
> Not a plenteous cork-crop: scarcely
>   Dare we hope oak-galls, I doubt:
> What's the Latin name for "parsley"?
>   What's the Greek name for "swine's snout"?

[1] *Latin for "Hail to thee!"*

You might have noticed some words set down in italics—these are prayers or bits of dialogue that seem ordinary but that contrast sharply with what the speaker is actually thinking. As an exercise, write a monologue of your own in which the character's actions and spoken words similarly contrast with his thoughts.

Lyric Poetry

The word *lyric* is derived from the word *lyre*, an ancient musical instrument used throughout Europe and the Middle East. Lyrics were the words written to accompany the music of the lyre and therefore were originally songs. Nowadays, a lyric poem is considered a short but intense moment of insight set down by the poet.

The lyric does not have to contain a narrative, though it may, and it does not have to be long, though it may stretch for several lines. But the lyric should focus on an experience that is unique to the vision of the poet. For the sake of discussion, you can classify many—but not all—lyric poems by the experiences they contain. Three main categories of lyrics are those that center on an image, those that center on an emotion, and those that center on an argument.

Imagery

To get an idea of how imagery works in poetry, consider your own face in a mirror. You may see the shape of your head, the fall of your hair, the tone of your skin, the color of your eyes, and so on. But remember that the image you see in the mirror is a reflection; you are actually seeing yourself backwards, and not as others see you. The quality of the glass in the mirror and its reflective materials will also affect the image you see. Distortions of light, shape, and dimension will occur no matter how close or far away you hold the mirror.

Writing poetry is like holding up a mirror to what you sense, remember, dream, or think; your poems are reflections of all those things, not the things themselves. However, the images you create in your poetry can be very powerful, and many lyric poems derive their meaning from a strong image placed directly in their center. William Blake's poem "The Tyger" is an effort to solve the mystery of that fierce animal's dreadful power. The tiger is obviously the central image, and the poet explores each feature of the tiger's body, asking what greater being could have created such a beast. In addition to the imagery, notice the meter and the rhyme, which reinforce the poem's message.

Tyger! Tyger! burning bright
In the forests of the night,
What immortal hand or eye
Could frame thy fearful symmetry?

In what distant deeps or skies
Burnt the fire of thine eyes?
On what wings dare he aspire?
What the hand, dare seize the fire?

And what shoulder, & what art,
Could twist the sinews of thy heart?
And when thy heart began to beat,
What dread hand? & what dread feet?

What the hammer? what the chain?
In what furnace was thy brain?
What the anvil? what dread grasp
Dare its deadly terrors clasp?

When the stars threw down their spears,
And water'd heaven with their tears,
Did he smile his work to see?
Did he who made the Lamb make thee?

Tyger! Tyger! burning bright
In the forests of the night,
What immortal hand or eye
Dare frame thy fearful symmetry?

As an exercise, you might try to focus on a similar image—one that instills fear or awe in you—as the subject of a poem. You'll notice that Blake proposes several questions in this poem. This is a great way to explore a subject. In your poem, you might consider using this method. Even if you don't come up with the answers to your questions, it might be a more exciting way to present the subject matter.

FACT

William Blake (1757–1827) was a forerunner of the Romantic school of poetry begun by William Wordsworth and Samuel Coleridge. His longer verses conceive an entire mythology of spirits and forces centered around the island of Albion. He was an accomplished artist, too, creating pictures for many of his lyrics.

Emotion

Lyrics based upon emotions can take readers through a wide range of human experiences. However, emotions can be even more difficult to evoke in poetry than images. Your reader must be able to recognize and feel the emotion using the small pieces of information offered by your words. A reader will not feel the exact same emotion you did when you began writing, but he will probably be able to sympathize with you by recalling a similar personal experience or feeling.

"On My First Son" by Ben Jonson is a strong example of emotion being the center of a lyric poem. In essence, the poem is a tender goodbye from a father who has lost his son. In the first line, Jonson uses the phrase "child of my right hand"—the translation of the Hebrew name Benjamin (his own and his son's name), to give final recognition to the relationship they shared.

Farewell, thou child of my right hand, and joy;
My sin was too much hope of thee, lov'd boy:
Seven years thou wert lent to me, and I thee pay,
Exacted by thy fate, on the just day[1].
Oh could I lose all father now! For why
Will man lament the state he should env'y,

To have so soon 'scaped world's and flesh's rage,
And, if no other misery, yet age?
Rest in soft peace, and asked, say, "Here doth lie
Ben Jonson his best piece of poetry."
For whose sake henceforth all his vows be such
As what he loves may never like too much.

[1] *That is, on the anniversary of the very day he was born*

FACT

Ben Jonson (1573–1637), like his contemporary William Shakespeare, was a poet and a playwright. His most famous play is *Volpone*, about a man who tricks his friends out of money and gifts. In 1619, Jonson was made the first poet laureate of England. Though Shakespeare is more widely recognized, his and Jonson's works share many similarities.

Jonson's poem is so compelling, in part, due to the extreme sadness of the subject matter. However, a poem doesn't have to focus on such strong material to effectively portray emotion. If you want to write a poem about a shattered dish or a dark storm cloud, you can still make it forceful and engaging. As long as you describe your feelings to your reader in great detail, the emotion will come through.

Argument

If you took a composition course in college, you may remember that an argument is a stance taken on an issue, with concrete details marshaled to support that stance. Many poems are written with this idea in mind—the speaker takes a stance on an issue and attempts to sway the reader, or a listener within the poem, toward his or her point of view.

A famous example of such a lyric is found in Robert Herrick's poem "To the Virgins, to Make Much of Time." In the poem, the speaker exhorts his listener to "go marry" and "be not coy" when she is young, for there is plenty of time for tarrying when one is old. Herrick sets out his argument in the first stanza of the poem, following:

> *Gather ye rosebuds while ye may:*
> *Old Time is still a-flying;*
> *And this same flower that smiles today,*
> *Tomorrow will be dying.*

The poetic form can help persuade your reader even further. While Herrick's poem will not convince all readers, the rhythm of the words and the rhyme he uses strengthens the argument. Even if you don't agree with his opinion on the subject, it's difficult not to be impressed by his skill. Try this method in your own poetry and see what responses you receive.

Present an argument within a poem of your own. To do this, you must select a controversial issue and support one side of it. You may choose to argue that both genders are equally intelligent, that dogs are better than cats, or that spring is a superior season to winter. Whatever your argument, be sure to support your claims thoroughly.

Open Form

An open-form poem is exactly what it sounds like. You can choose to use or not to use rhyme. You may follow a strict meter or vary your patterns to create different effects. Line breaks are not regulated by a certain number of feet or syllables, and the numbers of lines in a stanza, if you choose to use stanzas at all, can vary to suit your vision for the poem. The open form also allows you to move the lines around on the page. You can be creative with a poem's appearance, and even give it a certain shape on the paper. To help you understand open-form poetry, you may want to consider its most widespread form, *free verse*.

Elements of Free Verse

Though some free verse may look like prose, it actually carries more weight per word, due to compressed language. Using compressed language is a means of making fewer words do more. You can use several strategies and tools to create compressed language. Some of these include denotative and connotative meanings, figures of speech, symbolism, the repetition of key words, structures, images, and ideas, the altering of syntax, and the omission of words such as conjunctions, articles, and prepositions.

The aesthetics of a poem—the way it looks on a page—will also have an immediate effect upon a reader. You should thus be aware of the length of the lines, the line breaks and indentations (if any), the stanza breaks (if any), and the size of the page upon which the poem will appear. Some poets even choose to have the shape of a poem mimic a recognizable image, like a flower or a house, depending on the subject matter.

In free verse, poets must rely more strongly on language to move the energy of a poem from line to line. Ending lines with stressed syllables will help to create the energy you need to move your readers through your poem. Generally speaking, nouns and action verbs will always receive stress.

In free verse, each line should contain its own image or part of an image to make it distinct. To make each line stand out to the reader, you should create vivid descriptions to evoke specific responses. Careful readers should come away from each line with a sensory impression and with another piece of information to add to their understanding of the poem as a whole.

An Example of Free Verse

"*Tarzan* Episode 716: Jane Walks to the Watering Hole" by Todd Scott Moffett is an example of a free-verse poem. When you read the following first few lines of this poem, notice the arrangement of the lines and the effect of the separated lines acting almost like a second poem. Also, take note of the way each line ends, and the images contained within the lines.

The crazy chimpanzees spring
            like bandits

from the curtain of green trees.

> *She's too tired*

to scream anymore, the

> *humid jungle*

thickening her hair against

> *her glistening neck.*

Keeping this poem and the elements of free verse in mind, try an exercise. Take a favorite poem written by someone else, and explore its form to change its shape and rhythm. Don't alter the words or the order of the words—simply play with the line lengths, the line breaks, the stanza forms, and so on, to see how the poem looks in its new arrangement. Is it better or worse than the original?

Closed Form

Closed-form poetry dominated the canon for so many centuries that many people still think it is the only way to create poetry. Of course, this is not the case. But if you feel that free verse is too free for you, then you can also try the many closed forms available. You will learn about these forms in depth later in the book, but for now, take a look at the general ways closed-form poems may be classified:

- *Metered verse:* poems that fall under a metrical pattern like trochaic tetrameter or dactylic hexameter (*Blank verse*, a common form of metrical verse, is written in iambic pentameter.)
- *Rhymed verse:* poems that follow a strict rhyme scheme (Many rhymed verses will also follow a strict meter.)
- *Accentual verse:* poems that rely on a number of stressed syllables per line (These stressed syllables can be alliterated, usually three or four times per line, to form alliterative verse.)
- *Repeated verse:* poems that rely on a pattern of repeated words or lines
- *Syllabics:* poems that rely on a certain number of syllables in each line, or in the poem itself

Songs and Other Melodies

Though songs and poems follow similar forms and patterns, today they are often seen as very distinct. Songs are much more a part of popular culture, as they have the added effects of instrumentation and voice. Despite these distinctions, many poets try their hand at songwriting. For example, Ben Jonson wrote the following song, "Song: To Celia":

> Drink to me only with thine eyes
>> And I will pledge with mine;
> Or leave a kiss but in the cup,
>> And I'll not ask for wine.
> The thirst that from the soul doth rise
>> Doth ask a drink divine;
> But might I of Jove's nectar sup
>> I would not change for thine.
>
> I sent thee late a rosy wreath,
>> Not so much honoring thee
> As giving it a hope that there
>> It could not withered be
> But thou thereon didst only breath
>> And sent'st it back to me;
> Since when it grows and smells, I swear,
>> Not of itself but thee.

To hear this song performed, you might not recognize its poetic structure. But behind the melody are the same meter and rhyme scheme underlying the ballad form. This work is not actually a ballad—the song does not contain a narrative—but Jonson did use a popular song pattern. In fact, this pattern became so widespread that it even constitutes the basis of the songs people sing in church.

The Common Meter

If you attend a Christian church, you very likely sing songs from a hymnal during service. Many songs found in hymnals follow a pattern called *common meter*. This structure, like the ballad, organizes its lines in an 8-6-8-6 syllable pattern and divides the lines into quatrains. Also like the ballad, you have your choice of the ABAB or the XAXA rhyme schemes. Here is an example of the common meter from a well-known hymn:

Amazing Grace! How sweet the sound
That saved a wretch like me!
I once was lost, but now am found,
Was blind, but now I see.

Can you see the common meter structure within this song? For more practice with this form, write out the lyrics from other hymns and try to break them up into lines. Some children's songs may also follow this pattern.

Modern Music

In the last 120 years or so, songwriters have relied on another common pattern. Popular songs during this period, regulated largely by the storage space of phonograph records and by radio airtime, usually take three or four minutes to play. To meet this demand, the modern song is divided into four major portions, with one or two minor ones added here and there for variety.

The first minor portion is an introduction, which begins the song. The introduction can be an instrumental riff or vocal introduction by the singer that establishes a context for the song. The first major portion of the song, the first verse, usually follows the introduction. A refrain (a repeated line) or a chorus (a repeated stanza) follows the first verse. Immediately after the first verse comes the second verse, followed by its refrain or chorus. Musically, the first two verses are very similar; they use the same melody in the music, the same lines, and the same rhyme schemes.

The third major portion marks a break from the previous two. This section can be marked by a performer's solo, or it can be marked in the song itself by a change in the melody and in the line and rhyme patterns of the words. Following this break comes the final major portion, the fourth verse, which returns to the melody and line patterns established in the first two verses. Another minor portion—perhaps another solo, or another vocal interlude by the singer—will usually finish the song.

Of course, several variations upon this basic pattern occur. A song might begin with the chorus, for example, or jump right into the first verse. The solo may come in a different section, or it may be extended, as in a live performance, with different musicians taking turns. But in general, the variations are easy to track once you understand the basic pattern.

Chapter 8

Sonnets, Odes, and Ghazals

Three poetic forms with a long history in European and Middle Eastern literature are the *sonnet*, the *ode*, and the *ghazal*. Because they began as closed-form poems, they may strike you as formal in appearance and tone. Modern-day poetics, however, allow you to be more playful with the rules. Feel free to explore these forms in any way you like.

Little Songs

In Italian, the word *sonnet* literally means "little song." This translation is actually a good way to start a discussion about this popular form. Like a song, the traditional sonnet depends upon meter and rhyme to give energy to the lines. Also like a song, the traditional sonnet resolves itself by the final lines; it does not leave you with any open-ended questions to ponder.

The sonnet had been a popular form in Italy for at least 200 years before its introduction into English poetics during the Renaissance. The early English sonneteers discovered that the original sonnet form, as the Italians developed it, was hard to reproduce in English. The Italian language has many natural true rhymes, but in English, rhyming does not come as easily. The English sonneteers, therefore, developed their own rhyme pattern to accommodate the difficulties raised by their language.

The Italian (or Petrarchan) Rhyme Scheme

The Italian rhyme scheme, as it has been translated into English, has two parts: the *octave* (an eight-line scheme) and the *sestet* (a six-line scheme). The poem is therefore fourteen lines long and divided into unequal halves. In the octave, the lines rhyme like this: ABBAABBA. In the sestet, you have your choice of many schemes, including: CDECDE, CCDCCD, or CDCDCD. The content of the sonnet is organized around this division as well. Any images or ideas begun in the octave must be resolved so that a new set can be developed in the sestet. A turning point or transition word, called a *volta*, is often inserted at the beginning of the sestet to mark the division. The meter, too, is strictly regulated. Each line in the sonnet must be in iambic pentameter. While alternate feet may appear in the poem, the iamb is dominant and so establishes the rhythm of the poem.

Consider an example of the Italian sonnet form: "On First Looking into Chapman's Homer," by John Keats. Note that Keats uses the CDCDCD scheme in the sestet. Also, take note of his use of the word *then* in line nine as the volta.

Much have I travell'd in the realms of gold,
And many goodly states and kingdoms seen;

Round many western islands have I been
Which bards in fealty to Apollo hold.
Oft on one wide expanse had I been told
That deep-brow'd Homer ruled as his demesne;
Yet did I never breathe its pure serene
Till I heard Chapman speak out loud and bold:
Then felt I like some watcher of the skies
When a new planet swims into his ken;
Or like stout Cortez when with eagle eyes
He star'd at the Pacific—and all his men
Look'd at each other with a wild surmise—
Silent, upon a peak in Darien[1].

[1] *A region of Panama*

FACT

John Keats (1795–1821) was orphaned at a young age and trained to be a physician before dedicating his life to poetry. He is most famous for his odes and for his long poem *Endymion*. At the height of his poetic career, however, he was struck down by tuberculosis.

The English (or Shakespearean) Rhyme Scheme

The English version of the sonnet is also fourteen lines long, but the rhyme scheme divides the poem into four unequal parts. The first three parts are quatrains because they each consist of four lines. The last part is called a *couplet* because it consists of two lines. Taken together, the quatrains and the couplet create the following rhyme scheme: ABABCDCDEFEFGG.

Like the Italian sonnet, the English sonnet imposes its form upon the content of the poem. For anyone strictly following the standards, each quatrain in the poem should have its own image or idea. When a new quatrain begins, a new image or idea should start. A volta usually signals the transition along with the change in the rhyming words. The final couplet also has its own controlling idea, often one that comments upon the themes developed in the quatrains. The meter of the English sonnet, like the Italian, is strictly regulated. Iambic pentameter dominates the poem. Alternate feet, when they appear, provide a conversational rhythm or different shades of meaning for particular words.

The following is a Shakespearean sonnet (Sonnet 130) displaying this rhyme scheme. Pay close attention to the content of this sonnet as it provides a satiric look at a common sonnet convention—effusive praise of one's love.

My mistress' eyes are nothing like the sun;
Coral is far more red than her lips' red;
If snow be white, why then her breasts are dun,
If hairs be wires, black wires grow on her head.
I have seen roses damask'd red and white,
But no such roses see I in her cheeks;
And in some perfumes is there more delight
Than in the breath that from my mistress reeks.
I love to hear her speak, yet well I know,
That music hath a far more pleasing sound;
I grant I never saw a goddess go:
My mistress, when she walks, treads on the ground.
And yet, by heaven, I think my love as rare
As any she belied with false compare.

Build a Sonnet

Creating a sonnet is no easy task. Therefore, don't expect to produce a perfect sonnet on your first, second, or even third try. You must be patient with yourself while your skills develop. However, there are several tools you can use and exercises you can do to practice. To do these exercises properly you will need to give yourself plenty of time, limit your distractions, and work with them consistently over the course of several days. Also, remember that these exercises are only meant to familiarize you with the structure of a sonnet—the subject matter is entirely up to you.

Using Rhyme

A good place to start is the sound of the sonnet. Since you have two rhyme schemes to choose from, your first exercise will be to gather two groups of fourteen words. Arrange one set of words to form an Italian rhyme scheme, and arrange the other using the English rhyme scheme. The words do not have to make any sense when you put them together in this exercise; they simply have to rhyme. Consider the following example:

Rhyme Scheme Exercise	
Italian	**English**
oppose	sing
bend	book
defend	ring
repose	nook
impose	burn
end	day
send	return
suppose	play
store	reveal
ask	phone
seem	deal
ignore	blown
task	sense
redeem	intense

Once you have your lists, look at each word. Did you include words with more than one syllable? Did you use a lot of nouns and verbs? You need to be aware of your choices for two main reasons. Not only do these ending words have to rhyme, but, for the most part, they must also fall into the iambic foot pattern. You will be creating masculine or rising rhymes, so the stresses of any polysyllabic words should fall on the last syllable.

Constructing the Lines

Now, try an exercise for creating the lines of a sonnet. Begin by writing a descriptive passage of forty to seventy words. Use your surrounding environment, personal feelings, or a memory for inspiration. Here's an example:

A cloth doll is sitting on the sofa beside me. She has tan flannel skin that is soft to the touch. She is wearing a green felt dress over a yellow felt shirt and red felt booties. She has brown yarn hair tied in a pink flannel bow. She has black bead eyes, brown felt eyebrows, green felt cheeks, and lavender felt lips turned up in a smile.

The next step is to arrange this passage into lines of ten syllables each. Remember that the sonnet form calls for lines in iambic pentameter, meaning five two-syllable feet. At this point, you do not need to worry about foot patterns or rhymes. Just worry about getting the right number of syllables in the line. Here's how the previous passage looks when set into lines:

A cloth doll is sitting on the sofa
beside me. She has tan flannel skin that
is soft to the touch. She is wearing a
green felt dress over a yellow felt shirt
and red felt booties. She has brown yarn hair
tied in a pink flannel bow. She has black
bead eyes, brown felt eyebrows, pink felt cheeks, and
lavender felt lips turned up in a smile.

The example passage just happened to have enough syllables to create eight ten-syllable lines. But don't be discouraged if the passage you write does not have a perfect syllable count. When you write a real sonnet, these details will be more important; but this exercise is just for practice. And the more practice, the better. Try this exercise several more times with other descriptions you have written or with passages from books, magazines, or newspapers. The source is not important as long as the passage has fairly concrete details. Once you have done this exercise a number of times, you will notice your passages looking more and more like poems.

Finding Your Footing

The next step is to get used to the iambic foot pattern that dominates the sonnet form. A brief exercise will help you get started on this. First, create two lists: One list should contain single words of two or more syllables that have stress on the last syllable, and the second list should be made up of monosyllabic word pairs in which the second word receives the stress. These words do not have to rhyme.

ALERT!

When writing a sonnet you will inevitably need to move and change your words several times before you meet the requirements for the form. This being the case, you should always keep extra paper, erasers, and whiteout nearby so you can quickly make changes to your draft. It's also a good idea to periodically rewrite or type out the entire poem so you can continue working with a clean copy.

If you are not sure where the stresses fall, remember the rules of thumb you learned in Chapter 6. Also, listen to your voice as you say the words out loud. With stressed syllables, your voice goes up in pitch and volume, and you pronounce all the letters; with unstressed syllables, your voice goes down in pitch and volume, and you may dampen or omit the vowel sounds. As a last resort, look up the words in the dictionary to discover where their stresses lie. Here's an example:

Iambic Pattern Exercise	
Single Words	**Word Pairs**
above	in shock
delight	a sound
recede	by noon
enfold	the wall
transcribe	an egg

Iambic Pattern Exercise (continued)	
Single Words	**Word Pairs**
unleash	on time
believe	at school
dispel	its tail
incite	was tired
confuse	with love

A second exercise for training yourself in meter is a bit more complicated. Start with another forty- to seventy-word description, arrange the words so that ten syllables fall into each line, and then arrange or change the words so that the lines are dominated by the iambic foot pattern. Again, the words don't have to rhyme, and not every foot in each line has to be iambic, but most of the feet must have the unstressed-STRESSED pattern. Recalling the previous passage about the doll, consider the following:

> A doll is sitting on the sofa next
> to me. Her skin's a flannel tan that's soft
> to touch. She wears a green felt dress atop
> a yellow felt shirt, and red baby boot-
> ies. A pink flannel bow ties down her hair,
> the brown yarn strands cut short and neat. Brown felt
> eyebrows above her black bead eyes, pink felt
> cheeks. Her lavender felt lips curl a smile.

This time, your passage should have the same number of syllables in each line. But don't worry if it doesn't—if the last line of your earlier draft has fewer than ten syllables, you have space to make changes. Notice that many changes were needed to make this doll passage fit the meter, and it still isn't perfect.

If you scan these lines, you will notice that they aren't all in a perfect iambic pentameter. However, the iamb comes through enough to create a rhythm that works behind the surface beats of each line. Once you have completed this step for yourself, your lines will be in blank verse—unrhymed lines of ten syllables dominated by iambs.

The next step—which is significantly more difficult—is to try to make your lines rhyme. However, if you feel you're not quite ready for this challenge, you can try a simpler exercise to practice with rhyme and meter before returning to your blank verse. Go back to one of your rhyming lists, get another sheet of paper, and write lines of iambic pentameter, placing those rhyming words at the ends. The lines don't have to make sense when you put them together; they just have to obey the rhyme scheme.

About Odes

While the sonnet is an old form, the ode dates back even further. Forms of the ode appeared in ancient Greek plays and were originally sung by the chorus between the scenes. These ode forms involved a three-part structure: the *strophe*, during which the chorus danced to the left; the *antistrophe*, during which the chorus danced to the right; and the *epode*, during which the chorus stood still.

Another form of the ode was performed at public events, such as athletic games. One of the most famous poets of antiquity, Pindar, sang odes to the victors of wrestling matches, chariot races, foot races, and other events. Aside from glorifying the athlete, his family, and his trainer, Pindar was careful to speak highly of the gods and of the athlete's city of origin. Pindar also followed the three-part structure for the ode found in the Greek plays. The lengths of the stanzas and the lines could vary from poem to poem, but usually, within the same poem, the strophe and the antistrophe had the same stanza form and number of lines, while the epode had a different form and number.

FACT

Pindar (522–443 B.C.) came from a family that claimed descent from the founders of the city of Thebes, where the story of Oedipus takes place. Horace (65–8 B.C.) came from a family of freed slaves but worked his way into prominence in the fledgling Roman Empire.

The most famous writer of odes in Roman times, Horace, adjusted the form of the poem. He did not follow the older three-part structure but rather used quatrains that contained stricter line lengths and a regular rhyme scheme. Like Pindar, however, Horace continued to exalt the subjects of his poems and make many references to the gods.

The Romantic poets of England, particularly Wordsworth, Keats, and Shelley, created masterpieces with new renditions of the ode form. They experimented freely with rhyme schemes, lengths of lines, and lengths of stanzas, and they wrote about objects, people, and places that inspired a contemplative mood. The tone of the ode, as a result, became less overbearing and more refined.

Ode Form

As you have probably surmised, the form of the ode is not nearly as strict as that of the sonnet. Generally speaking, though, the ode should be long enough to be read aloud to an audience, without exceeding a length of about two pages. As far as content, you should offer praise for or a meditation on your subject, whether it's the president of the United States or a caterpillar. For this reason, the ode is usually a lyric, and it can center on imagery, emotion, or argument. Consider the following ode by John Keats, "Ode on a Grecian Urn":

> *Thou still unravish'd bride of quietness,*
> *Thou foster-child of Silence and slow Time,*
> *Sylvan historian, who canst thus express*
> *A flowery tale more sweetly than our rhyme:*
> *What leaf-fring'd legend haunts about thy shape*
> *Of deities or mortals, or of both,*
> *In Tempe or the dales of Arcady?*
> *What men or gods are these? What maidens loth?*
> *What mad pursuit? What struggle to escape?*
> *What pipes and timbrels? What wild ecstasy?*
>
> *Heard melodies are sweet, but those unheard*
> *Are sweeter; therefore, ye soft pipes, play on;*

Not to the sensual ear, but, more endear'd,
　　Pipe to the spirit ditties of no tone:
Fair youth, beneath the trees, thou canst not leave
　　Thy song, nor ever can those trees be bare;
　　　Bold Lover, never, never canst thou kiss,
Though winning near the goal—yet, do not grieve;
　　She cannot fade, though thou hast not thy bliss,
　　For ever wilt thou love, and she be fair!

Ah, happy, happy boughs! that cannot shed
　　Your leaves, nor ever bid the Spring adieu;
And, happy melodist, unwearièd,
　　For ever piping songs for ever new;
More happy love! more happy, happy love!
　　For ever warm and still to be enjoy'd,
　　　For ever panting, and for ever young;
All breathing human passion far above,
　　That leaves a heart high-sorrowful and cloy'd,
　　　A burning forehead, and a parching tongue.

Who are these coming to the sacrifice?
　　To what green altar, O mysterious priest,
Lead'st thou that heifer lowing at the skies,
　　And all her silken flanks with garlands drest?
What little town by river or sea-shore,
　　Or mountain-built with peaceful citadel,
　　　Is emptied of its folk, this pious morn?
And, little town, thy streets for evermore
　　Will silent be; and not a soul, to tell
　　　Why thou art desolate, can e'er return.

O Attic shape! fair attitude! with brede
　　Of marble men and maidens overwrought,
With forest branches and the trodden weed;
　　Thou, silent form! dost tease us out of thought
As doth eternity: Cold Pastoral!

> *When old age shall this generation waste,*
> *Thou shalt remain, in midst of other woe*
> *Than ours, a friend to man, to whom thou say'st,*
> *"Beauty is truth, truth beauty,"—that is all*
> *Ye know on earth, and all ye need to know.*

You may have noted that the speaker of Keats's poem addresses his subjects directly, sometimes beginning with the word *O*. This form of direct address, also known as the *vocative*, is a common feature of the ode and may be an element you include in odes of your own.

Build an Ode

As with the sonnet, there are several exercises that will help you create an ode. Since the ode is freer in form than the sonnet, the exercises will not be as structured. To begin, write a description of an object or person, as you did for the sonnet exercises. This time, however, you can experiment with the number of syllables in each line. Instead of the regular ten-syllable lines you created before, you might come up with a stanza that looks like this:

> *A cloth doll is*
> *sitting on the sofa beside*
> *me. She has tan*
> *flannel skin that is soft to the*
> *touch. She is wearing a*
> *green felt dress over a yellow*
> *felt shirt and red felt boot-*
> *ies. She has brown yarn hair tied in*
> *a pink flannel*
> *bow. She has black bead eyes, brown felt*
> *eyebrows, pink felt*
> *cheeks, and lavender felt lips turned*
> *up in a smile.*

In this example, a 4-8-4-8-6-8-6-8-4-8-4-8-4 syllable pattern is used, but you can choose any pattern that you wish. In fact, you should experiment with several syllable patterns to see how the lines look. Just comparing this exercise to the one created for the sonnet should show you how different a poem can look simply by changing the line lengths.

Because an ode generally offers praise for a certain subject, most odes use the title template "Ode to . . ." If you want to express your appreciation for your father, you could use the title "Ode to My Father." Even if you want to write about something minor or trivial, like ice cream or autumn leaves, you can still use this title. The title identifies your poem as an ode right from the start.

Once finished with this exercise, you can go in a couple of different directions. For example, if you want to practice the Pindaric ode, you will have to settle on a syllable pattern, then write a second stanza in the exact same pattern (the antistrophe), and then write a third (and final) stanza (the epode) with its own pattern. If you want to practice the Horatian ode, then you will have to form your lines into quatrains. You will also have to think about a meter. If you want to copy the ornate patterns created by Keats, Shelley, and others, then you will have to look over their poems closely to get a sense of their meter and rhyme scheme, and work with or against those patterns.

The Ghazal

The ghazal (pronounced like the word *guzzle*) developed in Persia (now Iran) some time during the tenth century. Originally written as a song of praise for a king, the form acquired other subjects over the centuries, among the most common being women and wine. As such, the subject matter has often been somewhat erotic. In modern times, however, the ghazal has been used as a song of protest, with highly charged political messages. Appropriately, the ghazal was adopted into American poetics during the 1960s.

Formal Requirements

The requirements for the ghazal, as it is still composed in the Middle East, make the poem quite a challenge in English—mostly because of the rhyme scheme. The entire poem is composed of five to twelve couplets. All of the couplets follow a strict syllable count—nineteen for each line. The first couplet of the poem must rhyme, and the last line of every following couplet must rhyme with this first stanza. Hence, for a five-stanza ghazal, you have the following rhyme scheme: AA BA CA DA EA.

ALERT!

In addition to the end rhymes, all of the rhyming lines in a ghazal have an internal rhyme. So, somewhere in the middle of those lines, you must have a word that rhymes with the word on the end. Therefore, in a five-couplet ghazal, you have to include twelve words that rhyme.

Despite the complex rhyme scheme, each couplet in the poem is a self-contained unit. Every couplet develops its own image or idea, almost as if it is a separate poem. The last couplet contains the poet's "signature"—her real name or pen name, and perhaps a message of a personal nature.

Informal Requirements

English-speaking poets have changed the requirements in order to make the ghazal more flexible. For example, some poets have modified the rhyme scheme so that the internal rhymes have been dropped and the end rhymes are limited to the couplets. The resulting rhyme scheme, AA BB CC, and so on, is far easier to manage in English. Some poets have even dropped the rhyme scheme altogether.

English-speaking poets have also done away with the syllable counts for the lines and the poet's signature in the final stanza. The requirement that each couplet be independent has become optional as well. The result of all these changes is a poem that retains only its reliance on five to twelve couplets. In this stripped-down version, the ghazal could be considered a free-verse poem.

Build a Ghazal

Because the ghazal has so many different requirements, it actually makes a good form with which to practice various exercises. First, you need to write out a 70- to 100-word description. You can borrow the one you wrote for the sonnet, but it would be good practice to write another one. Next, arrange your description into couplets. Here's how such an arrangement might look:

A cloth doll is sitting on the sofa beside me.
She has tan flannel skin that is soft to the touch.

She is wearing a green felt dress over a yellow felt shirt
and red felt booties. She has brown yarn hair tied in a pink flannel bow.

She has black bead eyes, brown felt eyebrows, green felt
cheeks, and lavender felt lips turned up in a smile.

Here the couplets are broken to keep one or two images intact in each line and to make each couplet end with a sense of completion. If you want, you can attempt to maintain the nineteen-syllable rule of the original form. The lines you create will be very long, but the length will allow for more detail.

If you use the description that you wrote for the sonnet, you should be able to see a clear distinction between the couplets you create for the ghazal and the ten-syllable lines you created for the sonnet. The couplets provide a greater sense of space, the longer lines being more sluggish and slow moving.

Also, pay attention to rhyme in your ghazal. You can try the rhyming couplet pattern that English-speaking poets have used (AA BB CC), or you can try the AA BA CA scheme and just stick to creating end rhymes. If you feel daring, however, you can try the AA BA CA scheme and attempt the internal rhymes called for in the original form. If you created three couplets with your description, as in the previous example, try to assemble three pairs of rhyming words for the first pattern, four rhyming words for the second, and eight words for the third.

An Example of the Ghazal

Here is an example of a modern ghazal written by Jeff Knorr called "What Would My Father Have Done?" Note that Knorr retains a flavor of the original rhyme scheme. He also retains the couplet form and the stanza count. However, he plays freely with the line lengths, and he does not force each couplet to contain its own image.

Coming out of the doctor's office, she's crying.
And there I am tossed against the shore, but

this is no shore because the sand,
that line where water meets land,

is a place for resting.
Logs wash up, glass floats

torn free of a net drift in from Japan.
I don't know what to do.

I know what I'll do later,
bring a bottle of wine,

two glasses upside down, clinking
with each step up stairs.

We'll drink on the bed until she's sleeping.
Later, when some foreign tide of wind recedes,

I'll go out into the backyard to fetch the dog,
and cry under the hopelessly descending moon.

Reprinted with the permission of the author.

Chapter 9

The Sestina, Pantoum, and Villanelle

The sestina, pantoum, and villanelle are three repeated verse forms from Europe and the Far East. As you explore these forms, pay attention to how the repeated lines and words affect the meaning of the poems, reinforce key images and themes, or create the sounds and rhythms that give the poems their musical quality. You should also be aware of how the poems come to a resolution, building upon the rhythms of the repetitions to reach a satisfying climax of meaning and sound in the final verses.

Poem of the Troubadours

Sometime during the 1200s in southern France, troubadours—traveling groups of singers and poets—created several verse forms, one of which is the modern *sestina*. The form of the sestina has changed little over the centuries. It contains six stanzas of six lines each, and a final tercet of three lines, called the *envoi* or "sendoff." Like the villanelle and the pantoum, the sestina does not rely on a meter. Unlike the villanelle and the pantoum, the sestina repeats only the end words, not the entire line, so you have more freedom to construct your verses.

ALERT!

The sestina form that you see here should not be confused with the sestet that you encountered with the sonnet. Though both get their names from the fact that they contain six lines, the sestina form does not depend on a rhyme scheme or a meter, while the sonnet's sestet has a very strict rhyme and meter.

The sestina has an intricate pattern for repeating the last words of the lines. It is not as simple to explain as the villanelle or the pantoum, so you will have to rely on the following chart to keep track of it. Remember that the letters in the chart stand for repeated end words, not for rhymes or lines.

Pattern of a Sestina	
Stanza	**End Words**
1	ABCDEF
2	FAEBDC
3	CFDABE
4	ECBFAD
5	DEACFB
6	BDFECA
7	B, E (first line); D, C (second line); F, A (third line)

The sestina rotates the end words until they appear in each position in a stanza. In the envoi, since that stanza has only three lines, two of the end words will appear in each line. However, one of the end words appears in the middle of the line while the other appears at the end. Hence, in the first line of the envoi, for example, end word *B* will appear somewhere in the middle of the line, and end word *E* will appear at the end.

As an example of the sestina form, consider Algernon Charles Swinburne's "Sestina." Using the chart here, follow through his poem to see how the end words appear and how he constructs his envoi.

I saw my soul at rest upon a day
As a bird sleeping in the nest of night,
Among soft leaves that give the starlight way
To touch its wings but not its eyes with light;
So that it knew as one in visions may,
And knew not as men waking, of delight.

This was the measure of my soul's delight;
It had no power of joy to fly by day,
Nor part in the large lordship of the light;
But in a secret moon-beholden way
Had all its will of dreams and pleasant night,
And all the love and life that sleepers may.

But such life's triumph as men waking may
It might not have to feed its faint delight
Between the stars by night and sun by day,
Shut up with green leaves and a little light;
Because its way was as a lost star's way,
A world's not wholly known of day or night.

All loves and dreams and sounds and gleams of night
Made it all music that such minstrels may,
And all they had they gave it of delight;
But in the full face of the fire of day
What place shall be for any starry light,
What part of heaven in all the wide sun's way?

Yet the soul woke not, sleeping by the way,
Watched as a nursling of the large-eyed night,
And sought no strength nor knowledge of the day,
Nor closer touch conclusive of delight,
Nor mightier joy nor truer than dreamers may,
Nor more of song than they, nor more of light.

For who sleeps once and sees the secret light
Whereby sleep shows the soul a fairer way
Between the rise and rest of day and night,
Shall care no more to fare as all men may,
But be his place of pain or of delight,
There shall he dwell, beholding night as day.

Song, have thy day and take thy fill of light
Before the night be fallen across thy way;
Sing while he may, man hath no long delight.

Swinburne has very ambitiously included a rhyme scheme for his end words, and he has brought each line into iambic pentameter. You, however, do not need to create a rhyme or keep to a meter. It is more important that the content of the poem seem natural rather than forced.

The Pantoum

The modern pantoum is based upon a Malayan form called the *pantun* that dates back to the fifteenth century. Like the villanelle and the sestina, the pantoum is not bound to a meter, but unlike the villanelle or the sestina, the pantoum does not have a length limit. It can be several stanzas long or only a couple, depending on your needs. As such, it makes an ideal poem for experimenting with closed forms in general and for practicing repeated verse.

The pantoum form is based on a few simple requirements. First, the entire poem is written in quatrains, the lines being of any reasonable length. Second, you may write with a rhyme scheme of ABAB, or you can avoid the rhyme altogether and work solely with the repetitions that are the basis of the form. Third, those repetitions follow an easy formula: The second and fourth lines (also called *refrains*) of one quatrain become the first and third lines of the following quatrain. Finally, the first and third lines of the opening quatrain are repeated in the final quatrain.

If you were writing a six-stanza pantoum, the scheme would look like this (remember that the letters indicate repeated lines, not rhymes): ABCD, BEDF, EGFH, GIHJ, IKJL, KCLA. Notice that in the closing quatrain, the lines that you repeat from the first stanza flip-flop in order. In other words, line three from the first stanza appears in the second line of the last stanza, while the opening line of the poem becomes the closing line. This graceful sequence makes the poem self-contained, with every line finding an echo somewhere later in the scheme. Several modern poets favor this form; some pantoums you might enjoy include Linda Pastan's "Something about the Trees," Thomas Lux's "All the Slaves," John Ashbery's "Pantoum," and Carolyn Kizer's "Parents' Pantoum."

Vive la Villanelle

As a poetic form, the villanelle passed from France to England sometime during the nineteenth century. American poets picked up the form soon after, and many well-known English-speaking poets have tried the form since. The villanelle is a short poem—only nineteen lines—but the form weaves repetition and rhyme in an intricate pattern. It is created out of three-lined stanzas called *tercets* and a four-lined quatrain. Here is the pattern for its rhyme and repetition: ABA, ABA (repeat line 1), ABA (repeat line 3), ABA (repeat line 1), ABA (repeat line 3), ABA (repeat line 1), A (repeat line 3). This pattern is easier to understand when considering an example.

You may notice that in many poems the first word of each line begins with a capital letter. This has been a poetic convention for centuries—a device used to distinguish poetry from prose—but you do not need to follow it. Poets like e.e. cummings have disregarded this convention and many other poetic principles in the past century.

If you feel the need, you may incorporate slant and eye rhymes, or make small changes to the repeated lines when they reappear, in order to add nuances to the poem. To give you an idea of how the villanelle form has been used by a professional poet, consider Edwin Arlington Robinson's "Villanelle of Change":

Since Persia fell at Marathon,
The yellow years have gathered fast:
Long centuries have come and gone.

And yet (they say) the place will don
A phantom fury of the past,
Since Persia fell at Marathon;

And as of old, when Helicon[1]
Trembled and swayed with rapture vast
(Long centuries have come and gone),

This ancient plain, when night comes on,
Shakes to a ghostly battle-blast,
Since Persia fell at Marathon.

But into soundless Acheron[2]
The glory of Greek shame was cast:
Long centuries have come and gone,

The suns of Hellas[3] have all shone,
The first has fallen to the last: —
Since Persia fell at Marathon,
Long centuries have come and gone.

[1] Mountain in Greece where the Muses, goddesses of the performing arts, would often gather
[2] Underworld river
[3] One of many names for the ancient Greeks

Variation One: The Terzanelle

There are two main variations of the villanelle form that you should be aware of. The first is the *terzanelle*. This form has the same number of lines and stanzas as the villanelle, but it uses a different pattern of repetition. As you will see, the middle line of one tercet is repeated as the refrain in the last line of the next tercet. The entire scheme for the poem looks like this: AB (refrain 1) A, BC (refrain 2) B (refrain 1), CD (refrain 3) C (refrain 2), DE (refrain 4) D (refrain 3), EF (refrain 5) E (refrain 4), FA (repeat line 1) F (refrain 5) A (repeat line 3). The last stanza of the terzanelle has an alternative scheme, FFAA, in which the first line continues the rhyme scheme started in the poem's fourteenth line, the second line repeats refrain 5, the third line repeats the first line of the poem, and the last line repeats the third line of the poem.

The terzanelle gets its name from the rhyme scheme called the *terza rima*, used in the tercets. As you can see from the scheme shown here, the terza rima involves an interlinking pattern—the middle line of one tercet rhymes with the first and last lines of the next tercet. This pattern gives you more resources for rhyming than the villanelle, which limits you to two rhymes. Fewer terzanelles than villanelles have been written, so examples are harder to find, but two that you might enjoy include "Terzanelle in Thunderweather" by Lewis Turco and "Terzanelle at Twilight" by Arpitha Raghunath.

FACT

The *terza rima* has a long and honorable history in Italian poetry. It is said that Dante Alighieri, who wrote *The Divine Comedy*, the masterpiece of the Middle Ages, invented the rhyme and the stanza to honor the Trinity in his work.

Variation Two: The Triolet

The *triolet*, another French form, found its way into English poetry sometime in the seventeenth century. It is a simpler form than the villanelle, and as such may be a good way to warm up to the more difficult form. The triolet is only eight lines long and is built around the repetition of two lines and two rhymes. Here is the scheme of the form: A (refrain 1), B (refrain 2), A (rhymes with line 1), A (refrain 1), A (rhymes with lines 1 and 3), B (rhymes with line 2), A (refrain 1), B (refrain 2).

The trick to the triolet is to add enough meaning to the rhyming lines so that the refrains don't simply repeat what you have said before (the same could be said about the villanelle and the terzanelle). Also, keep in mind that as with the villanelle and the terzanelle, you are not limited by a meter. However, you can work with one if you prefer.

Build a Sestina

Due to the reliance of the sestina, the pantoum, and the villanelle on repeated words or lines, you can practice with the same exercises for all three forms. Getting used to the schemes that govern the repetitions must be your first step in mastering these forms. The first exercise will be to practice the repeating pattern of the sestina. Take six words and arrange them into the pattern called for by the form. Your arrangement might look something like this:

Repetition Exercise						
1	**2**	**3**	**4**	**5**	**6**	**7**
grace	swell	wall	kind	air	yellow	yellow/kind
yellow	grace	swell	wall	kind	air	air/wall
wall	kind	air	yellow	grace	swell	swell/grace
air	yellow	grace	swell	wall	kind	
kind	air	yellow	grace	swell	wall	
swell	wall	kind	air	yellow	grace	

Remember that the last stanza (the envoi), in the form of a tercet, has a pair of the repeated words in each line—one in the middle of the line and one at the end. For example, *yellow* would come in the middle of the tercet's first line and *kind* at the end. In the tercet's second line, *air* would come somewhere in the middle and *wall* at the end. Starting with the list you created, you could write something like this for the first two stanzas:

In the end, it is only by the grace
of God that our souls don't turn yellow
or stumble like drunk monkeys into a wall.
Our words of supplication hold the air
still. If we speak louder, beg, a kind
of frozen chuckle, a swell

of the throat, chokes us. Oh, swell.
Our limbs, exhausted and grace-
less, offer no help. What kind
of gesture could we make anyway? Some yellow-
bellied genuflection, hands sweeping air,
eyes searching the paint on the wall?

This draft has varied the line lengths but maintained the pattern of repeated words. Notice, too, how function and category shift occurs with the words *grace* (noun) and *graceless* (adjective), and *swell* (noun) and *swell* (interjection). Notice also that the end of each line does not necessarily mean the end of a sentence or clause. Once you have your own opening pair of stanzas, you can press onward if you feel inspired, or you can set them aside and wait for more ideas to come.

Build a Pantoum

The next exercise you can try is to take the list of end words you made for the sestina and rearrange the words into the pantoum pattern. You need to remember that the pantoum is built with quatrains rather than the six-lined stanzas used in the sestina, so the words will take up different positions. Some of the words may not make it into the list at all. Remember, too, that the words at the ends of lines one and three in the opening stanza will reappear in lines two and four in the closing stanza, in reverse order. For simplicity's sake, here is one with four stanzas:

Pantoum Exercise			
1	**2**	**3**	**4**
grace	yellow	kind	rain
yellow	kind	rain	wall
wall	air	swell	power
air	swell	power	grace

For this exercise, take the word list that you just created and see if you can begin filling out the lines. Again, your lines don't have to conform to a meter or a rhyme scheme, though the lines shouldn't be so long that they take up the whole page. The exercise you generate might look like this:

In the end, it is only by the grace
of God that our souls don't turn yellow
or stumble like drunk monkeys into a wall.
Our words of supplication still the air.

Our souls don't turn yellow
only because God is kind.
Our words of supplication still the air
or stop the ocean's swell.

Only because God is kind
can we open our eyes, watch the rain,
or stop the ocean's swell.
That is the meaning of power.

Will we open our eyes, watch the rain,
stumble like drunk monkeys into a wall?
That is the meaning of power.
In the end, we live only by God's grace.

Your exercise may be rough and the word choice somewhat awkward, but don't be discouraged. The most important thing to look for is that, aside from a few small exceptions, the refrains repeat as they should throughout the poem. Remember to use enjambment to make some of the lines fit together more smoothly.

Build a Villanelle

Now, try a similar exercise for the villanelle by returning to your end-word lists. Remember: The villanelle gains most of its power through the repetition of lines, but the lines also have to rhyme. So, when you put together your list of ending words, you have to find rhymes for the key words as well. Here's how such a list might look:

Villanelle Exercise					
1	**2**	**3**	**4**	**5**	**6**
grace	race	place	space	brace	lace
kind	find	signed	remind	blind	mind
face	grace	face	grace	face	grace
					face

ALERT!

When you put your rhymes together for a villanelle, don't try to use fancy or unusual words. Surprise is good and necessary, but you will find it very difficult to sustain your rhymes in this form. Words used in ordinary speech will work best.

Now, work with the list you created for the villanelle. Here is an example of a completed exercise:

In the end, we live only by God's grace.
But when we pray, we want the kind
that keeps the pimples from our face.

that keeps our ball clubs in the race
for the pennant. Too late do we find
in the end, we live only by God's grace.

Who cares if there is a place
where the check is always signed?
It won't keep the pimples from our face.

Vain wishes are an empty space.
We need something else to remind
In the end, we live only by God's grace.

Perhaps a shock of cold water to brace
us, a soapy cloth that won't blind,
that keeps the pimples from our face.

The Greeks said our fate is a torn lace.
As we pass, keep this in mind:
In the end, we live only by God's grace,
the one who keeps the pimples from our face.

Because of the heavy repetitions and rhymes, enjambment is difficult to manage in the villanelle. End-stopped lines tend to dominate, creating an even heavier tone. Again, it is important to find natural-sounding words for your rhymes. Practice will only improve your ability to make sense of the lines once you understand the form.

As another exercise, you might take what you have created in your villanelle and shape it into a terzanelle and a triolet. To create the terzanelle, you will have to revise the rhyme scheme completely, and for the triolet, you will have to cut eleven lines. Following are the first seven lines of a terzanelle:

In the end, we live only by God's grace.
But when we pray, we want the kind
that keeps the pimples from our face.

As our vision darkens, too late do we find
that our hands can't grasp what we can't see.
But when we pray, we want the kind

of grace that keeps our lunches free.

Here is a complete triolet:

In the end, we live only by God's grace.
When our vision darkens, it's too hard to find
a soapy cloth to clear the pimples on our face.
In the end, we live only by God's grace.
Why care that our ball club's in the race?
Why care that the check is always signed?
In the end, we live only by God's grace.
When our vision darkens, it's too hard to find.

Other Exercises

There are some other quick exercises you can try to generate the three main forms discussed in this chapter. For example, with the sestina, instead of repeating the same end word over and over, try using sound-alikes instead. If the word *feel* appears as an end word in your first stanza, try using *fell*, *fail*, *fall*, *fill*, and *full* as the repeating words in the following stanzas. With the pantoum and the villanelle, you can try repeating only the last words of the lines instead of the entire lines. The feel and the sound of both poems will be vastly different when you are finished.

One variation you can work with in all three forms is function or category shift. You saw an example of it with the sestina and you can review the complete discussion of this element in Chapter 5. The word *face*, for example, is used as a noun in the phrase "a pretty face," as a verb in "she will face her accuser," and as an adjective in "at face value." These shifts can give you leeway in constructing your lines as well.

As you go through the exercises you have done, you might try to work with the other tools of the trade—meter, rhyme, and so on—to tighten up your lines. For example, you might revise your pantoum so that the end words rhyme. You might revise the sestina so that it follows an iambic pentameter. You could also work at the villanelle or its variations to regulate their meter. At all stages, you should experiment with the different forms and tools to see how they work together. And remember: You can never have too much practice!

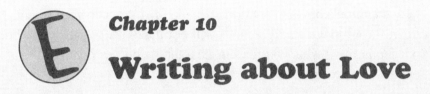

Chapter 10

Writing about Love

Love, in all its forms, is perhaps the most common subject of poetry. The emotion is so intense that it begs to be expressed. If he is brave, a poet might express his feelings to the object of his affection. If not, he may simply record his hopes and longings in a journal and in poems. If his love interest does not return his feelings, writing poetry may operate as a coping mechanism. But if the person does return his love, his poems may be triumphant and joyful.

Inquiring Minds Want to Know

While love will often bring you to the page to write about the joy or the suffering you are experiencing, you must remember that if you decide to shape those feelings into a poem for a reader, you have a responsibility to make the subject of your poem clear and engaging. Your reader needs to know the details of your situation so she can appreciate your poem. A chaotic gush of thoughts and feelings will not make sense to anyone but you. So, keep in mind what you read in Chapter 3, and use concrete details that appeal to the five senses.

Following Conventions

One convention of love poetry is that it describes in detail different aspects of the poet's beloved. If you choose to follow this convention, you can highlight a physical characteristic of your beloved or a character trait. For example, describe to your reader the long, soft hair, musical laugh, consistent generosity, or dimpled smile of the one you love. Use sensuous details to describe these traits. Do you remember how Shakespeare turned this convention inside out in his sonnet that begins "My mistress' eyes are nothing like the sun"? You can take Shakespeare's approach and then reveal your true intent at the conclusion, or you can follow a more straightforward path. Whatever method you choose, don't forget the details!

Using Drama

You can also write about your beloved as if describing him to one of your readers—perhaps a close friend. Address this friend as *you* throughout the poem, and in a chatty tone, write out the description using words from the list that you already set down; then turn the description into a dialogue by having this friend respond. This form of writing will help you establish your own voice and force you to write with specific detail. If this is successful, your reader should see your love interest just as you do.

If you prefer, you can make slight variations to this scenario. Perhaps you guess that if your friend meets this special person, she will fall in love, too. In this case, you may choose to downplay your side of the dialogue, understating your beloved's wonderful qualities to protect your own interests.

This and other variations will give your poem a greater sense of reality and create a more dramatic feel.

More on Monologue

Using monologue is another way to satisfy your reader's curiosity. The monologue, remember, can be written as if taking place within the mind of the speaker. Take another look at the information on the monologue in Chapter 7 and then write your own monologue. Consider the Robert Browning poem included in that section, "Soliloquy of the Spanish Cloister." As Browning's monologue is addressed to Brother Lawrence, you should address your love interest, a close friend, or even yourself in your monologue. You could also use the "fly on the wall" technique and imagine watching your loved one complete a series of ordinary actions. Your job will then be to supply description and commentary that make his or her actions seem extraordinary to the reader.

Surprise and Context

Finally, you might like to work with two ideas that poet Jeredith Merrin has named important elements of all love poetry: *surprise* and *context*. Using the method of surprise, you startle your reader with an observation, a rhyme, or a figure of speech. The surprise doesn't need to be earth shattering, but it should make your reader think of love in a new way. The idea of context will force you to make a connection between your feelings and the world around you. Perhaps some current event seen in a newspaper headline or a magazine article will remind you how your love fits into the big picture. Use this context to disclose your feelings in a new way.

Jeredith Merrin illustrates the idea of surprise by recalling the lyrics to Cole Porter's song "You're the Top." You might enjoy reading the lyrics and looking at the comparisons Porter makes between the loved one and many well-known cultural icons, such as the *Mona Lisa* and Mickey Mouse. Look, too, at the interesting rhyme combinations he uses.

Singing Praises

A poem that consists of a list of your beloved's best attributes, a discussion of those attributes with a friend, or a declaration of your love will set you within a time-honored tradition in English language poetry. Such poems tingle with newfound love or glow with love proven true over time. One of the most famous love poems in English expresses the latter feeling: Elizabeth Barrett Browning's "How Do I Love Thee?"

How do I love thee? Let me count the ways.
I love thee to the depth and breadth and height
My soul can reach, when feeling out of sight
For the ends of being and ideal grace.
I love thee to the level of every day's
Most quiet need, by sun and candle-light.
I love thee freely, as men strive for right.
I love thee purely, as they turn from praise.
I love thee with the passion put to use
In my old griefs, and with my childhood's faith.
I love thee with a love I seemed to lose
With my lost saints. I love with the breath,
Smiles, tears, of all my life; and, if God choose,
I shall but love thee better after death.

For practice, you might scan this poem to see how Browning has used rhyme and meter to shape the speaker's feelings. Then try to rewrite the poem in your own words using the same structure. You could also try the reverse: Keep Barrett Browning's words but change the form of the poem. These exercises might give you ideas on how to portray love in a poem of your own.

Longing

Having strong feelings for someone while lacking an outlet to express that feeling can lead to many a sleepless night. You want to be with that person, you want that person to love you, but something is preventing the two of you from being together. This feeling can arise especially when you know that the object of your affection is strictly off limits. In any of these cases, you are experiencing longing—a popular poetic topic.

The Shadow

Jeredith Merrin names a third element of love poetry that partially speaks to this feeling of longing: the *shade* or the *shadow*. The shadow is, in essence, an obstacle between you and love. Unrequited love is one such obstacle. This shadow, when it appears, can take pure love and give it a completely different shape.

Other obstacles that can create the shadow in love poetry are physical distance, time, infidelity, differences in background or culture, and objecting parents. Many books, plays, and movies, as well as poems, have been written about the shadows that can fall upon love. You, too, can use this element in your poetry.

How to Demonstrate Longing

One option is to use a traditional theme, the *aubade,* or morning poem. The aubade often involves the separation of lovers at the coming of the day. This prospect of separation can create a sense of longing even while one is still in the presence of one's lover. The following is an example of such a poem—Jeff Knorr's "Not an Ordinary Wednesday":

This morning my wife is up and showered
before me. She stands naked across the room
clinking past a watch, fountain pen, collecting
two earrings and inserting each with a tip of her head.
Her damp feet must be cold just beyond a shaft
of new light spreading like honey across the wood floor.
Wet hair touches her bony shoulders, then I follow
the line of her spine down, curving, and there
are drops of water on the back of her left thigh.
From the bed I try hard to bring her back.
What use is it to leave. The sun is not yet hot.
It'd be best to spend the next hours curled

tightly against each other like a peony
waiting to bloom in the afternoon heat.
And waking, we'll find each other's touch,
new, kissing until we are moving together
like wind entering trees, easing branches
west then east in sudden gusts.
I say, come on, climb in. To hell with work.
She laughs, dressed now, light in her face
as if she'd swallowed last night's melting stars.
One kiss, our hands together. They break.
As I stare into the space where we last touched,
a gentle thud, and the latch on the door clicks closed.
In the shaft of light, dust speckles the air, a long,
blonde hair spins in a small current and lands
on the foot of the bed. I will stay here listening
until I know she's as far away as the moon.

Reprinted with the permission of the author.

As an exercise, make a list of the things you are doing and thinking as you long for your beloved. If you are washing the dishes, describe the feeling of the water and the soap, the texture of the sponge and the towel, or the colors of the dishes. And if you are having a fantasy about this person, write it down in all its detail. Then write down a description of the obstacle keeping you apart. Once you have completed this preparation, write a poem about what you might do to break down that obstacle and how it would feel to find yourself with the person you love.

Rejection

Rejection is another common theme found in love poems. Whether you're being turned down by a new crush or by a longtime love, the effects of rejection can be devastating. Poets often choose to write about rejection, as it is a highly emotional topic that deserves plenty of description. You can write about this topic as a means of working through your pain or just to create art.

A Rejection Poem

Jeredith Merrin uses a rejection poem, Thomas Wyatt's "They Flee from Me," as an example of the shadow in love poetry. The first stanza in particular sets out a contrast, for the speaker, between how women once came to him and how they now avoid him:

> They flee from me that sometime did me seek
> With naked foot stalking in my chamber.
> I have seen them gentle, tame, and meek,
> That now are wild and do not remember
> That sometime they put themselves in danger
> To take bread at my hand; and now they range
> Busily seeking with a continual change.
>
> Thanked be fortune it hath been otherwise
> Twenty times better; but once in special,
> In thin array after a pleasant guise,
> When her loose gown from her shoulders did fall,
> And she me caught in her arms long and small;
> Therewith all sweetly did me kiss
> And softly said, "Dear heart, how like you this?"
>
> It was no dream: I lay broad waking.
> But all is turned through my gentleness
> Into a strange fashion of forsaking;
> And I have leave to go of her goodness,
> And she also to use newfangleness.
> But since that I so kindly am served
> I would fain know what she hath deserved.

Wyatt's poem is written in a verse form called *rime royal*, which includes a seven-line stanza and an ABABBCC rhyme scheme. His use of iambic pentameter is disguised by the modern spellings of many of the words here, some of which formerly had an unstressed *e* sound that filled the syllable count.

Writing about Rejection

As you can see from Wyatt's poem, the speaker doesn't simply wallow in his feelings. He uses specific details to talk about the women, describing expressions, gestures, and clothing, and recounting pieces of dialogue. You, too, must make use of specific details as you write about rejection. This will make your experience more real to the reader.

Your first step should be to think about a rejection, either real or imagined. Write down the place where it occurred, the time of year and time of day, the significant pieces of dialogue exchanged, the clothing worn, and the gestures and expressions used. Try to write as objectively as you can, without attaching any of your own feelings to it. Your emotions will inevitably come through, but trying to write objectively helps you focus on description.

Remember the general reasons for expressing yourself: change, discovery, and decision. Rejection in love is a moment when all three of these things may occur at once, so you should explore what is changing for the speaker, what discoveries are made, and what decisions are finally settled on.

The next step is to carefully consider the items in your description and attach to them specific emotional responses you may have had. Did your loved one make a facial expression that made you dread the conversation you were about to have? Did she put her hand in yours as if to say, "I'm sorry"? Did you feel anger, disappointment, or relief?

Also, don't forget the elements of surprise, context, and shadow. In the central stanza of his poem, with its dramatic turn to a particular memory, Wyatt gives the reader a poignant jolt of surprise. Having the speaker relate the incidents in retrospect provides context. Wyatt's theme of lost love includes and embodies the shadows of infidelity and the desire for revenge. As you can see, rejection can be just one part of a poem centering on larger issues.

Finally, you might consider including a continuation for the speaker in your poem. In other words, the speaker may have suffered this rejection, but where does he go from here? The speaker in Wyatt's poem complains that his life has not been the same. Will your speaker leave it at that, will he move on and find strength somewhere else to continue, or will the speaker plot revenge? Take another look at the Thomas Hardy poem "Neutral Tones" in Chapter 5 (page 62) as an example of how these steps can be used.

Carpe Diem

Some love poems attempt to coax a reluctant person into a commitment, either emotional or physical. Central to these poems is an argument known as *carpe diem*, meaning "seize the day" in Latin. The logic behind this argument is that today you have a chance to act on your love; tomorrow might bring a separation, an illness, or death, which can cut your time short. The argument also establishes the context of the poem—the one-sided relationship between the speaker and the listener.

A Carpe Diem Poem

One of the most famous carpe diem poems is Andrew Marvell's "To His Coy Mistress." He, like Shakespeare, begins by praising the lady's parts, saying that several hundred years should be devoted to a song about each. But with an ironic twist, he remarks that neither he nor his listener has enough time for such praises. He then uses some rather extreme imagery to support his argument, calling up dark, foreboding thoughts.

> *Had we but world enough, and time,*
> *This coyness, lady, were no crime.*
> *We would sit down and think which way*
> *To walk, and pass our long love's day;*
> *Thou by the Indian Ganges' side*
> *Shouldst rubies find; I by the tide*
> *Of Humber would complain. I would*
> *Love you ten years before the Flood;*
> *And you should, if you please, refuse*
> *Till the conversion of the Jews.*
> *My vegetable love should grow*

Vaster than empires, and more slow.
An hundred years should go to praise
Thine eyes, and on thy forehead gaze;
Two hundred to adore each breast,
But thirty thousand to the rest;
An age at least to every part,
And the last age should show your heart.
For, lady, you deserve this state,
Nor would I love at lower rate.
*   But at my back I always hear*
Time's wingèd chariot hurrying near;
And yonder all before us lie
Deserts of vast eternity.
Thy beauty shall no more be found,
Nor, in thy marble vault, shall sound
My echoing song; then worms shall try
That long preserv'd virginity,
And your quaint honour turn to dust,
And into ashes all my lust.
The grave's a fine and private place,
But none I think do there embrace.
*   Now therefore, while the youthful hue*
Sits on thy skin like morning dew,
And while thy willing soul transpires
At every pore with instant fires,
Now let us sport us while we may;
And now, like am'rous birds of prey,
Rather at once our time devour,
Than languish in his slow-chapt power.
Let us roll all our strength, and all
Our sweetness, up into one ball;
And tear our pleasures with rough strife
Through the iron gates of life.
Thus, though we cannot make our sun
Stand still, yet we will make him run.

With this description of the obstacles that will arise if they wait, the speaker of this poem hopes to convince the woman to accept his plea. As a reader, you might ask yourself how strong his argument is. Is it good enough to convince his listener? Does it convince you? Note the aspects of the poem that work well toward its purpose and recall them when you write your own carpe diem poem.

The Art of Persuasion

Since the argument laid out in a carpe diem poem is truly its central purpose, the images and figures of speech must give convincing reasons for the reluctant person to submit. The form of the poem, however, is for you to decide. Marvell uses iambic tetrameter and an AABB scheme, but you can try a sonnet, a pantoum, a sestina, free verse, or any other form you think will suit your goal.

To come up with subject matter, try a couple of exercises. First, describe the opportunity available to the speaker and the loved one. Perhaps they have a free weekend to take a trip, or a holiday that deserves celebration is approaching. Next, write down the obstacles—the shadows—that might arise if the speaker and the loved one wait too long to be together. Is one of them moving to a different city soon? Is one person ill?

Once these basics are established, a little flattery can't hurt. The speaker in Marvell's poem flatters the woman he loves, hoping to win her over. You can try this method in your carpe diem poem as well. What is your favorite feature of this person's face? Do you especially love the sound of her laugh or the way she smiles? If you prefer, you can begin your poem with flattery and then move into the specific aspects of the situation.

A Tempting Offer

A close relative of the carpe diem poem is the *temptation poem*. The temptation poem has the same purpose of coaxing a reluctant listener to grant the speaker's wish. However, the argument is different. Instead of the pressure—of time, place, or imminent shadow—set forth in the carpe diem poem, the temptation poem uses more subtle suggestions, hints, or even eroticism to appeal to the listener's desires.

Erotic Temptation

Eroticism in poetry does not generally allude to pornography or even explicit sex. While eroticism in a temptation poem calls upon the physical parts of love, passion, and the body, it does so in a manner that suggests mutual benefit for both lovers. The focus falls more on sensuality, beauty, and tenderness than a simple physical act.

To get a sense of the erotic in poetry, consider the following portion of a poem by John Donne, the last half of his "Elegy XIX: To His Mistress Going to Bed":

> License my roving hands, and let them go
> Before, behind, between, above, below.
> O my America! my new-found-land,
> My kingdom, safeliest when with one man manned,
> My mine of precious stones, my empery,
> How blest am I in this discovering thee!
> To enter in these bonds is to be free;
> Then where my hand is set, my seal shall be.
> Full nakedness! All joys are due to thee,
> As souls unbodied, bodies unclothed must be
> To taste whole joys. Gems which you women use
> Are like Atlanta's balls, cast in men's views,
> That when a fool's eye lighteth on a gem,
> His earthly soul may covet theirs, not them.
> Like pictures, or like books' gay coverings made
> For lay-men, are all women thus arrayed;
> Themselves are mystic books, which only we
> (Whom their imputed grace will dignify)
> Must see revealed. Then, since that I may know,
> As liberally as to a midwife, show
> Thyself: cast all, yea, this white linen hence,
> There is no penance due to innocence.
> To teach thee, I am naked first; why then,
> what needst thou have more covering than a man?

As you write your own temptation poem, consider the differences between men and women when it comes to love, passion, and sensuality. Investigate what tactics men and women use to tempt others. If you are a woman, try to write a temptation poem with a male speaker. And if you are a man, do the opposite. This exercise might provide insight into your own personal situation or an even broader topic.

Using Imagery

Some of the best temptation poetry walks the fine line between the suggestive and the erotic, alluding to but not completely revealing the physical aspects. As an exercise, make a catalog of body parts. Start with parts like the ankles or the elbows—parts that are not overtly sexual—and practice describing them in erotic terms.

For each body part on your list, imagine a way that it could be tempting. Describe the way the hem of a skirt might rest upon a woman's knee. Consider the way a shirt can reveal the ripples of a man's biceps. When you get around to writing a temptation poem, merely suggest these details without describing the action entirely. Your goal is not only to tempt the object of your affection, but also to tempt anyone who reads your poem.

Fulfillment

Fulfillment in love is one of the most satisfying feelings one can experience. Interestingly, fulfillment often comes in the aftermath of a relationship crisis or obstacle. For example, you might endure torturous months waiting for a guy in your office to notice you before he finally asks you to dinner. Or perhaps you agonize for weeks about asking the girl of your dreams to marry you. Just imagine your delight and relief when, after a romantic candlelit dinner, you offer her a ring and she says yes.

Many common crisis points that lead to fulfillment are firsts: first meetings, first dates, first kisses, etc. Therefore, when you write a poem about fulfillment, you may be returning to those firsts. If you kept a diary of those times as you experienced them, you have a valuable resource for ideas. If you didn't, then write out those times in narrative form first, making sure that you describe the events, people, places, and outcomes as accurately as you can. Don't wait too long, or you risk losing details that will affect the emotional tone of the poem.

QUESTION?

What is a crisis point?

Crisis points are moments in a story or poem—or in your own life—when the characters (or you) are faced with a major change, discovery, or decision. As happy as you are when these periods end well, there is also the possibility that they will not. Including a crisis point in your poem will add excitement and drama for the reader.

You might also look at the crisis points described in the poems by Hardy and Wyatt. The crisis points are followed by rejection, which is the dark side (the shadow) of the earlier fulfillment. But both poems rely on flashback—the speakers recalling past events—a technique you might use in your fulfillment poem.

Another kind of fulfillment results from a long, stable, happy relationship. This sort of relationship grows through the years and helps each individual within it to become a better person. Any problems that arise inside or outside of the relationship are overcome, making the relationship that much stronger.

A poem written about such a relationship will likely take all of those times into account, as if in summary. Such a poem is called an *occasional poem* because it is usually presented at a celebration of a special occasion, like an anniversary or a birthday. Traditionally, the ode form is used for this kind of poem.

Chapter 11

Writing about Family and Friends

It is natural to want to write about your father, mother, siblings, children, grandparents, aunts, uncles, friends, and acquaintances. These are the people who accompany you during the most important events of your life. These people also serve as role models and guide you through major decisions and experiences. Whether you choose to depict them realistically or shape them into characters, they will constantly affect your subject matter.

Word Portraits

As a poet writing about the people you love, you can work like a painter. The only difference is the tools you use to create portraits of your family members. You will be describing the clothing, hairstyles, expressions, postures, habits, and laughs that make these people who they are in your eyes—the details that make them memorable. In fact, you have a few extra tools at your disposal for this task.

Appearance

The first tool you have to re-create your loved ones is appearance. In this mode, you capture the external details of a person—just like a painter would. However, you have the option to describe the whole person based on dress, facial features, and so on, or you can concentrate on a single feature, describing it in such a way that it becomes symbolic of that person.

ALERT!

When describing the appearance of a person, don't forget to include his personal belongings—a favorite chair, a treasured book, a pair of eyeglasses perched on his nose. Recalling these items will not only create an identity for your reader to imagine, but it will also help you remember other memories and details about the person.

For example, perhaps the one thing you remember most about your father is his hands. You might recall how they slid around the leather-covered steering wheel of your family's car as you drove to church on Sundays, the knuckles whitening around the turns. Perhaps you identify your mother by her soft smile—a sight that reminded you in times of trouble that everything would turn out all right. Use enough description so that your reader can see these people the way you see them and get a sense of their personalities without having known them personally.

Actions

Closely related to the tool of appearance is that of action. To give the reader an even better picture of the loved one you are describing, show this person limping up a staircase, peeling potatoes over the kitchen sink, dancing in the family room, or shoveling the driveway. The description of a father's hands in the last section shows those hands in action, as well as in physical detail. Action and appearance should work together to show (and not tell) your reader about the person you are concentrating on. When you allow your readers to form impressions for themselves, you are adding to the pleasure they gain from reading your poems.

Having the tool of action at your disposal gives you an advantage over a painter. As a writer you can describe both the physical and emotional aspects of a person. To do this, you must remember the discussion in Chapter 3 about active verbs and active voice. Passive voice and linking verbs should be avoided in this case. You want the subject of your poem to jump out at the reader, almost as if she were watching a play or a movie.

Dialogue

Another tool you have for re-creating your relatives—one also not available to the painter—is *speech*. What a person says can reveal just as much as what a person wears or how a person acts. For example, if you have a relative who uses a lot of profanity, your readers will get a very strong impression of that person through the dialogue you include. Likewise, if you can accurately portray a person's accent to your reader, this may serve as a hint about the subject's heritage.

Speech can reinforce the impressions given by appearance and action—or create contrast. If a cousin consistently promises to return a borrowed item but never does, the reader will get a certain impression of the person. However, if the cousin keeps her promise, the reader will get a very different sense.

Using social, regional, and stylistic variation to capture the speech patterns of your relatives is a great tactic. An uncle who says "I ain't got" rather than "I don't have" has a certain social and educational background. A cousin who exclaims "Lord have mercy!" and "Bless his heart!" will very likely be associated with a particular region, culture, or age group. If one sibling speaks using only single words and another elaborates with clause after clause, the reader will get a very distinct, contrasting impression based solely on their stylistic differences.

Thoughts

One last tool available to you—and another that is not available to the painter—is thought. You can bring your reader into the minds of the people in your poems. To do this well, you must follow the same guidelines that fiction writers use when they create point of view. Early in your poem, you must establish a speaker—the voice through which a reader experiences the poem—and you must establish exactly how much information that speaker can reveal to the reader.

For example, if you begin the poem with the pronoun *I*, readers assume that the speaker is talking about herself. In most cases, this speaker will not be able to reveal the thoughts and the feelings of other characters. She can make guesses about them, based upon the surface details of appearance, action, and speech, but the speaker won't know definitively. The speaker will, however, be able to tell a reader what she is thinking or feeling. The monologue, discussed in Chapter 7, is a common method for such a speaker.

Here Comes the Bride

What is a better time to write about loved ones than after an event that has brought them together? Marriage is an experience that drastically changes one's life and one's lifestyle. While the couple getting married is obviously the most affected by such an occasion, the families and friends who attend a wedding are affected as well. With so many details and people included, the circumstances surrounding a wedding, or the event itself, can be a great subject for poetry.

A Traditional Approach

The traditional wedding poem, called an *epithalamion*, tends to be very long—possibly hundreds of lines. It also tends to be formal in tone, praising the bride and the groom and passing along the good wishes of the speaker in ornate language. The following portion of an epithalamion written by John Donne will give you a sense of the traditional form:

> *Hail Bishop Valentine, whose day this is;*
> *All the air is thy diocese,*
> *And all the chirping choristers*
> *And other birds are thy parishioners.*

A Modern Method

Joseph Millar presents a modern take on the marriage poem in "Dark Harvest." The poem sings praise but also includes a more solemn facet—the troubled pasts of both the speaker and the person he addresses. Consider the following selection from this poem:

> *You can come to me in the evening,*
> *with the fingers of former lovers*
> *fastened in your hair and their ghost lips*
> *opening over your body.*
> *They can be philosophers or musicians in long coats and colored shoes*
> *and they can be smarter than I am,*
> *whispering to each other*
> *when they look at us.*
> *You can come walking toward my window after dusk*
> *when I can't see past the lamplight in the glass,*
> *when the chipped plates rattle on the counter*
> *and the cinders*
> *dance on the cross-ties under the wheels of southbound freights.*
> *Bring children if you want, and the long wounds of sisters*
> *branching away*
> *behind you toward the sea.*

Bring your mother's tense distracted face
and the shoulders of plane mechanics
slumped in the Naugahyde booths of the airport diner,
waiting for you to bring their eggs.

I'll bring all the bottles of gin I drank by myself
and my cracked mouth opened partway
as I slept in the back of my blue Impala
dreaming of spiders.

From Overtime. Reprinted with the permissions of the publisher, Eastern Washington University Press (Spokane, Washington), and the author.

The traditional epithalamion is written in praise of someone. However, you can choose a different approach, as Millar does, and write your own distinct marriage poem. Praise your spouse, discuss your fears, illustrate your fulfillment, or express your worry about the future. People have all kinds of different feelings about marriage, and a poem is the perfect place to express yours without restriction.

And Baby Makes Three

Everyone has a different definition for a family. Some people consider friends a part of their families. Others treat their cats or dogs like siblings or children. And many people adopt children to start their families or broaden them. Traditionally, though, a family begins with the birth of children. A marriage marks the start of a joint life between two people, but the addition of children is often thought to complete a family.

If you are a father, you may have had the opportunity to see your baby enter the world or to deliver her yourself. This is an experience unlike any other, and a great subject for poetry. If you are a mother, these feelings are probably even stronger. You have carried your child for nine months. You have watched your body change to accommodate the life growing within you. Finally, you struggle for hours to bring your baby into the world. The emotions surrounding childbirth are overwhelming and provide a great inspiration for poetry.

Such emotions can be captured in poems, but chances are, you were so caught up in the moment itself that you forgot to remember details for later use. Do your best to recall the color of the bed sheets in the delivery room, the smell of the hospital, and the sounds of the machines around you. If you have a more unique situation, like adopting a child from another country or from a family member, work to recall the flight attendant on your plane as you traveled to get your baby or the sound of the pen on the documents as your child was legally made yours. These concrete details, in conjunction with your strong emotions, will create a realistic environment for your poem.

As an accompaniment to the list you make about the details of the birth, you can set down any worries and resentments you may feel. Hopefully, this list won't be long. However, it will give you the means to add complexity to your poem. A contrast of joys and worries, or a poem focusing on the uncertainties posed by future decisions, might be the result. Ask yourself important questions. What changed about the relationship between you and your partner when the baby arrived? How has having this first child affected your ideas about having more children? How do you envision your future now that you have a family?

Dealing with Divorce

Unfortunately, statistics show that about half of the marriages in the United States end in divorce. Like marriage and childbirth, divorce can create a great deal of change in your life. It might translate into the absence of family members, the acquisition of new roles, and even a relocation to a new place. Poetry will allow you to explore this new territory and express your feelings, both good and bad.

The Dark Side

Harsh feelings such as anger, resentment, bitterness, and inadequacy can accompany you through divorce proceedings and beyond. Very likely, these feelings surround the spouse that you have just left. Exploring these feelings in a journal or a series of free-writing exercises is the best way to prepare material for poems. Document your feelings, but also try to recall specific events that triggered these responses. For example, perhaps you were angriest with your spouse on the day she forgot to pick up the children from school. Or maybe you found yourself at the end of your rope the last time he made a mean comment about your appearance.

If you and your spouse have children, the situation will automatically become more complicated. They will feel confused and hurt, just as you will, but they will have more difficulty dealing with the situation. In your journals, it might be interesting to try writing about the divorce from the children's perspective. What is the most troubling thing about the divorce for them? What questions do they want answered? How are they choosing to deal with their feelings? Considering these questions will not only improve your poetry, but it will also help you do the best thing for your children.

A New Beginning

While divorce can be a complicated and upsetting mess, sometimes the event is needed and even welcomed by both members of a couple. If both people were unhappy in the marriage, maybe divorce is a necessary step toward finding happiness. If you are in an abusive relationship, divorce might be the one thing that can make you feel safe and comfortable again. So, divorce involves positives that you can explore just as deeply as the negatives. What are the benefits of the divorce? What are your prospects now you're on your own again? Consider these questions to find the silver lining of your situation.

And again, don't forget the details. Perhaps the day after your divorce you got your first full night's sleep in six months. Or maybe that menacing nauseous feeling in your stomach finally left for good. Did color return to your complexion and a smile to your face? Record these aspects in vivid detail and be sure to include them in your poetry.

Holidays

Holidays may be the only times that you see some of your friends and relatives. Because reunions are generally infrequent, occasions spent with family can also be awkward or uncomfortable. But seeing these people again can remind you how far your family extends and how many different lives it connects. You may have the chance to learn something new about your family at every meeting. Treasure these family legacies and stories, as they are also a part of your life and heritage.

A Time for Reflection

In the following poem by Jeff Knorr, "Winter Turkeys," the speaker relates his memories of his own family gatherings. The speaker is also documenting recollections made by his father—bits of stories that reconstruct the earlier times of the family.

There have been thirty-six turkeys
in my life, each near Christmas.
Two I have missed, in '86 and '88
and also missed the death of my father's mother.
That year in Vienna, I phoned
from a bar serving schnitzel. Then outside
the pale evening, as if a far off fire
heaved itself into the apricot dusk.

We eat well at these dinners: stuffings,
mulled berries, roasted turkey, many wines.
Our mother is getting so she shakes a bit
lifting the black, fat-spitting roaster.
Our father carves still with respectful
movements to the bird, feeling its curves
into neat slices of meat. This year he might
talk about the old Murray cabin up the road.
But that's as passing as the morning quail.
Instead he's telling me of a cousin he hasn't seen
since his mother's funeral. And this word
hangs, the f sticking on his lip
like the clot of fat and blood he wipes from the knife.
I nod, stand stupidly as a cow.

Later I'll leave him alone, jacket and brandy,
his half a snifter on the back deck.
He'll look a long way off into the sky and find
the railroad camps near Shasta,
our sister's ballet debut,
his first night with our mother cruising San Jose.
They tail like glowing meteors over the ridge.
In the morning we'll walk shoulder to shoulder
quietly through new snow
as though the stars had fallen to ashes overnight.

Reprinted with the permission of the author.

Writing about family during a holiday will provide you with a measure of the changes in your life. Compare a holiday when you were young to a celebration you attended last year. What has changed within the family? Who has left the group and who has arrived? Take careful note of all the differences. Are you better or worse for these changes?

The Good Times

While all families endure tragedies and hardships, most also experience good times. Recalling holiday celebrations is a great way to rediscover these happy days. Though your impulse may be to focus on the negative aspects of your family's past, don't forget to relish the joyful memories you have. Be sure to recall Easter egg hunts with your cousins, pool parties at your aunt's house, and picnics you had with your parents and siblings. Create poetry to present to your family, to honor a loved one who has passed away, or just to reflect on your life experiences.

Enduring Loss

Death is an inevitable part of life. However, though everyone knows it's coming, it is still heartbreaking to lose a loved one. Most individuals also feel awe, fear, or dread when they consider how death will come to them. Poetry about death can run a wide gamut, and can highlight any of the many aspects of this universal fate.

The traditional poem about someone else's passing is the *elegy*. This form features the speaker's sadness but also includes praise for the departed. The tone is usually somber but some memories about the departed can bring a measure of contentment. In a well-known elegy by Thomas Gray, "Elegy Written in a Country Churchyard," the speaker contemplates with wonder the many lives of the people buried in a churchyard.

Writing about someone's death is bound to stir very strong emotions within you. However, try not to let these feelings dominate the poem. As with other topics, you must concentrate on concrete details to make the experience more real for your reader. Focus on the physical aspects: location, clothing, sounds, and foods, for example.

Many other poems on this subject tend to be more personal than Gray's. They often focus on the speaker's emotions and on some key events shared by the speaker and the departed. Ben Jonson's poem about his son's death, discussed in Chapter 7 (page 88), is an example. To write about the death of a person close to you, you must let your own feelings be your guide. Are you devastated? Are you angry? Are you even a little bit relieved? Describe any emotions you felt during the experience, and then write out the events that triggered each emotion.

Treasured Relationships

The person you are today is a result of the influences that friends and family have had upon you throughout your life. You may have chosen to embrace these people and make them a part of your daily routine, or you may have broken all of the ties that once linked you. Regardless of your true situation, you can always reflect on your family in your writing.

The Importance of Childhood

When you were a child, your parents and siblings offered you your first taste of love, comfort, trust, and companionship. They trained you on how to interact with other people and gave you a view of the world that you likely held into adolescence. Your family might also have been your first source of pain and betrayal, possibly giving you a negative view of relationships.

FACT

One popular theory holds that the relationships men have with their fathers determines the relations they have with coworkers, while the relationships men have with their mothers determines the relations they have with friends and lovers. For women, it's the opposite.

As you get older, your friends help to shape your life as much as, and sometimes more than, your family. During your teenage years you likely spent lots of time with your friends. During your college years and young adulthood, your friends likely seemed to take the place of your family. Unfortunately, friends, like family, can cause you pain. Even though you might have endured hard times when you were young, you shouldn't forget them completely as you move on in your life. These memories continue to shape your present self and will help you create stronger poetry.

Hanging On

You hold friends and family close for two opposing reasons—for the love, laughter, and good times they bring, and for the bitterness, regret, and anger that you cannot let go of. Through your interactions with these people, you have learned how the world operates, but you have also learned many valuable lessons about yourself. Those three essential elements of inspiration—change, discovery, and decision—will mark points in your personal development, but your interactions with others will help you see how you have grown. In other words, try to think of these people as your mirror.

Including details of memories in your poems helps create a bond between you and your reader. It is difficult to create realistic stories and situations with your imagination alone. Pulling from personal experience is a much better method.

As an exercise, write down a list of things you have learned with the help of your family. Next, write down a list of things you have learned with friends. Finally, try to think of lessons you have learned completely on your own. You will likely find that others had an influence on you during almost every major stage of your life.

Ideas for Writing

As an exercise, write an ode recalling one of the things your friends or relatives have done for you. You can follow the traditional ode guidelines and make it a song of praise, or you can give it an ironic twist and concentrate on the negative. The elements of love poetry discussed in Chapter 10—Jeredith Merrin's ideas about surprise, context, and shadow—can help you here. For example, you can choose a surprising event, set it in the context of what you were doing at that time in your life, and give it shadow by exploring any obstacles or negative aspects that existed.

Another good exercise to try is to write a poem to one of your friends or relatives about any anxiety you are currently having. You can write the poem as a monologue or as a dialogue, but be sure to address this friend or relative as "you" throughout the poem. To get started with this idea, come up with a list of words that describe the anxiety you feel. You can construct a sestina with the list as end words or you can turn the list into refrains for a pantoum or villanelle.

You might also start with another descriptive passage of forty to seventy words, as you did for the sonnet. The subject matter can be a description of your mother's appearance, a loving memory of your son's first steps, or an angry reply to a friend who betrayed you. If you find yourself going over seventy words, don't stop—continue until you have expressed the entire thought. Then, as before, break the passage into lines using a syllable count. Next, try different stanza patterns (couplets, tercets, quatrains, etc.), and then work with a foot pattern and rhyme scheme, if appropriate.

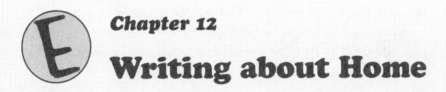

Chapter 12

Writing about Home

All aspects of one's home—the rooms, furniture, decor, appliances, etc.— can be the subjects of poems or the settings for poems about other subjects. The word *home* can have several different meanings as well. It can represent a hometown, a birthplace, or a place you visited for only a short time. Therefore, home doesn't have to be restricted to the place where you live now. It can be a combination of all the places from which you draw your identity or into which you retreat for privacy and strength.

Starting Outdoors

Using your home as the subject or the setting of a poem will force you to pay attention to your surroundings. Do you live on a street bordered by sidewalks, lit by streetlights, and populated by passing cars, or is your home on a dirt road surrounded by fields and grazing livestock? Does your house perch on the side of a cliff overlooking ocean waves, or does it sit in a quiet, green valley brightened by wildflowers? The atmosphere of your home is created by its appearance against its environment, so pay attention to both of these aspects when you write about this place.

FACT

One popular form of literature, called *gothic*, depends a great deal upon a house and its appearance. The house is often raised to the level of a character that acts, communicates, and even seems to show emotion. Think of the house in *The Addams Family* television show and movies, for example.

As you describe the house and its locale, use concrete details—the height of the house, the building materials, paint colors, window and door placement, balconies, gardens, terraces, porches, garage, and so on. Pay attention, also, to the time of day. Your house will look one way in daylight and another at night. During the day, does sunlight reflect off the front windows, or does your house sit beneath the shadow of trees? At night, is your house dim and silent, or is it brightly lit by lamps and candles, with smoke curling up from the chimney?

Stepping Inside

Once you have examined the appearance of your house from the outside, go to the entrance of the house. Is it welcoming or does it give the house an inhospitable feel? The entrance gives a visitor (or reader) his first impression of the house, so you must describe it in detail.

Secondly, what room do you enter when you step into the house? Do you find yourself in the midst of a chaotic family room, littered with dolls, toy cars, and dress-up clothes? Are you standing in a foyer complete with a coat rack, shoe collection, and bucket of umbrellas? Or is there a stiff wooden bench and a stack of magazines, as if you're in the waiting room of a doctor's office?

One room to explore in detail is the kitchen. In many homes, the kitchen is the center of family life—the place where the day begins and ends. An example of a poem with a kitchen setting is Theodore Roethke's "My Papa's Waltz," in which a young boy and his drunken father lurch through a dance before a disapproving mother. If you're writing about the kitchen in your house, be sure to give the details of the furniture and appliances, the food that is served there, and the view from the window.

Roman orators used the objects of their houses as mnemonic devices to remember long speeches they gave in public. The orators mentally walked through their houses and visualized objects as they memorized the opening sentence of a passage. When it came time to recall the speech, they would remember the objects in order and thereby recall the passages.

Beyond the entryway and kitchen, you have other areas to explore—the basement, attic, dining room, office, bathroom, and bedrooms—and you have many objects to consider as well. What furnishings, tools, and belongings are present? How are they arranged? What passageways and entrances lead to these rooms? You want to provide an experience for your reader as she travels through your poem. Another poem you might consider reading as you explore the complexities of a house is Theodore Roethke's "Root Cellar," which paints a chaotic picture of the objects kept in a storage basement.

Exercises

Once you have toured your house, you should try several exercises in your journal. Take the time to go over each part of the house—inside and outside, upstairs and downstairs, during the day and at night—and write out

THE EVERYTHING WRITING POETRY BOOK

descriptive passages about what you've found. Even minor objects deserve significant consideration as you focus your attention on the details.

For example, if you want to describe one of the shoes in your closet, begin not with the general shape and color of the shoe but with the small spot of mud on the toe. The spot may be no larger than a penny, but it is a detail that you can describe and possibly attribute to a particular memory. After you have described the spot of mud, continue with the shoelaces, tongue, sole, and even the inside of the shoe, until you have given a complete description. Don't forget to use your five senses as you write. What does the material of the shoe feel like when you touch it with your fingertips? Does the sole look worn or is it still strong and shapely? Can you smell the aroma of new leather or the stench of sweat and dirt?

Public and Private Places

Two themes to investigate as you write about your home depend on the ideas of public and private space. The difference between the two can be identified fairly easily. For example, would you feel more comfortable encountering a complete stranger on the sidewalk outside your house or in your living room? Chances are, you'd prefer the former. Similarly, you would likely feel more comfortable spending time with guests in your dining room as opposed to your bathtub.

City Versus Wilderness

The distinction between the known and the unknown is a staple of literature. In general, people are comfortable with the things that are familiar and common, and fearful of unidentified or mysterious people, places, or objects. In ancient literature, this distinction is depicted through images of the city (the familiar) and the wilderness (the mysterious).

Cavemen kept a fire burning at night for a good reason—to deter any animals lurking in the darkness from approaching. As humans developed, clans grew into villages, villages became cities, and walls and other fortifications were built for protection. The city was a place of refuge, law, civility, and culture, while the wilderness outside contained danger, chaos, lawlessness, wild animals, and criminals.

By whatever means it occurs, the crossing of the boundary between the city and the wilderness represents a crisis. Many ancient stories illustrate what happens when the wilderness breaks in upon civilization. For example, in the epic poem *Beowulf,* a monster called Grendel terrorizes the meeting hall of the Danes. In literature, humans who venture into the wilderness often face extreme dangers as well. Think of all the monsters Odysseus encounters on his voyage, for example.

FACT

From the beginnings of U.S. industrialization straight through to the present day, some Americans have valued urban development for economic and social reasons, while others have treasured the calm and safety of the countryside. Consider this distinction in your poetry. Which do you prefer?

Home as a Refuge

On a personal level, your house is like your very own city. It is a place where you rest and recuperate, where you share your heritage, memories, and dreams with your family, and where your basic needs of life are taken care of. Everything outside your home can be perceived like the wilderness; it can be a place of danger, of mystery, and of temptation. To gain more insight into the dynamic of city and wilderness, read *The Odyssey* by Homer. The story follows Odysseus through his ten-year struggle to return from the fighting at Troy. This tale of the physical and psychological challenges he faces, and his final relief to return home to his wife, is as poignant today as it was nearly 3,000 years ago.

For an exercise, make a list of the dangers in the "wilderness" outside your home. If you live in the country, your list will probably contain many natural dangers, and if you live in a city, you will list more manmade threats. Keeping these hazards in mind, write about the characteristics of your home that make you feel safe.

Public and Private Space Within Your Home

Inside your home, you make a distinction between spaces where you allow guests, spaces you share only with family, and spaces where you would only feel comfortable with a spouse or partner. With the growing availability of larger homes and personal bedrooms for each member of a household, the distinction between public or family space and private space has undergone a significant change in recent decades. In America, the old image of an entire family sleeping together in a single bed or sharing bathwater has been relegated to the past or to certain regions or social classes.

The beloved stories of pioneer life written by Laura Ingalls Wilder present us with lasting images of how families managed space in the 1800s. The book *Little House in the Big Woods* describes how the father, then the mother, and then the children would take their weekly baths—without changing water—and how the family left the woods when they became "too crowded."

The division between city and wilderness, or interior and exterior, can, in a sense, be internalized inside the house. For example, if you are throwing a party in your house, you might prepare the living room, dining room, kitchen, and perhaps a family room for your guests. A guest bathroom close to one of these rooms may also be used for the party. Private rooms such as bedrooms, family bathrooms, offices, and so forth would probably be off-limits, differentiated by closed doors and extinguished lights.

Guests who are invited to stay overnight are afforded a special sleeping area and bathroom—either a guest room or a family member's room converted for the purpose. Guests and family members respect the temporary boundaries drawn between them. Family members, too, understand that there are boundaries within the house even when no guests are present. For example, bedrooms and bathrooms are not to be entered when the doors are closed.

As a result of these factors, poems set within different areas of a house include varying levels of intimacy, privacy, or exposure. Theodore Roethke's poem "My Papa's Waltz," for example, gives a private look at the family unit—how they behave when they are not around other people. Similarly, Jeff Knorr's poem "Not an Ordinary Wednesday," included in Chapter 10 (page 131), is set in a bedroom and provides an intimate look at a husband and wife.

As an exercise, put the name of each room in your house at the top of a page and then begin a list of activities you do in each room. Which do you do with family? Which do you do with guests? Which do you do by yourself? Looking at the results of these lists will give you a sense of how public or private space is broken up within your home.

To write poetry set in these rooms, look at the actions on your list. Try for an element of surprise, playing against the conventions of public and private space. Set a poem about eating birthday cake in the basement. Or write about a complete stranger who appears in your bathroom. Why have the boundaries been broken, and what are the results?

You Are Where You Live

You have very likely heard the expression "You are what you eat." Similarly, it's quite possible that others identify you according to the place where you live. Your home, and the city in which (or near which) you live, can give others a strong impression of who you are as a person. This impression may be right or wrong, but it still occurs. The same impression, dependent upon the way you describe a home in a poem, can be elicited from your reader about your characters.

Identity and Society

In the movie *Cheaper by the Dozen*, the oldest son of the Baker family, Charlie, has trouble signing up for the football team of his new school. Though he was close to earning a scholarship as the quarterback of his old team at Midland, the coaches of his new team relegate him to defensive back. Because he is in a new environment unlike the one he came from, the new people he meets make immediate judgments about him. He is also repeatedly mocked for having come from the country. These responses and comments are based solely on first impressions, and those impressions create an identity for Charlie that differs from the way he sees himself.

FACT

The conflict between city slickers and country folk is as old as civilization, and many examples of it appear in literature. In fact, many languages are bursting with vocabulary that can be used to describe one or the other lifestyle. Look up the meanings and the origins of the words *civil, urbane, polite, rustic, bucolic,* and *pastoral* to see which category they fall under.

As an exercise, write down the name of the city where you live—or to which you live closest—and then write down the reputations that the city and its people have. Los Angeles, for example, is known as a sprawling, car-congested city, overflowing with movie stars. New York is supposedly the "city that never sleeps" and is identified by overwhelming skyscrapers and historical monuments like the Statue of Liberty. Right or wrong, these impressions will appear on your list and may provide helpful insight for your poem.

As another exercise, go to the library and research the history of the city or the area where you live. Who lived there before you? Did any historical events take place there? Did any famous people live there? What was the landscape like before the buildings (if any) went up? Once you have the answers to these questions, you can then incorporate some of that history into a poem. These tidbits of reality will help you create identities for your characters.

Identity and Home

In a more specific and personal way, your home will establish your identity in the eyes of your friends and guests. For example, if you keep a spotless home and a guest comes over for a visit, that guest will likely leave with a certain opinion of you based upon your house's appearance. If you live in a one-room wooden cabin with a dirt floor and a corrugated tin roof, then your guest is going to gain a vastly different impression of you.

Identities can be established for each person within a home by the way he keeps his private space. Try to recall the details of the private spaces your family members kept when you were growing up. Once you have assembled these details, you can use them to construct realistic characters for your poetry. For example, if your older sister kept a mound of clothes on the floor of her bedroom, a swamp of school papers on the desk, and an assortment of makeup products all over the dresser, you can use these elements of her living space to construct a similar character personality. Even if your sister eventually became an accountant, you can use the details of her life to create an artist or a lawyer character.

As you describe your living space, don't forget your pets! They have belongings and private spaces, just like the family. The type of pet will determine the interaction it has with the humans in the house. A dog, for example, will likely have access to several parts of the house, but a fish will be restricted to its tank.

Remembering Your Birthplace

Clearly, your identity begins at birth, and throughout your life it is undeniably linked to your birthplace. Some spend their early years living in the same house and never leave that neighborhood, city, or state. This sustained familiarity gives a person an acute sense of belonging to an environment— its culture and its landscape. In this situation, you come to know the smell of its seasons, the sounds of its traffic, the tastes of its foods, and the sights of its skyline.

Those Who Stay

If you remain in your birthplace past childhood, writing about it comes naturally. This place has contributed to who you are, so writing about it is just like describing an essential part of your personality. And since you have grown along with your environment, it's not too difficult to look back beyond your own experience and imagine your hometown at the time of your birth—or even before. There are reminders of your growth and the growth of your birthplace everywhere you look. You have photographs, keepsakes, and memorabilia to help you trace this evolution.

If you are still in contact with your birthplace, you may want to try to write a series of poems that re-create the stages of your life set against this landscape. How did you mature with your birthplace? Has the neighborhood grown in strength and stability since your birth, or has it settled into a steady decline?

You may also want to identify what brought your family to this town or city in the first place. Why have your relatives felt such a strong connection to the area throughout the past century? Who has this place allowed you to become? How has it disappointed or helped you? Answering these questions may generate ideas for multiple poems.

Those Who Move Away

While many find themselves deeply connected to their birthplaces, other individuals spend their lives traveling to distant places. If you are one of these wandering souls, returning to your birthplace can be emotional, awkward, or even scary. If there's nothing natural about your return, you will have to exert extra effort to revisit it and study it. In order to write about your birthplace you must investigate it thoroughly.

You may have very few concrete records of your time spent in your childhood home. The photographs, memorabilia, and heirlooms may be few, and the memories even fewer. In these situations, your poetic imagination along with your research will allow you to fill in the gaps. If you can't speak with your parents about your old home, try to imagine how they might respond to your questions. Envision the thoughts of your parents as they chose this place to begin your life as a family.

Perhaps the most important question to ask yourself is "Why did I leave this place?" Were you fleeing from a broken home? Were you bored with your surroundings? Did you travel far away in search of an education, a job, or a partner? By forcing yourself to uncover your feelings about the place you came from, you will find a wealth of poetic inspiration.

Chapter 13

E Writing about Environment

There are countless different environments in the world from which to draw inspiration. Many writers choose to focus on nature; they might describe a favorite tree or personify a mountain. Some write about the pleasures of travel and the discoveries they make in distant lands. Still others document details of the cities in which they live or the rolling hills that fill the view from their window. And there is also the environment that exists in each person's mind—a place of wonder that one visits in daydreams and hopes to encounter in the future.

Nature as a Subject

In some ancient cultures, people personified the elements of their natural environment as gods and goddesses. At other times throughout history, writers have created literature revering nature, not necessarily as the work of deities, but as the purest part of life. Contrastingly, some have condemned nature for its harsh, wild ways.

In a famous nature poem, William Wordsworth's "The Daffodils," the speaker imagines himself moving like a cloud and spying a group of daffodils:

I wandered lonely as a cloud
That floats on high o'er vales and hills,
When all at once I saw a crowd,
A host, of golden daffodils;
Beside the lake, beneath the trees,
Fluttering and dancing in the breeze.

Continuous as the stars that shine
And twinkle on the Milky Way,
They stretched in never-ending line
Along the margin of a bay:
Ten thousand saw I at a glance,
Tossing their heads in sprightly dance.

The waves beside them danced; but they
Out-did the sparkling waves in glee:
A poet could not but be gay,
In such a jocund company:
I gazed—and gazed—but little thought
What wealth the show to me had brought:

For oft, when on my couch I lie
In vacant or in pensive mood,
They flash upon that inward eye
Which is the bliss of solitude;

And then my heart with pleasure fills,
And dances with the daffodils.

In "The Daffodils" Wordsworth uses *personification* to bring the flowers and the ocean to life. When a writer uses personification he gives non-human objects human attributes or actions. In this case, the daffodils and the waves are dancing—an action that only humans can perform.

There are many exercises that you can do to help yourself create nature poetry. Beginning with descriptions of features such as hills, streams, and seashores will get you in tune with the physical aspects of nature. Free-writing and journal entries devoted simply to descriptions focusing on your five senses will give you a store of images from which to draw. The best exercise you can do simply involves visiting that hill, stream, or seashore and enjoying the place you wish to write about. However, you should also pay attention to the feelings that such landscapes instill in you. Are you at peace? Do you feel sad? Be careful not to forget the three elements of change, discovery, and decision. An encounter with some aspect of nature can lead to one or more of these three events. In Wordsworth's poem, the speaker is clearly marking a change in his life, being recollected some time afterward. Your visit with nature could bring about something similar. Perhaps spending time at a lake will inspire you to relocate closer to a body of water.

Writing about Weather

Along with specific natural features, poets have also written about the weather. At one time, deities were thought to control these forces, too. Poets would thereby address their works to a deity, or personify the weather, just as Wordsworth personified the flowers and the ocean.

In modern poems, the weather may be the subject matter, or it may be a setting that strongly influences the work. Neide Messer's poem "Hold On" works with weather to bring the speaker to the point of discovery:

A mid-November wind blusters up
and suddenly the city crackles
with the sound of leaves
above the rooftops.
They scudder down sidewalks,
quarrel in doorways—
all things thinner, more brittle
in these drought years.

Suddenly I imagine people in flight
holding their hats, scarves
twirling and coats billowed out
like big umbrellas.
The wind buffets them against
fences and along ditch banks,
sends them dancing in the blue.
Thin and weightless, their faces
bear a startled look, eyes wide,
lips shaped like O.

How fragile we become
traversing uncertain ground,
the weight of indelible yesterday
in every pocket, and I understand
what strength it takes
to hold ourselves down, to live
each day knowing one true emotion
could blow us away.

The wind flings the car door wide
when I get out, and it takes
both my hands to close it.
I grab my keys and dash for the porch,
feel the wind's cold breath
creep under my coat.

The speaker makes her discovery in the third stanza—that we are "fragile" and must "hold ourselves down" against emotions that can batter us about as the wind batters her. To come up with your own weather poem, follow the exercises set out in this section for nature poetry. Start with descriptions, concentrate on the five senses, get in touch with your feelings, and see what changes, discoveries, or decisions you are led to.

FACT

Neide Messer was writer-in-residence for the state of Idaho in 1990 and 1991. Her first book of poems, *In Far Corners*, was published by Confluence Press. Her poem "One Blessed Thing" was nominated for a Pushcart Prize. Her work also appears in *Circle of Women*, a Viking anthology of Western women writers.

Travel Poetry

Travel writing, believe it or not, is probably the oldest form in Western literature. *The Epic of Gilgamesh*, first set down in written form between 3,500 and 4,500 years ago, relates the life of a wandering strongman, Gilgamesh, who becomes king of Uruk and undertakes two important quests: one to defeat Humbaba, the guardian of the cedar forests; and one to find Utnapishtim, the one-time mortal who holds the secret of immortality. Some written works, like *The Epic of Gilgamesh*, have followed the travels of heroes on wondrous quests, while others are more down to earth and involve more personal matters.

The Travel Log

The act of traveling often causes you to enter unfamiliar territory—physical, emotional, or spiritual. This kind of journey can lead you to many insights about yourself. Poems may deal with the changes, discoveries, and decisions that come with travel, they may involve the speaker's feelings as he is traveling, or they may simply explore new sights and experiences. The idea of travel and the act of traveling itself offer you, at the very least, a sense of change and excitement that can add spice to your poems.

In one travel poem, Neide Messer's "Flying Home Late," the speaker is traveling home and anticipates a reunion with her family:

Circling above the city lights,
the moving ribbons and intermittent flashes,
I attempt to find home, the exact location,
the one light raised against the boundless
black gesture of night.

Later, near the rotating baggage claim, I wait
impatiently, stare at the poster of vanished
children. I can't get home fast enough,
the way I couldn't wait to get away.

Driving home I imagine my own sons
asleep, one curled like a question,
arms anchored around a pillow,
the other with arms flung wide like a king
or an eagle riding high wind.

Under the lamplight I unlock the door
and slip soundlessly inside. I tip-toe
through the quiet dark, check each sleeping son,
like two halves of a contrary longing,
the one curled close, the one flying.

From In Far Corners, Confluence Press, 1990. Reprinted with the permission of the author.

The speaker, knowing her sons well, imagines the positions they take during their sleep as she returns home. Her guesses are proven true when she finally sees them. While the overt discovery has to do with her sons, the speaker is discovering something about herself too—namely, the "contrary longing" she expresses in the next to last line. Her sons have become symbols of the two desires she expresses at the end of the second stanza: "I can't get home fast enough, / the way I couldn't wait to get away." Messer, in quick, easy strokes, is describing feelings many people have. Though you may periodically have intense impulses to travel far away, you are probably always relieved to return home again.

Bright City Lights

The city was initially regarded as a center of civilization—a place of law, religion, and culture. Early cities contained temples, churches, castles, meeting halls, and other structures to house the ruling classes and awe the common folk. Today, cities carry much of the same purpose and influence, though they have expanded to house great populations of people and thriving businesses. Inhabitants continue to take pride in their cities and the variety of cultures, foods, entertainment, and housing available there. Excited by urban progress, people even hold ceremonies to celebrate the groundbreaking and completion of new building projects.

Big City Dreams

If you have ever been to the top of a tall building like the Empire State Building, the Eiffel Tower, or the Space Needle, you know that you have been treated to a rare sight. The cityscape stretched out below you—the bright lights, the people, the cars, the buildings—is an incredible sight. If you have visited the museums, libraries, theaters, stadiums, and arenas in a particular city, you have had the privilege of experiencing the cultural opportunities that the city has to offer. All of these aspects of a city can inspire your poetry.

It is said that you can read the values of a people by finding the largest buildings in their cities. In ancient times, the largest buildings were temples and churches. During the European Renaissance, the biggest buildings belonged to the kings and their governments. Nowadays, the largest buildings tend to house corporations.

With so many different kinds of people from so many distinct cultures, there seems to be endless writing material in a city. You can write about a discussion you had with a homeless person on a subway, a group of pigeons you watched in a park, or a fantastic restaurant where you ate one evening. You can also explore a dream or wish you have had about a city. Perhaps when you were younger you wished to see some marvel in a far-off city, like Big Ben in London, England, or the Sydney Opera House in Australia. Did you ever fulfill that dream when you got older? If so, what was the trip like? Did it meet your expectations? If not, why haven't you gone to visit that site? Do you plan to go in the future?

If you live in a city that has received wide literary attention, you might want to write about a less popular landmark. Instead of discussing Seattle's Space Needle, for example, describe the Pike Place Market. Instead of writing about southern California's Disneyland, explore the Modjeska Historic House and Gardens. This will help you create more unique poetry for yourself and for your readers.

The Quiet Side of Cities

Of course, a city is not only about traffic jams and skyscrapers; it has its quiet places as well. These are great spots from which to gain inspiration. Perhaps you will see a young boy sailing a model boat on a pond or a little girl flying a kite in a park. Watching the wildlife in a city can give you good ideas as well. Take note of the birds that nibble on fallen crumbs as you sip coffee outside of a café. Locate a squirrel in a tree carefully watching the passersby. Describing these moments will give your city poetry a unique spin.

The "fly on the wall" technique is also useful in cities—some call this "people watching." You can draw a comparison between the people you see walking down the streets and those who are working in the shops. Contrast the people riding the subway to work early in the morning and those taking it to a club at night. One exercise to try is a series of brief descriptions that capture the people you see around you. Focus on their actions and appearances, record the bits of dialogue you hear, and try to create a strong impression of these people without speaking to them.

To give your city poetry a really quiet atmosphere, try doing writing exercises without using the sense of sound. How would you describe a truck rumbling by without the rumble? How would you describe a jackhammer without the rhythmic pounding and cracking? Focus on the visual aspects of the scenes around you.

Take note of the same details of the cityscape around you. Describe the buildings, the streets, the sidewalks, the cars—all of the features you can see, hear, smell, and touch. Then go back to the descriptions of nature that you made before and compare your notes. Locate any similarities or wildly opposing details that you can juxtapose in your own poem. Read your poetry aloud to yourself. Does it capture the feel of the city?

The Downside of Cities

Since cities attract people from all walks of life and press them together into a confined space, problems inevitably arise. A brief walk through the heart of any major city will take you through a number of situations, intense and trivial, tragic and frustrating, overwhelming and upsetting. Generations of poets have confronted these problems with their verses, storing images that are familiar to many. In the late 1700s, William Blake wrote a poem called "London" that captures the misery of the people trapped in the city:

I wander thro' each charter'd street,
Near where the charter'd Thames does flow,
And mark in every face I meet
Marks of weakness, marks of woe.

In every cry of every man,
In every Infant's cry of fear,
In every voice; in every ban,
The mind-forg'd manacles I hear.

How the Chimney-sweeper's cry
Every black'ning Church appalls,
And the hapless Soldier's sigh
Runs in blood down Palace walls.

But most thro' midnight streets I hear
How the youthful Harlot's curse
Blasts the new-born Infant's tear
And blights with plagues the Marriage hearse.

ALERT!

If you're having trouble beginning a poem about the negative sides of a city, try using the immediate problems confronting you personally as a start. Focus on the broken bottles that litter the sidewalks outside of your apartment, the graffiti on the walls of the train you take to work, or the gravel that scratches up your windshield when you're driving.

To write a poem about the downside of a city, you do not need to overwhelm your readers with a list of existing problems. Instead, you should focus on creating images through the use of detail, as Blake does. Write out descriptions of the homeless man who stands in traffic with his tin cup, the mountain of stinking garbage in the alley behind your office, or the woman clutching her arm after a mugger has torn away her purse. These small pictures will say more to your reader than any blatant denunciations of homelessness, pollution, and crime.

Imagining the Ideal

One of the pleasures of daydreaming is imagining an ideal place. For one person, this place could be a deserted beach with sunlight reflecting off the waves. For another, the perfect spot might be a mountain cabin with a crackling fire and a comfy overstuffed chair. Or your ideal place might not even exist in the world. Perhaps you imagine a new nation, a new planet, or a new universe. Even if the place doesn't exist anywhere else but in your mind, you should still describe it as though it is tangible and real. In fact, you should pay even more attention to your descriptions of imaginary places than real ones. Since the place does not exist, you must bring it to life using sensory impressions and believable details.

Capturing Your Place

The imaginary place you create is special to you. Perhaps you are the king or queen of an imagined empire, or maybe you are a visitor to a distant land. Your ideal place might resemble one you have experienced before, but the subtle variations you add make it more magical. Over the centuries, a great deal of literature has been written about idealized or invented places, such as Camelot, Brigadoon, Narnia, Middle Earth, Oz, Shangri-la, Dilmun, and the Elysian Fields. The word *utopia* is used for such places, where readers are drawn to follow the heroes and travelers they admire.

To write about your own imaginary place, you must work through several journals or free-writes. You won't capture anything beyond the barest essence of this place if you write only one description of it. Take several days. Turn the place over in your mind and observe it from all angles. What does it look like? Who are its inhabitants? What is their currency? How do they dress? Travel to the boundaries of this place and describe what you see, hear, smell, feel, and taste at every step. And don't simply describe a place once—you must describe it during different seasons, at different times of day, and under different weather conditions.

Don't forget that your invented dream place is unattainable for a reason. Consider this fact, and ask yourself why a place like this could never exist on Earth. What about human nature, animal instinct, or the environment would not accommodate your utopia? This idea might add shadow (see the discussion of *shadow* in Chapter 10) to your poem.

Once you have begun your descriptions, you can set out a list of reasons why you visit this place. Is it the beauty of the landscape? Is it a place where you find peace and solitude? Has the place helped you find a new facet of yourself—a desire for adventure, a new motivation, or a strength of character you never knew you had? Have you fallen in love with someone there? Have you located relatives or friends in this place?

Two ideas that you may wish to incorporate into your poem about your ideal place are beauty and longing. For example, this place may be so beautiful that you long for it even when you aren't imagining it. You can't, however, simply use the words *beautiful* and *longing* and expect your readers to experience what you have envisioned. Work diligently to bring these feelings to life using simple and clear details.

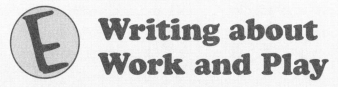

Chapter 14

Writing about Work and Play

S ince the majority of your waking hours are likely spent working at a job, it's inevitable that many of your ideas for poems will be inspired by your workplace. Whether you work in an office, in the outdoors, or in your home, you have plenty of material to draw from. Fortunately, life is not all about work. During your hours off and on the weekends you can devote your energy to family, friends, and personal hobbies. These activities can generate material for poems just as easily as your job.

What You Do

It's impossible to escape one basic fact: The major reason why most people work is to support themselves. While a job provides you with income, it also hopefully gives you a sense of accomplishment and purpose. Whether you have dug a hole for a swimming pool, balanced a complex business account, or waited on 100 dinner guests in a single evening, knowing that your skills are useful and appreciated is a gratifying feeling.

Like your home and your family, your job says a great deal about who you are as a person. Right or wrong, people perceive you based upon the job you hold, and they create an identity for you this way. As an exercise, make a list of occupations and then write a number of your own preconceived notions about them. Are your ideas accurate or stereotypical?

A significant part of this satisfaction comes from the dignity of the work you do. If you work as a counselor at a high school, a sanitation worker for your city, or a lawyer who protects the innocent, you are providing a valuable service to your fellow citizens. That basic satisfaction you feel about your work can be very useful in your poetry. Conversely, your job might just be a way to earn money, or perhaps you were forced into the job by a parent or spouse. Whatever your situation, the work you do can give you great ideas for poetry.

William Wordsworth's well-known poem "The Solitary Reaper" takes the "fly on the wall" approach to the subject of work. The speaker of the poem spies a woman working in a field and listens to her as she sings:

> *Behold her, single in the field,*
> > *Yon solitary Highland Lass!*
> *Reaping and singing by herself;*
> > *Stop here, or gently pass!*
> *Alone she cuts and binds the grain,*
> *And sings a melancholy strain;*

O listen! for the Vale profound
Is overflowing with the sound.

No Nightingale did ever chaunt
*   More welcome notes to weary bands*
Of travellers in some shady haunt,
*   Among Arabian sands:*
A voice so thrilling ne'er was heard
In spring-time from the Cuckoo-bird,
Breaking the silence of the seas
Among the farthest Hebrides.

Will no one tell me what she sings?—
*   Perhaps the plaintive numbers flow*
For old, unhappy, far-off things,
*   And battles long ago:*
Or is it some more humble lay,
Familiar matter of to-day?
Some natural sorrow, loss, or pain,
That has been, and may be again?

Whate'er the theme, the Maiden sang
*   As if her song could have no ending;*
I saw her singing at her work,
*   And o'er the sickle bending;—*
I listen'd, motionless and still;
And, as I mounted up the hill,
The music in my heart I bore,
Long after it was heard no more.

Wordsworth's speaker tries to pinpoint the source of the woman's song. Is it a "melancholy strain"? Does she sing of "sorrow, loss, or pain"? The speaker admires this woman's song and the difficult work she does, and she intrigues him. By choosing concrete details about your job, you can intrigue your reader in a similar way.

Textures of the Workplace

If you sit at a desk at work, examine it closely for a few minutes. What material is it made out of? Is it littered with papers or clean and organized? Is there a computer, a calculator, a stapler? If you work at a restaurant, do you have your own cubby or locker where you keep your personal things? If you own a landscaping company, do you drive a truck filled with tools or a car with your logo on the side? These details create a texture that makes your workplace different from your home.

If there is a cafeteria or break room at your workplace, take the time to examine it. Since this place likely has tables, chairs, a sofa, and perhaps a TV, microwave, and refrigerator, it would most likely compare to the kitchen or living room in your own home. Are there any differences? Which space is more comfortable? Why?

Invisible Elements

Generally speaking, the workplace is designed to be functional, and your home is designed to be comfortable. The details of furniture, decoration, and lighting contribute to the comfort level of a space. Revisit the break room in your workplace. Is the sofa lumpy, or is the upholstery too rough, too cold, or too slick? How does your sofa at home feel in comparison? Also, what is the temperature like in your workplace as compared with your home? Is your office kept cold by central air conditioning, while your home is warmer due to a fireplace?

Write a poem about the different textures of your workplace and your home. Describe how a similar object in both places feels to you. Write down key descriptors, such as fabrics, colors, and temperatures. Also, describe the things you see at work that you don't see at home—filing cabinets, uniforms, or heavy machinery.

Though they are not in the majority, some people feel more comfortable at work. For example, if you live in a very small, modestly furnished apartment in a city, you may enjoy the comfort of your leather office chair, the wall-to-wall office carpeting, and the art hanging on the walls of your office. Companies often provide their employees with extra benefits so that they may do their jobs more efficiently. If you sit in a chair cozier than any chair you have at home, you probably favor your work environment.

If you work at home, take a look at the area you have set aside for your job. Does it have a feel different from that which you find in the rest of the house? How do you set up boundaries to keep the work area distinct? Do you keep a separate work area at all? Compare the elements of working from home with jobs you have had in the past. Do you prefer working from home or do you miss the companionship of coworkers? Do you find it easier or more difficult to motivate yourself in your home environment?

Textures of Relationships

The relationships you have with your coworkers are similar to the other relationships you have in your life. You must share a particular space with your coworkers, just like you once did with siblings and roommates. However, these people do not necessarily come from the same background that you do, and they are likely to say and do things that you are not used to. But you will generally share interests and skills with these people, as you all hold similar jobs in a single location.

Your boss, if you have one, probably acts a bit like a parent. She may train you in your job tasks and in the work culture of your company, and very likely she will set policies for your dress code, your workspace, your deadlines, and your meal times. Similarly, if you have people working under you, they may seem a bit like your children. You set certain guidelines for them to follow and you give them particular responsibilities.

However, there is a large difference between your work mates and your family members. You can, in some cases, pause your work relationships the moment that you leave your job for the day. And when you quit or lose your job, you don't have to retain any ties with the company or the people with whom you worked. Family relationships, on the other hand, are always with you. For example, you probably have pictures of family members at work, but you likely don't keep pictures of your boss and coworkers at home.

How can relationships be illustrated in poetry?
Since poems are not acted out or accompanied by instrumentation, it takes skill and practice to realistically express a relationship. Perhaps the most important element of creating a relationship within a poem has to do with the point of view of your speaker. The speaker can address a reader, another character, or himself. What language does he use, who does he address, and what is his opinion of the subject of the poem?

This difference in relationships leads you to behave differently in your work and home environments. Unless you know your coworkers well, you probably don't allow them to see parts of your personality that you would allow your family to see. At work, you may come across as shy and reserved, but at home, you might be fun-loving and open. But occasionally, you might find the boundaries between work and home being crossed. Perhaps you will one day marry a coworker. Maybe your office mate will become the godparent of your first child. Explore these relationships and highlight the similarities and differences between your home life and your work life. These ideas and themes could make for fascinating poetry.

Chores

You probably spend some portion of your life maintaining and repairing the areas where you live, work, and play. In many ways, the chores you take on define your role in your family and create an identity for you, much like your job. Daily and weekly chores can become such a routine part of life that you might not even notice when you're doing them. Less frequent chores, like seasonal ones, generally require more effort, planning, and materials. Reflecting on your chores and the way you feel about them can provide you with strong poetic material.

Living on Your Own

If you live by yourself, then you will have to take care of all the chores around your home. However, you will likely have a list of chores that you prefer to do, those that you don't like to do, and those that you will (or must) pay someone else to do for you. Your chore strategy will reveal much about your personality, and this pattern can be one that you use when creating a character within a poem.

For example, say you have a character in a poem who lives in a messy bedroom but who spends two hours each evening preparing a meal, eating it, and cleaning the pots and the dishes. That person's priority is clearly placed on having a well-cooked meal as opposed to a neat living space, and a reader will gain a certain impression about that person. If a character keeps a manicured lawn, trimmed trees, and crystal-clear pool but doesn't pick up the newspapers cluttering the dining room, a reader will identify a different sort of person. Characters who live alone drive readers to question that status. Why does the character live by herself as opposed to with roommates? Why has the character never married? These details will help you create an intriguing image in your poem.

Living with Others

When you live with others, whether with roommates or family, you will likely divide the chores between the residents. The chores each person chooses to do—or those that the person will accept if assigned—will give insight into that person's personality and skill level. For example, one person in the house might be good with plumbing and will therefore fix any leaks or other plumbing problems that arise. An artistic person might choose to create seasonal decorations, sew curtains for all the windows, and buy pieces of art for the walls. Someone who enjoys cooking might volunteer to prepare the meals for the other members of the household.

This division of labor might be handy, but it also establishes an identity for each person living in the home. If these identities are not altered or switched every once in a while, some members may become dependent on others, and some might get frustrated with their responsibility. Brainstorm about these dynamics for your poetry. Draw from your own experiences and from others that you have read about in books, magazines, or newspapers. Also, it might be a good idea to steer clear of traditional or clichéd chore assignments. A female character need not always be the stay-at-home parent or laundry person, and a male character should not always be given the tasks of outdoor chores and household repairs. If you mix it up a little the characters will be more interesting for your reader.

Repetitive Tasks

If you are performing a repetitive, manual chore such as lawn mowing, you may find your thoughts wandering. It is very possible that you will have an idea for a poem as you are doing your yard work or some other tedious task. Don't ignore these thoughts! Even a seemingly unrelated thought could be useful in a poem. For example, Jeanie French's "Thinning" explores an act the speaker has done countless times but which she suddenly perceives in a new light. French takes the action of gardening, a hobby associated with nurturing and life, and turns it around by recasting the gardener in the role of killer.

Reluctant, I sit down between rows
faint lines of valiant green marching
between aisles of straw, the sun hot
on my head, burning the tips of my ears
and the back of my neck. I separate
the seedlings gently with my fingertips
feeling for the strongest, thickest shoot
in the clutch of tiny succulent leaves,
for that is the one which will survive
my tender care. I can't wear gloves—
I need all the delicacy of unimpeded touch,
nothing but the ridges of my fingerprints
and the pulpy-soft, new-sprung stalks.
I grasp a spindly clump of seedlings and pull
gently, sever roots from nurturing earth,
lay them aside to die in the strong spring sun.

Murder lives in my cells
as I reach for the next sacrifice.

Reprinted with permission of the author.

One good idea for a poem would be to make a chore a metaphor for another action. For example, write about mopping the floor as though holding back a disastrous flood. Or write about washing your windows as a way of seeing things more clearly and changing your perspective on life.

Tinkering with Tools

Your job and chores have their own rhythms, from the clack-clack of a keyboard to the squeal of an electric drill and the grumbling of a lawnmower. Capturing the music of these rhythms in your poems will require a good ear, a strong feel for the sounds of words, and a good grasp of the metric forms discussed earlier.

A Child's Perspective

As a child you were likely fascinated by tools, gadgets, and machines. They can look funny, frightening, or fantastic. Jeff Knorr, in his poem "Taking Notes on Storytelling," exemplifies this childhood fascination:

The tractor down the road is stopped, cold.
It has been here empty for two days now.
My son and I break from my work
and go out in the cold in his wagon.
He bellows, tractor, as we come close.
Wide-eyed and pleased as a colt
in an open, spring pasture,
he drives his eyes over the machine.
He steals grace from the engine,
from fat tires caked with mud and hay.
We bounce down the road,
so he looks over his shoulder, smiles,
and begins the unintelligible story of tractors
while tracing the veins of a single maple leaf
flaming red in his hands.

Reprinted with the permission of the author.

Knorr is careful with his rhythms as he portrays the child's emotions. The first line, for example, rolls the reader into the poem on an iambic beat. A comma replaces a missing unstressed syllable in front of the final word, *cold*. This forces the reader into a pause to make up for the dropped beat. In describing the child's reaction to the tractor he begins critical lines with the same iambic beat: "He bellows, *tractor*"; "he drives his eyes."

The mystery of machines can offer a poet boundless opportunity for writing. What machines fascinated you as a child? Take a trip back to your childhood and recall one machine as vividly as you can from your innocent perspective. Then look at the same object with your adult eyes. What does the machine mean to you now?

Knorr also pays close attention to the sounds of the words. Note, for example, in the line "He bellows, *tractor*, as we come close" how "bellows" and "close" repeat the long *o* sound—almost as if reproducing the long "Oh!" exclamation of a wonder-struck child. The words "drives his eyes" repeat the long *i* sound as if to emphasize what the eyes are seeing and doing. The last two lines repeat the long *a* sound—"tracing," "veins," "maple," "flaming"—to reinforce the shift in attention from the tractor to the leaf.

Finding the Rhythm

Perhaps the best thing about tools and machines, however, is that they make weird and impressive noises. Walt Whitman, in his poem "To a Locomotive in Winter," expresses a childlike joy at the sounds of a train:

Thee for my recitative!
Thee in the driving storm, even as now, the snow, the winter-day declining,
Thee in thy panoply, thy measured dual throbbing, and thy beat convulsive,
Thy black cylindric body, golden brass and silvery steel,
Thy ponderous side-bars, parallel and connecting rods, gyrating, shuttling
  at thy sides,
Thy metrical, now swelling pant and roar, now tapering in the distance,

Thy great protruding head-light fix'd in front,
Thy long, pale, floating vapor-pennants, tinged with delicate purple,
The dense and murky clouds out-belching from thy smoke-stack,
Thy knitted frame, thy springs and valves, the tremulous twinkle of thy
    wheels,
Thy train of cars behind, obedient, merrily-following,
Through gale or calm, now swift, now slack, yet steadily careering;
Type of the modern! emblem of motion and power! pulse of the continent!
For once come serve the Muse, and merge in verse, even as here I see thee,
With storm and buffeting gusts of wind and falling snow,
By day thy warning ringing bell to sound its notes,
By night, thy silent signal lamps to swing.

Fierce-throated beauty!
Roll through my chant with all thy lawless music! thy swinging lamps at night,
Thy madly-whistled laughter! echoing, rumbling like an earthquake, rousing
    all!
Law of thyself complete, thine own track firmly holding,
(No sweetness debonair of tearful harp or glib piano thine,)
Thy trills of shrieks by rocks and hills return'd,
Launch'd o'er the prairies wide, across the lakes,
To the free skies unpent and glad and strong.

Like Knorr, Whitman is also sensitive to the rhythms of his verses. The heavy repetitions at the beginnings of his opening lines (called *anaphora*), for example, echo the chug-chugging sounds of the train. He also depends on iambics to gather steam in many of his lines: "By night, thy silent signal lamps to swing"; "with all thy lawless music, thy swinging lamps at night." Most notable, though, are the long, languid lines themselves, which mimic the echoing sounds of the train and even the length of the train itself.

Whitman also takes full advantage of the sounds of his words. He makes ample use of alliteration: The *s* sounds in "silvery steel" and "smoke-stack" echo the hiss of steam, the *t* sounds in "tremulous twinkle" echo the sound and the flash of the wheels, the *r* sounds in "rumbling" and "rousing" mimic the "earthquake" created by the train's passing. He also chooses words, such as "throbbing" and "shuttling," that imitate the sounds he is re-creating (onomatopoeia). It's clear that the speaker in Whitman's poem takes great delight in reproducing the sounds he hears.

> To re-create sounds in your poetry, mimic them with your mouth first—hiss like a steam engine or growl like a motorcycle—and pay attention to the positions of your tongue, lips, and teeth. What letters would you normally produce in those positions? Write them down and create words to generate those sounds.

Pleasures and Pastimes

Working knowledge of your pastime can go a long way toward creating poems that you will enjoy just as much as the pastime itself. Say, for example, that you enjoy sewing quilts. Each scrap of cloth gathered from a favorite dress, a child's pajamas, or a father's handkerchief, stands as a reminder of that time in your life and opens a floodgate of memories.

Example Poems

The following poem about quilting is called "A Fixed Celestial," by Neide Messer:

> *Snip thread, guide it*
> *through the needle's eye,*
> *knot the end. Pull*
> *the quilt hoop close*
> *and stitch. The last two*
> *I pull out, try again.*
> *This time three stitches,*
> *then three more. Soon*
> *they come quick and even, in and out,*
> *along the edge of each piece*
> *in a thrifty star pattern.*
> *A collision of florals and solids*

in hues of rose, navy, bone,
the shapes run into one another.

Like stars years ago
in a box canyon. A swath of lights
edge to edge in crystalline
winter shimmered in our eyes
as we gazed upward at Hubble's discovery,
the expanding universe, all
celestial masses moving farther apart
forever—galaxies, constellations,
the north star, Pluto and Mars—
even Orion
spinning slowly from us.

This is not a distance
I comprehend—light years away
already, but I know about
separation, all our heavenly
bodies on this blue-green earth, bound
by gravity and promises, yet
disconnected. We hover,
drift away, leave alone.
Here in this sewing room
I piece together what I can,
not people and planets but this
milky way of fabric.
With thimble, needle and thread,
one by one, my hands
stitch the star down.

Reprinted with the permission of the author.

Any reminders you have from your pastimes—fabric pieces, photographs, ticket stubs, autographs—make excellent beginning points for poems. To work toward the creation of a poem, first write a narrative about the details of the reminder. Did you wear that shirt to your very first football game? Was that photo taken on your ninth birthday? Once you have established a narrative, take out concrete details that appeal to the senses and work them into a poem.

Another poem, "Camping, Northern California," by Chad Lietz, describes a moment of awareness that overcomes the speaker while looking into the night sky:

We drop dried flesh into our mouths & chew
the night's wide scope into a tunneled pulse,
a geodesic dome of insect sight.

Head thrown back you wait along the road
& watch the stars explode or spin, fractals
of sky & grainy jagged light; I'm lost
behind, among the same, slackjawed & smiling.
Only a breath from that far space to here.

The grove begins to sag like Joseph sheaves
in dreams. I pull a string & bend the trees.
Arbored arms unbind the sky & wrap
themselves around this spot where earth revolves
beneath our feet. This flesh we share in touch
explodes, competes with stars in fractured light.

From Red Rock Review, *Issue 16 (Fall 2004). Reprinted with the permission of the author.*

Don't simply talk to yourself when you work with your own memories. The memories may be vivid to you, but your reader was probably not there with you at the time. Like Lietz, you must include significant details to bring your reader into your experience.

Writing about Your Pastimes

Pastimes, like jobs, can be performed with tools, gadgets, and machines. A sewing machine, for example, makes a special hum-click sound as the needle works through the cloth. A butane stove used at a campsite makes a distinct hiss. The wheels of a skateboard rumble one way when you ride on concrete and another when you ride on wood. Be sure to include the music of these tools and machines when you write about your pastimes.

You can also try a "what if" poem. For example, if you are a fan of the Chicago Cubs baseball team you probably know that the team has not won a World Series since 1908. What would it be like if the team finally won? Describe how the winning moment would play out on the field, where you would be at the time, and what you would do to celebrate.

Another topic for writing could be the moment you learned how to perform your hobby. Say, for example, that you tried to paint a watercolor of the bowl of fruit on your dining-room table. However, in every attempt, you ended up blending the oranges, apples, and bananas into a brown mess. But one day, something magical happened. The colors stayed in their places, the shapes held, and the fruit bowl appeared! What a feeling of triumph! This is the sort of moment to describe in detail in your poetry. This moment may also have taught you something about yourself as a person. A new-found skill, strength, or talent is something you can work into the context of your poem.

Chapter 15

Writing about Culture

The aspects of a culture communicate to others what is important to a particular group of people. It shows how they live now, how their forefathers lived, what they fight for, and what they believe in. Writing about your culture's popular trends, history, music, foods, and religions not only gives voice to your own perspectives but also, in a small way, redefines what they mean. In other words, you are helping to shape your culture by writing about it.

Popular Culture

Pop culture is always reinventing itself. The music, clothing, hairstyles, and movies that are popular one day will be outdated the next. Though trends disappear as quickly as they arrive, they often make comebacks at later times. On the one hand, such change is dizzying and disorienting. People often feel they are losing track of these changes if they do not read every newspaper, magazine, or book and watch every program on television.

QUESTION?

What is popular culture?
Also known simply as pop culture, this term embodies the contemporary lifestyles, fashions, and products that are generally accepted by a given population of people. Pop culture can also include cultural trends and patterns, including those related to food, religion, and travel.

On the other hand, cultural change can signify positive progress. Long gone are the days when women could not vote, when it took mail several months to be delivered, and when people were forced into their parents' professions. Now, women not only vote but also hold public office, e-mail sends your messages instantly, and, with the right education, you can choose any profession you want.

Current Events

To write about pop culture, you must keep informed about current events. You can read and write about new technology, like the iPod or hybrid cars, or the latest toys popular among kids. You can also read and write about more serious matters, such as war, disease, and poverty. All of these events, both good and bad, make up the culture in which you live.

Charles Harper Webb's poem "Political Poem" takes a look at some of the serious events transpiring in Latin America. The speaker holds a cynical view toward the prospect of changing things for the better, but the woman he speaks to holds fast to her ideals. The compromise they work out at the end of the poem is amusingly personal.

Fog blew over us, alone on the dark pier.
As waves rolled by with the nonstop consistency
of wars, you talked about your politics,
using words like desaparecidos, campesinos,
Chile (pronounced Cheé-lay). "I love the passion

of Latinos," you said, "though the men see my mind
as a drawback—a headache after a good drunk."
You called me "a gringo cynic"; I obliged
with "All rulers stand on the crushed backs of someone.
My politics is to avoid the bottom of the pile."

I've seen your starving Indios *in cardboard shacks,*
skeletal dogs and stick-limbed niños
limping naked through mud streets.
I know your politics spring from a good heart,
just as I know your sympathy for the oppressed

comes from oppression; your rage at cruelty,
from cruelty to you. Altruism often
springs from private pain; I know that's true,
just as I know you needed me to voice your doubts.
I'd work with you for "social justice"

if I thought change would do more
than shift the cattle prods and atom bombs
to new oppressors' hands, shoving new victims
under revolution's wheel. I don't know what,
besides dying, will stop the pain that we all feel.

But I know this: we walked to my room
from the pier, undressed each other,
and all night did for the cause of justice,
liberty, and love, the best
that, in this tortured world, two bodies can.

From Red Rock Review. *Reprinted with the permission of the author.*

The speaker in Webb's poem states that "Altruism often / springs from private pain." Look at an issue that you have a personal stake in, or an object that you own, and use it as the springboard for your own commentary on modern culture. For example, if you own a lot of books, try to isolate the reason why you read so much. Do you read for personal entertainment or are you pursuing knowledge? Why does your culture read so many (or so few) books? Do your private practices match or oppose those of your culture?

History

As often as a culture reinvents itself, many ideas, trends, and values a culture holds come from deep within its history. History, however, does not only live within books, newspapers, and films. Many of the buildings, foods, and people around you draw from history as well. In fact, you can sometimes interact with these histories without knowing it. When you pass by a fire hydrant, do you ever wonder who invented it? When you eat a piece of candy, do you ever try to guess where it originated? Asking these questions and finding their answers can start you on the path toward great historical poetry.

Choosing Events

Historical events and people have always provided inspiration for poets and writers. You have already read one historical poem: Edwin Arlington Robinson's "Villanelle of Change" (page 118), which deals with the battle between the Greeks and Persians at Marathon. Poets also occasionally write poems to commemorate the anniversaries of memorable events. Many poets, for example, have already written verses in remembrance of the September 11 terrorist attacks. Countless poems have been written about the wars, politics, art, and music that have appeared throughout history. The key to getting started is choosing a historical event to focus on.

To write a historical poem, identify an event, place, or person that intrigues you. For example, perhaps Susan B. Anthony and her work for women's suffrage have always fascinated you. In this case, you can learn about her upbringing, the political action she took, and her other interests. Write a poem from her point of view as a child. Or imagine what she would think of the current state of women's rights if she were alive today.

Writing Personal Histories

If you ask any person in America about his or her family history, you will likely hear stories of immigration, of hardships back in a home country, and of acclimation into American culture. If you look hard enough at your own family history, you will find similar stories. Perhaps you will find that your ancestors were slaves. They might have fought in the First or Second World War. Or maybe they fled pogroms in the Soviet Union.

Jeff Knorr, in his poem "Keep Your Dog Quiet," examines the decades-old conflict of Latinos and Anglos in the Southwest through the two main characters in the poem. The speaker, an Anglo, recalls a friendship he had with a Mexican-American boy. Consider the following selection from the poem:

> It is raining and late October.
> The dog and I have chased the leaves
> nearly back to home for an easy two miles.
> As we pass a gate, low and Spanish
> wrought iron, the black dog on the other side
> wheezes at us like an inner tube being stomped on.
> He lunges off all four paws, huffing harder and harder
> for a moment stopping then starting again the life,
> what matters most right now, cut out of him—debarked.
> He keeps at it. We cross the road and come up
> in front of the quiet house with a flagpole,
> stainless steel flying stars and stripes.
>
> I'm drifting in the clouds racing past
> the blue square and red stripes,
> maple and sycamore leaves like flames swirling our feet.
> It's eighth grade again, that fall rainy afternoon
> when Jesse Gallegos and I sit in social studies,
> the teacher flexing against us asked,
> "Who can tell us about Mexicans in California?"
> Then he points a finger like a gun at Jesse
> and pops, "And I don't want to hear from you."
> We sit through the timelines that look like arrows,

lame talk of missions, of land grants, of Mexican
cowboys—vaqueros, Jesse whispers—our
history the moments of conquest.
These weren't the Mexicans I knew.

Reprinted with the permission of the author.

To write a personal history like the one in Knorr's poem, take a look at two cultures that are living side by side. What tensions exist between them? How have those tensions surfaced in the community? What personal involvement have you had in those tensions? Write out your answers to these questions in as much detail as you can before working with a poetic form.

Traditions

Another way to look at culture is through the traditions you carry forth within your family, community, or nation. Comparing the different holidays that separate countries celebrate is one way to look at traditions. For example, though England, Canada, and America are all English-speaking countries, they don't all celebrate the same holidays. England and Canada celebrate Boxing Day on December 26, and Americans don't celebrate it at all. Similarly, Americans celebrate Thanksgiving in November, but Canadians celebrate it in October.

One idea for a poem would be to research one of these different holidays to find out why it is celebrated. For example, have you ever heard of Guy Fawkes Day? This is an actual holiday celebrated every year in England on November 5. You could write a poem about the man, the events surrounding his life, and the traditional celebrations held in his memory.

Another idea would be to look at how one of your own celebrations has changed over the years. For example, if you have seen the movie *Meet Me in St. Louis*, you may remember that on Halloween, the children don't go trick-or-treating. Instead, they build bonfires and play pranks all through the town. Do you celebrate this holiday differently? Likewise, does your family do something unique to celebrate a certain holiday or people's birthdays? Use these special details to create an interesting poem.

Traditions at Home

Home life is filled with traditions that would make interesting topics for poems, too. For instance, your mother may always use the best china, silver, and linen for Sunday dinner. Perhaps your family vacations at a secluded beach every August. Or maybe your father and uncle go deer hunting every winter. If you don't know the reasons and stories behind these events, ask! These are the details that will add color to your poetry.

Make sure you ask more than one person about your family's traditions so you can view them from different perspectives. Your brother may remember Sunday dinners with details you forgot, or your aunt might recall what gifts were given at birthday parties over the years. You might even choose to write a poem about those different perspectives.

Once you have learned the details about a particular family tradition, write a poem about it. Perhaps your mother uses the fine dinnerware on Sundays to continue her own mother's tradition. Maybe your mother and father choose the same beach each year because it is the place where they spent their honeymoon. And your father and uncle might hunt every year because their father took them hunting when they were younger.

War and Warriors

Unfortunately, as long as there have been cultures, there have been wars. And as long as there have been wars, writers have written about them. Nearly 2,500 years ago, Aeschylus, in his play *Agamemnon*, portrayed the joy one soldier felt upon his return home from the Trojan War. He also described the harsh conditions under which the common soldiers lived. If you have fought in a war or lived through wartime, you probably have a wealth of memories charged with strong emotion and imagery.

The Honor of Fighting

Many poets over the centuries have written about the honor of fighting well, even if it leads to the death of the warrior. Alfred, Lord Tennyson's famous poem "The Charge of the Light Brigade" describes the charge of 600 horsemen armed with sabers into a position defended by guns and cannon. Many of the horsemen fell, but Tennyson emphasizes the glory, not the slaughter, in the last stanza of this poem:

> When can their glory fade?
> O the wild charge they made!
>   All the world wonder'd.
> Honour the charge they made!
> Honour the Light Brigade,
>   Noble six hundred!

The Horror of War

Wilfred Owen, a soldier in World War I, described war differently from Tennyson in his poem "Dulce et Decorum Est." Note the detail with which he portrays the weariness and the raggedness of the retreating men. Note also how the scene changes when the gas explodes in their ranks:

> Bent double, like old beggars under sacks,
> Knock-kneed, coughing like hags, we cursed through sludge,
> Till on the haunting flares we turned our backs
> And towards our distant rest began to trudge.
> Men marched asleep. Many had lost their boots
> But limped on, blood-shod. All went lame; all blind;
> Drunk with fatigue; deaf even to the hoots
> Of tired, outstripped Five-Nines that dropped behind.
>
> Gas! Gas! Quick, boys!—An ecstasy of fumbling,
> Fitting the clumsy helmets just in time;
> But someone still was yelling out and stumbling,
> And flound'ring like a man in fire or lime . . .

Dim, through the misty panes and thick green light,
As under a green sea, I saw him drowning.

In all my dreams, before my helpless sight,
He plunges at me, guttering, choking, drowning.

If in some smothering dreams you too could pace
Behind the wagon that we flung him in,
And watch the white eyes writhing in his face,
His hanging face, like a devil's sick of sin;
If you could hear, at every jolt, the blood
Come gargling from the froth-corrupted lungs,
Obscene as cancer, bitter as the cud
Of vile, incurable sores on innocent tongues,—
My friend, you would not tell with such high zest
To children ardent for some desperate glory,
The old Lie: Dulce et decorum est
Pro patria mori.[1]

[1] *It is sweet and fitting to die for one's country*

Whatever your judgment of war, you cannot simply state your opinion in your poetry. The result will be passionate but not necessarily poetic. If you have personal experiences to draw from, then do so. Like Tennyson and Owen, you must find details that re-create the experience for your reader.

The Subject of Faith

Faith is another strong part of many cultures. Over the centuries, poets have created countless verses in honor and praise of their deities. Whether in supplication, prayer, or reflection, many have centered their poetry on the heavenly being they feel guides their lives. The speakers of these poems have usually encountered a challenge or problem in their lives that they cannot overcome alone. This is the point at which they turn to faith.

Communication

George Herbert's poem "Easter Wings" is one such poem that deals with faith. Because the speaker feels unworthy of God's love and attention, he asks for God's help. Note the form of the poem, which was originally printed sideways to look like a pair of wings:

Lord, who createdst man in wealth and store,
Though foolishly he lost the same,
Decaying more and more,
Till he became
Most poore:
With thee
O let me rise
As larks, harmoniously,
And sing this day thy victories:
Then shall the fall further the flight in me.

My tender age in sorrow did beginne:
And still with sicknesses and shame
Thou didst so punish sinne,
That I became
Most thinne.
With thee
Let me combine,
And feel this day thy victorie:
For, if I imp my wing on thine,
Affliction shall advance the flight in me.

Searching

Some poets and mystics aren't content to pray or meditate to talk to God. Many will go on a quest to seek their deities. The poems that result can be narratives in the form of a quest, they can be lyrics that describe how the writer feels when he or she finds God, or they can be desperate searches for reasons for their failure.

Two symbols that will appear frequently in poems about faith are the mountain and the tree. Sometimes a related image will appear—a ladder, a rope, a stair, a pole, a column—but these derive from the two main symbols. The mountain and the tree represent a pathway between cosmic zones— upper, middle, and lower—that the mystic travels. The journey on the path is always dangerous, with many obstacles and forces bent on turning him or her back.

FACT

If you are interested in reading more about the symbolism of the mountain and the tree, you might enjoy the works of Mircea Eliade, who explores their meanings in many contexts, and whose ideas are mentioned in this book. A good book to start with is *The Myth of the Eternal Return*.

A very famous poem of the Middle Ages, Dante Alighieri's *The Divine Comedy*, features a hero who veers from the pathway to heaven. When he tries to climb the Mount of Joy, three beasts chase him away. He is then forced to travel a longer mountain route through hell and purgatory to reach his final destination. Echoes of the mountain and the tree appear in many secular works, too. The images, however, are derived from the spiritual journeys that gave them birth.

Visions and Spirits

Praying to or otherwise communicating with a deity is not the only way to experience the realms of faith and belief in poetry. Some poems are filled with very spiritual moments that do not involve God at all. Perhaps you will see something so wonderful and awe-inspiring that the vision takes on the feeling of a religious experience. The speaker of your poem can impart this experience to your reader.

The Fantastic

A famous visionary poem, Samuel Taylor Coleridge's "Kubla Khan," borrows the name of the Mongol emperor and describes a fantastic pleasure-dome. Coleridge's poem seems to be about the imagination itself. The imagination gives rise to amazing constructs like the pleasure-dome, but like the river, it can disappear again, taking inspiration with it.

In Xanadu did Kubla Khan
A stately pleasure-dome decree:
Where Alph, the sacred river, ran
Through caverns measureless to man
    Down to a sunless sea.
So twice five miles of fertile ground
With walls and towers were girdled round:
And here were gardens bright with sinuous rills
Where blossomed many an incense-bearing tree;
And here were forests ancient as the hills,
Enfolding sunny spots of greenery.

But oh! that deep romantic chasm which slanted
Down the green hill athwart a cedarn cover!
A savage place! As holy and enchanted
As e'er beneath a waning moon was haunted
By woman wailing for her demon-lover!
And from this chasm, with ceaseless turmoil seething,
As if this earth in fast thick pants were breathing,
A mighty fountain momently was forced;
Amid whose swift half-intermitted burst
Huge fragments vaulted like rebounding hail,
Or chaffy grain beneath the thresher's flail:
And 'mid these dancing rocks at once and ever
It flung up momently the sacred river.
Five miles meandering with a mazy motion
Through wood and dale the sacred river ran,
Then reached the caverns measureless to man,

And sank in tumult to a lifeless ocean:
And 'mid this tumult Kubla heard from far
Ancestral voices prophesying war!
  The shadow of the dome of pleasure
  Floated midway on the waves:
  Where was heard the mingled measure
  From the fountain and the caves.
It was a miracle of rare device,
A sunny pleasure-dome with caves of ice!

  A damsel with a dulcimer
  In a vision once I saw:
  It was an Abyssinian maid,
  And on her dulcimer she played,
  Singing of Mount Abora.
  Could I revive within me
  Her symphony and song,
To such a deep delight 'twould win me
That with music loud and long,
I would build that dome in air,
That sunny dome! Those caves of ice!
And all who heard should see them there,
And all should cry, Beware! Beware!
His flashing eyes, his floating hair!
Weave a circle round him thrice,
And close your eyes with holy dread,
For he on honey-dew hath fed,
And drunk the milk of Paradise.

To record your own visions, pay attention to experiences you have had that seem out of the ordinary. Since visions of this sort bring you into contact with other powers, they should stand out. Write out in detail what you have seen. Record any insights you have learned about yourself, too.

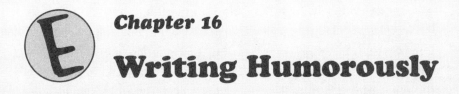

Chapter 16

Writing Humorously

Though poetry is generally a serious genre of writing, many poets have chosen to use humor in their work. Poems can satirize people, places, and objects, or take an ironic look at life. Some poems exaggerate for an absurd effect, and others tone down hilarious events to create a sense of irony. Poems can be witty, charming, hysterical, or riotous—the choice is entirely up to you.

Satire and Parody

Satire traditionally centers on the weaknesses, vices, or mistakes of a person or a particular group of people. That weakness is exposed to the public with the intent that it be addressed and perhaps corrected. The satire can become cruel, but usually it is lighthearted enough to make even its subject smile.

Parody is closely linked to satire, satire often being the purpose of parody. A good parody gets its message across by pretending to be the very thing it makes fun of. For instance, a parody of a science fiction movie follows the rules and conventions of sci-fi movies. A parody of a romance novel follows the rules and conventions of romance novels. A parody of a love sonnet follows the rules concerning meter, foot patterns, line lengths, and content.

How to Create a Satire

People in prominent positions are often the subjects of satire simply because of their visibility. A president, a governor, a movie star, even your boss at work—all are in plain sight of the people around and below them. Any misstep they make instantly becomes the topic of gossip and ridicule. Though these people are good subjects for satire, almost any person, place, or thing will do.

A subject may already be so ridiculous that it begs to be the subject of a satirical poem. Perhaps a loathed enemy's new hairstyle is all the material you need. In this case, don't overstate the obvious. Simply isolate strong details and relate them realistically to your reader. Your description should speak for itself.

To write a satire, you need an appropriate subject. You don't have to go after a president or somebody famous, though he may deserve it. You just need to choose someone, or something, that has gotten your attention. For example, perhaps the copy machine at work has devoured yet another of your expense reports. The copy machine has gotten your attention, and its malfunctioning behavior is the aspect you can mock.

A Look at Parody

Here is a parody of Coleridge's well-known ode "Dejection: An Ode," written by Charles Harper Webb, entitled "Dejection: Not Even an Ode":

After a month in hospital, what cancer patient
still has dignity? After years in solitary,
who is lonely any more? "I'm past caring,"
the farmer tells his bank after the fourth dry spring.

My love for music—even Little Richard
and Zeppelin, Tchaikovsky and Bach—erodes
each day. A chocolate malt's not what it was.
Once I chugged down women by the case;

now I lack stomach for one. After so many
rainbow trout, their glimmer dulls, their fight
fades like a message carried on kite string.
My bench press steadily declines. Only

so many times a man can shoo the cat, or tell
a grandchild, "Stay out of the street," and care.
Only so many drive-by shootings will bring tears.
At 15, I thought old people were fear-crazed

all the time, staring at death's empty eyes.
Now I know why, in those Kleenex-clutcher movies
I despised, Grannie smiles out of her pain,
and whispers, "I'm tired. Blow out the candles, dears."

From Red Rock Review. *Reprinted with the permission of the author.*

The humor is very dark but understandable if you read Coleridge's poem. Coleridge's speaker anxiously anticipates a storm. Webb exaggerates this aspect: His speaker paints a bleaker picture of life than Coleridge's speaker could ever dream. He also makes fun of Coleridge's somber intent in the title; the words "not even" suggest the poem is too depressing to be an ode.

Irony

Irony is created when intent and outcome do not match. For example, imagine you want to impress your date with a candlelit dinner. You make reservations at a fancy restaurant, buy a new outfit, and get a haircut. Even the weather cooperates. Everything is going great when the maitre d' seats you at a secluded table. The waiter brings you champagne to start you off, but then . . . the cork explodes out of the bottle and smacks your date in the eye! After a half-hour of holding an ice pack to the injury, your date can proceed with dinner. However, the mood is ruined. All of the preparations you made for the date, contrasted with the immediate disaster, create irony.

Irony can be used to create humorous or serious effects, and both can be found in poems. A humorous effect occurs when the outcome is both surprising and amusing. More serious forms of irony cause a reader to think deeply about a subject. In all, you have four types of irony to work with: *verbal irony*, *dramatic irony*, *situational irony*, and *cosmic irony*.

Verbal Irony

Verbal irony occurs when you say one thing but mean another. If your roommate leaves her dirty laundry all over the house, you might call her a neat freak to draw her attention to her sloppiness. This is an example of verbal irony, and it occurs all the time, in everyday speech. This sort of irony can lead to *sarcasm* if it has an edge to it.

Often you will say ironic things on purpose, but occasionally you will say them by accident. These instances can be great for use in poetry. Keep your ears open (and use the "fly on the wall" technique) when you're in public places. Listen for dialogue that you can use in an ironic poem. Perhaps you'll hear a child tell her parent to grow up or a wife beg her husband not to buy her diamonds. Record these unconventional instances and explore them in your writing.

Dramatic Irony

Dramatic irony occurs when the characters do not know what the audience knows. For example, in the original film *The Parent Trap*, one of the twin sisters cuts the back of the other's dress as she is going to an elegant party. The audience can see the cut running all the way to her hips, but the girl herself isn't aware of it right away. In a humorous situation, part of the fun is watching the character's surprise when she catches up with the audience.

Consider a poem by Dayvid Figler, "The Infinite Wisdom of the Father," which makes ample use of dramatic irony. The speaker of the poem creates the irony by filling in the meanings behind what the father says. The father remains ignorant of these meanings—hence, the irony.

I.

Sprawled out across Father's knee to
Receive what I deserved (oh, when good prayers go wrong),
He said, "This is going to hurt me more than you."

Did he mean his arthritis?

I said, "Dad, despite your proclamation, you cannot
*   literally beat some sense into anyone."*

"OWWW!" (I was 27).

II.

"If you don't stop your crying, I'll give you something to cry about."

What eight-year-old wants something to cry about?
What eight-year-old can stop crying?

"That's it," he said, "I'm going outside to kill your dog."

He grabbed a serrated steak knife.

Tears kept flowing, but now changed color.
We didn't own a dog.
The neighbors did.

III.

Father would abandon us
To go out on gambling binges in the name
Of seeking
A loaf of bread.
Sometimes gone for days at a time,
Mom would forgive him if he came home a winner.

"Who can really complain?" Mom would whisper counting her share.

Was I a love child?

"The only reason your mother and I
*   never got a divorce*
*   was because of you kids*
*   . . . neither one of us wanted custody."*

They stayed together till the end of time.
We all did.
Who can really complain?

Reprinted with the permission of the author.

Note that Figler is also writing a satire about some of society's preconceived notions of behavior. Parent-child relations, divorce, custody, gambling, abuse, and animal cruelty receive Figler's attention. Despite the seriousness of these issues, Figler uses irony to allow the reader to laugh at them.

Situational Irony

Situational irony is like verbal irony except with actions instead of words. One action may be intended, but the outcome may be completely unexpected. The example given at the beginning of this section, in which the wine cork hits your date in the eye, is an example of situational irony. A romantic dinner date was intended, but the outcome was a black eye.

To create your own situational irony, you can work from experience or imagination. Have you ever had an embarrassing experience? Have a series of unfortunate occurrences ever happened one right after another? Explore the circumstances and details of these incidents. Were they ironic? If you don't have experience to draw from, you can create your own story. Describe the scene, the intent of the characters, and the outcome of the action.

Cosmic Irony

Cosmic irony occurs when you have a sense that the entire universe is working against a character. No matter how hard that character struggles, the Powers That Be bring him or her to a contrary result. For example, in the Coyote and Road Runner cartoons, Wile E. Coyote toils relentlessly to catch Road Runner. However, every gadget he uses and every trap he builds malfunctions at the critical time. In every episode, the coyote ends up falling from a humongous cliff, getting smashed by giant boulders, or being blown up by dynamite—the list of failures goes on and on.

Hyperbole and Understatement

Another way to inspire laughter with your poems is by using *hyperbole* and *understatement*. These figures of speech are opposite ends of the same scale. Hyperbole means exaggeration—going over the top. Understatement is just the opposite—toning down a situation.

Making a Mountain out of a Molehill

To create hyperbole, take something ordinary and exaggerate it. Perhaps you agree to meet a friend for lunch and he arrives ten minutes late. When he arrives, you say, "I've been waiting here for days!" While many people use hyperbole on purpose to make a point, others use it unknowingly all the time. Do you ever use the expression "Let's eat—I'm *starving*"? If so, then you might use hyperbole more often than you think.

ALERT!

To make hyperbole humorous, you can't simply exaggerate. If you say, "He is as big as a house," you are exaggerating, but not cleverly. Instead, if you say, "He is as big as an elephant's rear end," the comparison is more unusual and, therefore, more comical. If you find it difficult to come up with unusual exaggerations right away, start with something more common and work your way up.

Hyperbole is behind the humor of Andrew Kiraly's poem "Superworld High, 1987." In it, he exaggerates (and thereby parodies) the descriptions he finds in a high school yearbook:

From left: St. Craig,
Patron of Perpetually Interesting Hair;
Our Veiled Lady
Of Fortuitous Distraction;
Saint Mandi, Patron of the
Neverending Seafood Event,
Limited Time (plush
cartoon lobsters conspiring in the gym
to make America have fun) Only;
Saint Fran, Patron
Of Dour Librarians Whose 10:18
Snack Is Cheerios in a Sandwich Bag;

(A miracle:) all voted Most
Likely to (<u>verb</u>),
Superworld High, 1987.

(Not pictured: Saint Sarah,
Patron of the Cavalier,
But Principled—and Charming—
Misdeed.)

Printed with the permission of the author.

To practice hyperbole, take a few common actions, people, or things and make them much more than they really are. Here are some ideas to start with: a tall man, a fluffy cloud, a deep pool, a firm handshake, a pleasant song. You have two general strategies you can follow to make your hyperboles. First, you can compare the item to something else. To do so, use the configuration *as (adjective) as* or *(adjective)-er than*. For example: "He is *as big as* an elephant's rear end" or "He is *bigger than* an elephant's rear end."

Second, you can increase the size or number. For example, if there are 5 ants crawling in your kitchen, you can exaggerate by saying there are 1,000. If a person's cheeks are flushed, you can say they are deep crimson, like the color of red wine. You can exaggerate lengths of time, quantities of items, physical descriptions—almost anything you can think of.

Making a Molehill out of a Mountain

Whereas hyperbole takes something ordinary and exaggerates it, understatement can take something outrageous and make it seem ordinary. For instance, if you were standing on the deck of the *Titanic* as it was sinking, and said, "Well, this is a bit of bad luck," you would be understating a very serious situation.

There are actually two forms of understatement you can use. One is the downplaying method, as in the previous example, and the other is called *litotes*. In this second form, you create a double negative. For example, if you ask your friend how she is feeling today and she replies, "I'm not unwell, thank you," the double negative *not unwell* creates a litotes.

When creating understatement, be sure to write with irony in mind. Understatement and irony can work together to create the humor in a statement. In *Style and Statement,* Corbett and Connors say that understatement should not deceive the listener. The irony lets the listener know that you are not attempting to deceive.

Your double negative will almost always involve a verb and an adjective or adverb. In the example "I'm not unwell, thank you," the word *not* negates the verb *am* (*I'm* equals *I am*), and the *un-* prefix negates the adjective *well*. You should therefore begin with a statement having a verb and an adverb or adjective that will take a prefix like *un-* or *in-* or *dis-* or *a-* to make it negative.

Hot Cross Puns

As noted in Chapter 5, a *pun* is a play on words. Specifically, this means you are playing with the meanings or the sounds of the words you use. For example, if you say you "saw" a log, it could mean you have seen it with your eyes or cut it with a saw. Puns can be very useful in your poetry to create humor, broaden meaning, or simply display the versatility of language.

Puns in Action

Though puns have generally been considered a low form of humor, it actually takes quite a bit of skill to create clever puns. Consider the poem "The Embarrassing Episode of Little Miss Muffet" by Guy Wetmore Carryl, which takes a comical look at a conversation between the spider and the famous Little Miss Muffet. The poem concludes with the following stanza:

And the Moral is this: Be it madam or miss
To whom you have something to say,
You are only absurd when you get in the curd
But you're rude when you get in the whey.

To get a feel for puns, write a list of words in which each has more than one meaning. For example, your list could include words like *dough* (bread dough/money), *coat* (jacket/coat of paint), and *nuts* (crazy/food). Also, write out pairs of words that sound the same but mean different things. These are called *homonyms*. Some examples of homonyms are *dough/doe*, *heal/heel*, and *sail/sale*.

Types of Puns

Following is a list of the types of puns available to you, as appears in the book *Style and Statement*, by Corbett and Connors. Don't be thrown off by the Greek names. You don't have to remember them. The important thing is to understand the puns themselves and to learn how to use them.

- *Antanaclasis:* a word repeated in two different senses
- *Paronomasia:* words that sound alike but have different meanings
- *Syllepsis:* two senses given to a word by the other words around it

Here are examples of the three types of puns:

- *Antanaclasis:* He buttered me up with butter cookies.
- *Paronomasia:* She's an author looking for the write stuff.
- *Syllepsis:* He lost his jacket and his mind.

The pun in Guy Wetmore Carryl's poem about Little Miss Muffet would be considered paronomasia. Corbett and Connors cite the following two lines from Alexander Pope's *The Rape of the Lock* as an example of syllepsis in poetry:

Here thou, great Anna! whom three realms obey
Dost sometimes counsel take—and sometimes tea.

Limerick and Clerihew

Two verse forms that can be used to create humor are the *limerick* and the *clerihew.* The first is probably well known to you, but the second may be new. Both are easy to learn and will provide you with plenty of ways to impress and entertain your readers.

The Limerick

A limerick consists of nonsensical verse that pokes fun at its subject. Despite its humorous purpose, the limerick does have a few formal requirements. First, it has five lines. Second, it has a rhyme scheme. Third, it has a meter or syllable count for each line. The rhyme scheme is easy to follow: AABBA. The meter, however, can be strict or loose, depending on your needs. If you want it to be strict, then your limerick should have a dominant anapestic foot (da da DUM). You should have three anapests in lines one, two, and five, and only two in lines three and four.

If you want to be loose, then you don't have to follow the requirement for the anapest. However, you do need to have three stressed syllables in lines one, two, and five, and two stressed syllables in lines three and four. The stresses should add a lilt to the limerick, and lines three and four should remain shorter than the others. That way, you will build energy for the punch in the final line.

Here are two limericks created as examples. The first follows the strict requirements, and the second follows the loose. Read and reread both to see the difference.

> *There was once a young girl in row three*
> *who grew fond of the scab on her knee.*
> *She would scratch and would scratch*
> *until one day it hatched!*
> *And a bird of pink skin fluttered free!*

> *A boy on the playground today*
> *had something he wanted to say*
> *to the girl on the swing*
> *—a pretty li'l thing—*
> *but instead he just let out a "Hey!"*

Whether you make your limerick strict or loose, you should be aware of a three-part structure beneath its form. The first two lines set up the premise of the poem. The next two lines often introduce a second element. The final line delivers the punch, usually an amusing connection between parts one and two.

The Clerihew

The clerihew is named after the poet Edmund Clerihew Bentley, who used the form early in the last century. Its requirements are even simpler than the limerick's. It has four lines, it states the subject of the poem as the very first line, and the rhyme scheme is AABB. Here is an example:

ice cream cone
will comfort you when you're alone.
But be sure in the end
you don't mistake it for a friend.

Since the clerihew has fewer rules you may find it an easier form to work with than the limerick. Try writing a series of clerihews about different subjects, such as your favorite food, the daily weather, a family member, or a pet.

Epigrams

The word *epigram*, "to inscribe," comes from the Greek and is often confused with the word *epitaph* (a message carved on a gravestone). Throughout its long history, the epigram has been used to set forth wise sayings, good advice, or personal ridicule. In some cases, epigrams are like little flashes of wit and venom; they are short in length so that the speaker can make a quick escape before a victim has the chance to respond.

Epigrams do not always rhyme, so such well-known sayings as "He who hesitates is lost" and "Good things come to those who wait" are sometimes categorized as epigrams. However, a good epigram is often written as a rhyming couplet, such as these from Benjamin Franklin's *Poor Richard's Almanac*:

He who longs for glass without the G,
Take off L and that is he.

If you would reap praise, you must sow the seeds:
Gentle words and useful deeds.

Franklin's *Poor Richard's Almanac* was widely popular in colonial America and came out in several editions. Any one of them will yield several epigrams for you. William Blake wrote a long poem, *Auguries of Innocence,* that can be dissected into a series of epigrams.

Make Epigrams Work for You

To begin writing epigrams, you might want to begin with another list. This time, you should write down the names of people who really annoy you—bad drivers, gossips, or slobs, for example. These people will be the basis of "He Who" or "She Who" epigrams like the one given earlier.

Another way to begin would be to write down any wise lessons you have learned from personal experience. You can think of something serious like "A man in motion is either chasing or fleeing," or you can write something funny like "Don't mistake your iron for your phone." Then see if you can make them jingle and ring using rhyme.

Finally, you should look over the figures of speech included in Chapter 5. Most of the figures listed there will turn your sayings into well-crafted epigrams. Antimetabole—reversing the word order of a pair of phrases—is used in these two sayings from Benjamin Franklin:

'Tis against some men's principle to pay interest,
and seems against others' interest to pay the principal.

He that is of the opinion money will do everything,
may well be suspected of doing everything for money.

Another exercise would be to write epigrams to or about your friends or family. Try to capture some aspect of each person in two lines. Remember: The lines should rhyme or use one of the figures of speech mentioned in Chapter 5. Just be prepared to receive the same treatment in return!

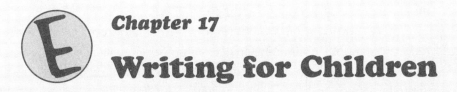

Chapter 17

Writing for Children

Children, perhaps even more so than adults, love to hear the music of language. They also love to hear poems about unusual people, places, and animals. As children listen to these verses, however, they are not just being entertained. They are learning about the language itself, its sounds and its rhythms. What they learn in these early poems will carry over into their language skills as they become educated and grow into adults. Reading poetry to children, or helping them create their own poems, is a fun way to enhance their language skills.

Stories in Verse

To write stories in verse for children, review what you read in Chapter 7 about narrative poetry. The narrative poem, remember, includes a story told by a narrator (or speaker), and that narrator could be you (the writer) or one of the characters in the poem. You also have to pay attention to the elements of plot, character, and setting.

You've learned a bit about creating settings and characters, and you'll read more about characters in this chapter. However, you have not yet learned very much about creating a plot. The works of Dr. Seuss and Shel Silverstein (among others) are excellent models for creating simple but interesting plots for young readers. The two kinds of plots that will probably work best for you are the *episodic plot* and the *dramatic plot*.

The Episodic Plot

The episodic plot consists of a series of events strung together. The events may or may not be related by cause; in other words, the first event may or may not cause the second to happen, and the second may or may not cause the third to happen. Many picture books are laid out in this manner; one page may show a character staring into an empty refrigerator and the next may show her purchasing food at a market. Or the events could be more random: A character is shown petting a dog on one page and sitting in a classroom on the next.

Perhaps the best examples of episodic plot are found in your newspaper's comic section. Each day, you can read a brief episode involving the characters of a particular comic strip. The episodes are strung together over time without a strong causal relationship, and the characters themselves show little or no change.

The advantage of the episodic plot is that it is easy for very young readers to understand. At a young age, a child is probably more interested in the colors, pictures, and tone of your voice than the story itself. A complicated plot will only confuse and distract a young child. The goal is to keep the child's attention without overwhelming her.

The Dramatic Plot

The dramatic plot is based upon the model set out for you in Chapter 7. Characters are presented with a problem to be solved, or they may have a conflict among themselves that is causing strife. The purpose of the dramatic plot is to see how the characters deal with and resolve their problems.

Unlike the events of the episodic plot, the events of the dramatic plot are causally related. This means if something happens in the poem, it will cause something else to happen. A character who finds that she has an ant problem in her house, for example, will decide to call an exterminator to take care of the problem.

The dramatic plot, because it involves more complexity, will work best when you are writing for older readers. Because the events of the dramatic plot are causally related, you can add complications to the narrative that will appeal to children who like adventure and action. However, younger children may still enjoy simple dramatic plots. The conflict in Dr. Seuss's *Green Eggs and Ham*, for example, is basic enough for preschoolers to follow and enjoy.

ALERT!

In shaping the dramatic plot, don't forget about change, discovery, and decision. These three ideas form many of the important events in the dramatic plot, including the climax—the point at which the conflict or problem is solved. Be sure to include the decisions that were made as a result of the changes or discoveries.

A Narrative Poem

One great narrative poem for children is Edward Lear's "The Owl and the Pussycat." The plot involves a journey made by the two main characters. Read the poem carefully to decide whether Lear has used an episodic or a dramatic plot.

The Owl and the Pussycat went to sea
　　In a beautiful pea-green boat;
They took some honey, and plenty of money
　　Wrapped up in a five-pound note.
The Owl looked up to the stars above,
　　And sang to a small guitar,
"O lovely Pussy! O Pussy, my love,
　　What a beautiful Pussy you are,
　　　　You are,
　　　　You are!
　　What a beautiful Pussy you are!"

Pussy said to the Owl, "You elegant fowl!
　　How charmingly sweet you sing!
Oh! Let us be married! Too long we have tarried:
　　But what shall we do for a ring?"
They sailed away, for a year and a day,
　　To the land where the bong-tree grows,
And there in a wood a Piggy-wig stood,
　　With a ring at the end of his nose,
　　　　His nose,
　　　　His nose,
　　With a ring at the end of his nose.

"Dear pig, are you willing to sell for one shilling
　　Your ring?" Said the Piggy, "I will."
So they took it away, and were married next day
　　By the Turkey who lives on the hill.
They dined on mince and slices of quince,
　　Which they ate with a runcible spoon;
And hand in hand, on the edge of the sand,
　　They danced by the light of the moon,
　　　　The moon,
　　　　The moon,
　　They danced by the light of the moon.

You might have noticed that this poem depends a great deal on repetition at the end of each stanza. Can you guess why? Read the poem aloud or sing it with a melody and see what effect the repetition might have on children as they listen.

Characters for Kids

The characters in children's poetry are not like the characters in poetry written for adults. The example of "The Owl and the Pussycat" in the last section shows that many characters may be animals that display human intelligence. Stories like *Winnie the Pooh*, which features a cast of a child's toys, and TV shows like *Sesame Street*, whose characters are imagined puppet creatures, show that the range of characters for children can be far broader than that of characters for adults.

With your human characters, you will also have to decide on their ages. Children will respond in one way to adult characters, whom they will judge to be authority figures, and in another way to child characters, whom they will accept as peers. Once you have determined the ages of your characters, be sure that their actions match these identities.

Even the human characters in children's poems behave differently. Mother Goose's verses, for example, feature an old woman living in a shoe, a wife who is put in a pumpkin, and a person eating a pie filled with blackbirds. Adults may find these characters nonsensical, but children have delighted in them for decades.

Creating the Characters

As with characters you draw from family and friends and from people you observe in public places, you must pay attention to the details. You do not have to describe the characters completely, but you should include a significant detail or two to bring the characters to life. In "The Owl and the

Pussycat," the Owl has a guitar, and he and the Pussycat set sail in a pea-green boat. The child does not need to know where the Owl was born or whether or not the Pussycat has siblings. The only details a child is concerned with are those that are pertinent to the plot. For example, the Piggy-wig is included in the poem because he has the ring the Owl and the Pussycat will use for their engagement.

Creating Animal Characters

Creating animal characters can be easier or more difficult than creating human characters. On the one hand, animals of all kinds are of interest to youngsters—even those that adults dislike, such as bats and spiders. So, you can be sure that animal characters will arouse enthusiasm among your readers. On the other hand, you must decide how intelligent your animal characters will be. Will they be able to speak and think as humans do? Will they show intelligence in their actions but be unable to speak? The more you personify your animal characters, the better children will relate to them.

Furthermore, you must also be aware of the roles some animals play in traditional children's stories. The owl, for instance, is usually a wise character, the eagle is strong and noble, the fox is quick-witted and sly, and the wolf is villainous. Whether or not you abide by these guidelines will affect a young reader's response. While a dim-witted owl and a kindhearted wolf may be unique and intriguing characters, their unusual personalities may only confuse a young reader.

Characters and Setting

Another way to excite your young readers is to have the characters of your poem—human and animal—visit strange and wonderful places. Children will be curious to know how the characters will act in these unfamiliar places. This is part of the attraction behind "The Owl and the Pussycat." It is also the reason for the popularity of another children's poem, Eugene Field's "Wynken, Blynken, and Nod":

Wynken, Blynken, and Nod one night
Sailed off in a wooden shoe—
Sailed on a river of crystal light,

Into a sea of dew.
"Where are you going, and what do you wish?"
    The old moon asked the three.
"We have come to fish for the herring fish
    That live in this beautiful sea;
    Nets of silver and gold have we!"
      Said Wynken,
      Blynken,
      And Nod.

The old moon laughed and sang a song,
    As they rocked in the wooden shoe,
And the wind that sped them all night long
    Ruffled the waves of dew.
The little stars were the herring fish
    That lived in that beautiful sea—
"Now cast your nets wherever you wish—
    Never afeard are we";
So cried the stars to the fishermen three:
      Wynken,
      Blynken,
      And Nod.

All night long their nets they threw
    To the stars in the twinkling foam—
Then down from the skies came the wooden shoe,
    Bringing the fishermen home;
'Twas all so pretty a sail it seemed
    As if it could not be,
And some folks thought 'twas a dream they'd dreamed
    Of sailing that beautiful sea—
    But I shall name you the fishermen three:
      Wynken,
      Blynken,
      And Nod.

Wynken and Blynken are two little eyes,
*   And Nod is a little head,*
And the wooden shoe that sailed the skies
*   Is a wee one's trundle-bed.*
So shut your eyes while mother sings
*   Of wonderful sights that be,*
And you shall see the beautiful things
*   As you rock in the misty sea,*
*   Where the old shoe rocked the fishermen three:*
*   Wynken,*
*   Blynken,*
*   And Nod.*

Another character type to consider is the inanimate object. The moon in Field's poem speaks and sings to the characters. A dish and a spoon are characters in the nursery rhyme "Hey, Diddle Diddle." You will also have to establish the intelligence and human traits of these objects if you choose to use them.

Poems for the Little Ones

Children enjoy poetry simply for its musical quality and its exciting stories. The adventures taken by the Owl and the Pussycat and Wynken, Blynken, and Nod were created with the purpose of entertaining young listeners. Children can visualize the images a poem sets forth, without relying upon corresponding pictures or film. The bounce of the rhyme and the meter can have them tapping their toes or rocking their heads in time with the rhythm.

ALERT!

Don't write about things so extraordinary that you use too many complicated or unfamiliar words. Your vocabulary should remain simple and accessible for a young reader; use only one- and two-syllable words that name everyday objects and actions. You can incorporate more unique words once in a while to create a surprising effect.

If you are a parent, you probably know how effective rhythms and melodies are at lulling your children to sleep. For infants, the rocking of a cradle and the rhythm of a lullaby create a soothing atmosphere that helps them drift off to sleep. A poem by Alfred, Lord Tennyson, "Sweet and Low," illustrates this; it is a lullaby sung by a mother to her child. It gives the listening child images to visualize, and it uses several rhymes and repetitions to create its rhythms:

Sweet and low, sweet and low,
    Wind of the western sea!
Low, low, breathe and blow,
    Wind of the Western sea!
Over the rolling waters go,
Come from the dying moon, and blow,
    Blow him again to me;
While my little one, while my pretty one sleeps.

Sleep and rest, sleep and rest,
    Father will come to thee soon;
Rest, rest, on Mother's breast,
    Father will come to thee soon;
Father will come to his babe in the nest,
Silver sails all out of the west
    Under the silver moon:
Sleep, my little one, sleep, my pretty one, sleep.

Learning Poems

Due to the power of poetic language, children tend to remember verses and songs quite easily. If a poem entertains youngsters, they will read it over and over again until they have memorized it. Poets and teachers have taken advantage of this fact and written verses that help children remember educational and life lessons. Poems have been written to teach youngsters everything from the parts of the body to the names of the planets. Songs as simple as "This Little Piggy" and "Here's the Church" make infants aware of their fingers and toes. "One, Two, Buckle My Shoe" teaches toddlers about numbers. "Thirty Days Hath September" is a verse that helps children remember how many days are in each month.

To write poems that teach basic lessons, you have to keep the word *simple* in the front of your mind. The topics can't be too complex, and the poems themselves can't be too long or complicated. Otherwise, the children will not understand or be able to memorize what you have written. One poem by Sara Coleridge called "The Months" teaches children the names of the months and about the turning of the seasons:

January brings the snow,
Makes our feet and fingers glow.

February brings the rain,
Thaws the frozen lake again.

March brings breezes loud and shrill,
Stirs the dancing daffodil.

April brings the primrose sweet,
Scatters daisies at our feet.

May brings flocks of pretty lambs,
Skipping by their fleecy dams.

June brings tulips, lilies, roses,
Fills the children's hands with posies.

Hot July brings cooling showers,
Apricots and gillyflowers.

August brings the sheaves of corn;
Then the harvest home is borne.

Warm September brings the fruit;
Sportsmen then begin to shoot.

Fresh October brings the pheasant;
Then to gather nuts is pleasant.

Dull November brings the blast,
Then the leaves are whirling fast.

Chill December brings the sleet,
Blazing fires and Christmas treat.

The interaction these songs encourage between parent and child also aids in the process of bonding, an important psychological step for children. The more you interact with your children at this stage of their lives, the better your chances of having a healthy relationship with them later.

Haiku

The haiku is a Japanese verse form made popular during the seventeenth century as a party game. That's right—people would go to parties and entertain themselves by writing poetry! However, because of its short length and simple content, the haiku is also an excellent way of teaching children about the art of writing poetry. Even children in second grade can master the form and create some touching—and amusing—poems.

Haiku Form and Content

The haiku's original requirements have been stretched as poets have experimented with the form. Teaching children the original requirements, however, will help them gain an understanding of counting and syllabification. The haiku is only three lines long and originally required seventeen syllables. The first line took five syllables, the second seven, and the third five again.

With children, the subject matter of the haiku can be left open to whatever you think will interest them. However, if you want to teach them another of the original requirements, you can attempt to have the children include a *sentinel word* in the haiku. Traditionally, the haiku captures a sudden, extreme flash of emotion through a concrete image. This image is expressed in the sentinel word.

Sentinel words aren't simply feeling words, such as *anger, love*, and *joy*. Instead, they name an animal or a plant that evokes the image of a season or a time of day. In turn, the season or time of day creates the mood that expresses the poem's emotion.

The haiku was not originally a rhyming verse. However, many haiku now written in English work with a rhyme, often in the first and last lines. Having your children use a rhyme will hone their language skills, but if you feel this is too difficult, hold off on the rhyme requirement until they are older.

For example, if you think of summer, what animals or plants do you imagine? Perhaps where you live, the most widely recognized summer plant is the sunflower. The sunflower, therefore, may act as a sentinel to identify the season and express the emotion within the haiku. What do you see most frequently in the winter? If you see a lot of maple trees with bare branches, then those bare-branched maples might be the sentinel words in your haiku.

Haiku Exercises

Have the children list the animals, plants, weather patterns, or natural features that make up the landscape where you live. If you live in farm country, the children will likely choose animals like cows or pigs and edible plants like corn and potatoes. Don't limit the children to things that you (or they) think are pretty or poetic. Have them take a notebook and a pencil on a walk and jot down everything that they encounter—not just the aesthetically appealing.

The next activity for the children is to draw pictures of the words they listed. Encourage them to draw the bird, the trash can, or the stream they found just as they remember it or as they fancy it. Have them look carefully at their drawings to see what the bird or the trash can or the stream is doing. For instance, is the bird flying through a blue sky, building a nest in a tree, or perched on a telephone wire? A bird in flight, its wings and feathers spread, usually suggests freedom or high spirits, while a bird in a tree or on a wire, wings and feathers tucked close to its body, suggests inaction and, perhaps, contemplation.

The next exercise is to have the children begin writing haiku about the pictures they have drawn. You may also work with the sentinel/contrast pairs you have created if you are trying the form. The task at this stage is to set down each image in succinct detail. The children should not explain the images to their readers. Any emotions or meanings must be implied by the images themselves. They should also try to maintain the five-seven-five syllable count to give themselves a feel for the form.

Here are two haiku written by seventh graders based upon these exercises:

The raindrops pull down
a daisy's weak white petals.
Playground bullies laugh.

Black roses growing
through the cracks of ghetto streets.
White snow covers them.

Within the syllable count, the students chose flowers—a daisy and roses—to function as their sentinel words but juxtaposed them with images—bullies, rain, and snow—that work against the hope usually promised by the spring season. The students also used the tools of the trade: The first poem repeats the long *a* sound near the start of all three lines and alliterates *weak* and *white*; the second poem repeats the long *o* sound throughout and makes liberal use of hard consonants.

For good examples of this form, have the children read haiku written by the Japanese masters Matsuo Basho, Taniguchi Buson, and Kobayashi Issa. Consult a good poetry anthology, or look for the collected works of these writers. The children should also read haiku produced by English-speaking poets. There are a number of haiku anthologies available.

Bouts-Rimés

Another poetic form that began as a party game is *bouts-rimés*, which translates literally from the French as "end rhymes." Despite this translation, the form does not necessarily have to include rhymes. Its basis is a list of words that you place at the ends of each line. For example, if your word list is *table*, *blackbird*, *sundae*, *grease*, *green*, the first line of the poem will end with *table*, the second with *blackbird*, and so on. Because the list has five words, the poem will have five lines.

Where does the list come from? This is the fun of the form. The list can be generated during a quick walk through a neighborhood, from vocabulary words selected from assigned readings, or by several quick-witted children at a party. It is a form easily adaptable to the skill levels and the needs of young writers.

You may add a twist or two to this basic setup. For example, if you want to teach the children about rhymes, your end words can rhyme using the pattern AABB or ABAB or XAXA, or you can create internal rhymes with your end words. You can also impose rules upon the foot patterns and meters you allow the children to use. The number of words on the list is not restricted either. You could have as few as two or as many as twenty-five—or more—depending on how much you feel the children can handle.

Examples of Bouts-Rimés

Since bouts-rimés have no limitations on line length, meter, or rhyme, the first exercise—perhaps the only one you need—is for the children to generate the list. Aside from nouns and verbs, you might also consider having the children include words that will allow them to use function and category shift. For example, the word *quarter* might appear on the list, but the word may be used as a noun ("I need change for a quarter"), a verb ("She should quarter the pie"), or an adjective ("Give the wheel a quarter turn"). Just remember that one of the rules of the game is that you cannot change the spelling of the word as it appears on the list—you can't change *quarter* to *quarters* or *quartered*.

Another exercise for older children is to use enjambment for all but the final line of the poem. Enjambment, remember, means that the end of a line in your poem is not the end of a sentence or a phrase (ending each line where a sentence or phrase ends is called *end-stopping*). For example, if you started with the previous example list and created end-stopped lines, you could write something like this:

The two of us sat at a table.
You turned and smiled at a blackbird.
I finished eating my sundae.
The bottom of my bowl filled with ice cream grease.
The skin on my knuckles turned green.

Such an effort will feel like you're deliberately writing toward your list of words (and it probably won't produce good poetry either). Enjambment will give the poem more flow and hide your word list better. Here's the same list used in a poem with enjambment:

As we sat at the table
I noticed through the window a blackbird
perched quietly. I ate my sundae
slowly, but it felt like grease
on my tongue. The bird turned green.

You should see by comparing the two that the second has a better flow to it and a sharper energy that moves you from line to line. The content of the poem doesn't make very much sense because the words were chosen at random. Choosing words randomly can provide you with more of a challenge, but you can also select words that you know will go together well. Practicing the enjambment exercise will help children not only with bouts-rimés but with other forms as well—even those that have rhymes. After a while, the children will get a better sense of when to use enjambment and when to use end-stops.

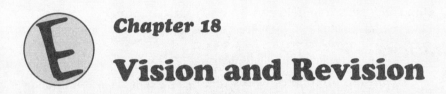

Chapter 18

Vision and Revision

You may feel that revision will spoil the inspiration that brought you to the page. Or you may feel that poems, being so short, don't need a lot of revision. However, neither of these worries is valid. Even professional poets use a drafting process to improve their work. They may make it look easy, but you can be sure that most of the published poems you read are the result of hours of thought. This chapter will give you the tools you need to create your own revision process.

Clause Patterns I: Nontransitive

In Chapter 3, you read about different phrase patterns—participles, absolutes, and prepositional phrases—that you can use to liven up your details. For your revisions to be successful, you should have a working knowledge of the basic clause patterns used to create sentences. First, you must understand the distinction between a phrase and a clause.

Definitions

A *phrase* is a group of words that form a unit. This unit, however, cannot stand on its own as a sentence. For instance, the word groups *in the driveway*, *spinning its wheels*, and *windshield covered with ice* cannot be set off as sentences—that is, beginning with a capital letter and ending with a period.

ALERT!

Watch out for nouns that appear after prepositions. The preposition plus noun group—the prepositional phrase—modifies a verb or another noun elsewhere in a sentence. Therefore, the sentence "She walked through the park" is an intransitive clause pattern.

A *clause* is also a group of words that form a unit. But the clause differs from the phrase in two important ways. First, the clause always has a subject/verb pair at its heart. Second, many clauses can stand on their own as sentences. "She is the smartest girl in the class" and "We ate the whole pizza in ten minutes," are clauses that can be punctuated as sentences.

The Intransitive Pattern

In Chapter 5, you read briefly about the noun/verb/noun pattern that creates clauses. Sometimes this noun/verb/noun pattern creates a *nontransitive clause* pattern. This means either that the subject is the only one affected by the action of the verb or that the verb names a state of being rather than an action.

When the subject is the only one affected by the action of the verb, the subject/verb pattern is *intransitive*. Sentences like "She is walking very quickly" or "He went upstairs" are built upon this pattern. The subjects of the two sentences, *she* and *he*, are performing the actions named by the verbs *walking* and *went*, and no one else is involved. You might have noticed that the second noun in the noun/verb/noun pattern has disappeared. The disappearance of the second noun is common in the intransitive pattern.

The Linking Verb Pattern

When the verb names a state of being instead of an action, then the subject/verb pair forms a *linking verb* pattern. This usually means that whatever follows the verb renames or describes the subject. Sentences like "She is a police officer" or "He became a nurse," follow the noun/verb/noun pattern (she/is/police officer; he/became/nurse), and the second noun renames the first. In other words, both nouns refer to the same person.

This pattern can be altered by replacing the second noun with an adjective. In the sentences "She is brave" and "He became dizzy," *brave* and *dizzy* are both adjectives that describe the state of being of the subject. Traditionally, the main elements in both forms of the linking verb pattern are labeled subject/linking verb/complement.

Sometimes a quick look at the verb will tell you which pattern you are using. Verbs such as *come, go,* and *walk* frequently create intransitive patterns, and verbs like *be, become, seem,* and *appear* often create linking verb patterns.

Clause Patterns II: Transitive

Sometimes the noun/verb/noun pattern creates a transitive clause pattern. This means two—sometimes three—entities can be affected by the action that the verb names. The subject is the starting point of that action, and the direct object is usually the end point of that action.

The Basic Pattern

In the sentence "She is walking her dog," the subject *she* performs the action named by the verb *walking*. The word *dog* rounds out the action named by the verb, making it the direct object. Notice that this noun/verb/noun pattern is different from the one in the linking verb pattern. In the linking verb pattern, the two nouns (she/police officer; he/nurse) refer to the same person. In the transitive pattern, however, the two nouns (she/dog) refer to different entities.

FACT

Some verbs can create both the nontransitive and the transitive patterns. "She walked through the park" is intransitive, but "She walked her dog" is transitive. "He smelled awful" is a linking verb pattern, but "He smelled the pie" is transitive.

Variations to the Pattern

The transitive pattern can also be altered. One way to do so is by adding an *indirect object*. For example, in the sentence "She gave the teacher an apple," you have a subject (*she*) which starts the action, and a direct object (*apple*) that the indirect object (*teacher*) receives. In this sentence, there are three nouns (she/teacher/apple) that refer to different things.

You can also alter the pattern by adding an *object complement*, a noun that renames the direct object. For example, in the sentence "We elected him president," *we* is the subject and *him* is the direct object, but the word *president* tells us what the direct object became. *Him* and *president* refer to the same person.

We can alter the pattern yet again by making the object complement an adjective. For example, in the sentence "The fumes made her dizzy," *fumes* is the subject, *her* is the direct object, and *dizzy* is an adjective that tells us what the direct object became. However, no matter what variation you make in the transitive clause pattern, you must always have a direct object present.

Clause Patterns III: Independent and Dependent

Clauses can be distinguished further by their ability to stand on their own as sentences. Clauses that can stand alone are called independent. Those that can't stand alone are called dependent. Both types have the subject/verb pairs required of all clauses. Dependent clauses, however, are independent clauses that have been changed so that they can be embedded within yet another clause.

The Adverbial Clause

Consider the clause "She is a police officer." You can punctuate it as a sentence because it can stand on its own. However, by putting a subordinating conjunction before it (*because she is a police officer*), you turn it into an *adverbial clause*. It still has a subject/verb pair in it, but it can no longer stand on its own as a sentence. It must now be joined to an independent clause (*Because she is a police officer, she has had training with firearms*) and in this case describes the verb of that clause.

FACT

A list of subordinating conjunctions, words like *because, since, if,* and *while,* can be found in any English handbook. These conjunctions not only turn independent clauses into dependent clauses but also tell you what relationship they have with the clauses they join: time, place, reason, cause, and others.

The Noun Clause

If you add *that, whether,* or *if* in front of an independent clause, or if you change one of the nouns to *who, that, what,* or *which,* you can create a *noun clause.* The noun clause fills one of the noun slots in the noun/verb/noun pattern. For instance, if you turn the previous sample sentence into *that she is a police officer* or *who is a police officer,* you can embed both new noun clauses in the second slot: *I know that she is a police officer* or *I know who is a police officer.*

The Relative Clause

If you change one of the nouns in an independent clause into the word *who, whom, that,* or *which,* you can create a *relative clause.* The relative clause works like an adjective—it describes a noun. For example, in the sentence "My daughter, who is a police officer, lives in Los Angeles," *daughter* is a noun. It is also the subject of the independent clause *my daughter lives in Los Angeles.* The clause *who is a police officer* describes the word *daughter.*

FACT

The noun clause and the relative clause look similar, but they have different functions. The noun clause fills the place that a simple noun can fill, usually the subject or object slots in a sentence. The relative clause always describes a noun and usually comes directly after the noun it describes.

Punctuation

Punctuation separates word groups but it can also tell you what sorts of word groups are being separated. For example, when you use a period, you are signaling that what comes before the period is a complete thought or, grammatically, a complete sentence. If you use a period to set off a word group that is not complete, you have created a sentence fragment. To tell if a word group is complete, look first for one of the subject/verb patterns described above.

Two other punctuation marks, the exclamation point and the question mark, also signal the end of a complete thought. The thought may be a clause ("What a nice boy he is!"; "Is he a nice boy?"), an exclamation ("What a nice boy!"), or a question ("Which boy?"). The exclamation point and the question mark are not used as often as the period.

Many inexperienced poets believe that the exclamation point must be used to express an extreme emotion. They feel that the reader will miss the emotion without the signal given by the punctuation. Try instead to choose words and images that express the emotion, without relying on the punctuation. It's easy to overuse the exclamation point, so be careful not to depend upon it too often.

Marking Separation

Three punctuation marks create varying degrees of separation: the semicolon, the colon, and the dash. They do not create total separation like the period, the exclamation point, and the question mark. The semicolon can separate complete thoughts but does so in a manner that suggests that the thoughts are closely related. If you write, for example, "He went to the bank. She went to the store," the period shows total separation between the two statements. However, if you write "He went to the bank; she went to the store," the semicolon implies a link between the two actions—perhaps she went to the store because he went to the bank, or they acted at the same time.

When a colon separates complete thoughts, the word group before the colon anticipates the word group after it. For instance, take a look at the following: "The sergeant made a new rule: No enlisted man was to leave the barracks on weekends." Here, the first part, "The sergeant made a new rule," anticipates the second part. You might also say that the second part explains the first part. In this case, what comes after the colon explains what the new rule stipulated.

The dash is more visible than the colon and semicolon and creates more separation between two phrases. Therefore, it gives more emphasis to the two phrases it sets apart. Compare the following examples of these three punctuation marks:

- I was wrong; she would go on to be a great singer.
- I was wrong: She would go on to be a great singer.
- I was wrong—she would go on to be a great singer.

The dash seems to give more impact to what follows than the other two marks. Now compare these three to the total separation signaled by the period: "I was wrong. She would go on to be a great singer." The tone, the meaning, and the style of each sentence are altered by the punctuation chosen.

But remember, there is not always a right or wrong answer when it comes to choosing between these forms of punctuation. There are some cases in which a dash or a colon would work, and others in which a semicolon is the only appropriate punctuation.

Semicolons, colons, and dashes are also used to create lists. The colon and the dash introduce the list, and the semicolon separates the items on the list. However, only use the colon and the dash when an independent clause comes before the list. Use the semicolon only when the items in the list are broken down further with commas.

The Comma

The comma separates phrases from clauses, makes lists, and marks the boundary of clauses joined by *and*, *but*, and *or*. However, because of its many uses, the comma tends to cause the most trouble for writers. But you need not despair. There are a few rules you can easily learn to make sure you are using the comma correctly. For instance, assess the use of the comma in this example: "I was wrong, she would go on to be a great singer." Since *I was wrong* is a complete thought and *she would go on to be a great singer* is a complete thought, the comma is misused here.

Now consider this sentence: "After the game we went to the pub to celebrate." There seem to be two distinct word groups here: *after the game* and *we went to the pub to celebrate*. The first group, *after the game*, is not a complete thought. For this reason, it should be set off from the rest of the sentence with a comma: *After the game, we went to the pub to celebrate.*

When commas appear in lists, they may separate all of the items: *We bought peas, carrots, and celery*—this usage is called *serial commas*. The following is also correct: *We bought peas, carrots and celery*. It is only important that these usages are consistent. Only when the list contains two items does the comma not appear: *We bought peas and celery*.

Now take a look at this sentence: "People, who live in glass houses, should not throw stones." It looks awkward, doesn't it? It seems more natural to leave the commas out: "People who live in glass houses should not throw stones." Another problem arises in this sentence: "The football team which stayed at the hotel, won the game." The commas in such a case have to go on both sides of the word group *which stayed at the hotel*—or not appear at all. The rule "Two or none but never one" applies here.

Line by Line

Once you have completed a few drafts of a poem, you should do a *line edit* to make sure your sentences are clean. Line editing means that you go through your poem line by line to correct any errors you see. The process can be laborious, but it will add polish that a careful reader will appreciate. Consider the following three suggestions to make your line-editing process smooth and helpful.

First, find the subjects and the verbs of your sentences. Seventy-five percent of all errors can be corrected by following this step. For example, look at the following sentences:

- <u>Sarah</u> <u><u>pours</u></u> the water into the simmering pot and <u><u>begins</u></u> to boil.
- Different <u>syrups</u> <u><u>were lined</u></u> up on the counter next to the espresso machine, such as vanilla, amaretto, and coconut.

The subjects of the sentences are underlined once, and the verbs are underlined twice. By reading aloud just the subject and the verbs of the first sentence, you can detect a major error—Sarah can't possibly be boiling herself. The following is one revision you could make:

- <u>Sarah</u> <u><u>pours</u></u> the water into the simmering pot and the <u>water</u> <u><u>begins</u></u> to boil.

Adding a second subject to the sentence *(water)* creates a sentence that logically connects the actions of the verbs to those performing the actions.

The problem in the second sentence arises from the use of passive voice. Passive voice tells the reader that the subject of the sentence is receiving rather than doing the action of the verb. However, in this sentence, the syrups are indeed performing the action—they are lining the counter. To revise the sentence, you might write:

- Different <u>syrups</u> <u>lined</u> the counter next to the espresso machine, such as vanilla, amaretto, and coconut.

Second, make sure the modifiers are placed where they should be. Modifiers include adjectives, adverbs, prepositional phrases, participles, infinitives, and relative clauses. Generally, modifiers should be placed next to the words they modify, either directly before or directly after. The sentences used in the previous examples have unnecessary modifiers or modifiers placed in the wrong positions:

- <u>Sarah</u> <u>pours</u> the water into the simmering pot and the <u>water</u> <u>begins</u> to boil.
- Different <u>syrups</u> <u>lined</u> the counter next to the espresso machine, such as vanilla, amaretto, and coconut.

In the first sentence, the adjective *simmering* is not used accurately. Pots don't simmer; the contents of a pot simmer. Hence, you can delete it:

- <u>Sarah</u> <u>pours</u> the water into the pot and the <u>water</u> <u>begins</u> to boil.

In the second sentence, the list beginning with the phrase *such as* has been placed next to *machine*, as if the machine itself could come in different flavors. The list should be placed next to the word *syrups*:

- Different <u>syrups</u>, such as vanilla, amaretto, and coconut <u>lined</u> the counter next to the espresso machine.

Third, make sure your punctuation goes where it should. Addressing the first two suggestions first will help you to find and correct many common punctuation errors. In the example sentences above, some punctuation is missing or unnecessary. They should read as follows:

- Sarah <u>pours</u> the water into the pot, and the <u>water</u> <u>begins</u> to boil.
- Different <u>syrups</u> such as vanilla, amaretto, and coconut <u>lined</u> the counter next to the espresso machine.

In the first sentence, the comma marks the boundary between clauses joined with *and*. In the second sentence, the phrase "such as vanilla, amaretto, and coconut" comes between the subject *syrups* and the verb *lined*. Remember the comma rules you learned. The phrase must be set off with two commas or no commas. Removing the comma in front of the word *such* makes the most sense.

Yet even this is not quite accurate. Syrup can't really line a counter unless it has been spilled there. You can improve the sentence further as follows:

- Next to the espresso machine, <u>bottles</u> of different syrups such as vanilla, amaretto, and coconut <u>lined</u> the counter.

Now that the syrups are in containers, this version of the sentence can stand, without need of more revision. Following are more sentences you can use to practice finding and fixing errors:

- Various creatures could be seen out of the corner of the eye scurrying away.
- Tomatoes, corn, cucumbers, and the sweet scent of watermelon permeate the air.
- Large teardrops traced the edge of her glasses as they ran down her face and fell to her lap in a small puddle.

What's Your Style?

Another exercise that will help you with your revision process is doing a style analysis of poems you read or write. To do a style analysis, you will have to have a good grasp of grammar and sentence construction. You should also keep a calculator handy. To give you an idea of how to do a style analysis, consider the following poem by Joseph Millar, "Telephone Repairman." The style analysis follows the poem.

All morning in the February light
he has been mending cable,
splicing the pairs of wires together
according to their colors,
white-blue to white-blue
violet-slate to violet-slate,
in the warehouse attic by the river.

When he is finished
the messages will flow along the line:
thank you for the gift,
please come to the baptism,
the bill is now past due:
voices that flicker and gleam back and forth
across the tracer-colored wires.

We live so much of our lives
without telling anyone,
going out before dawn,
working all day by ourselves,
shaking our heads in silence
at the news on the radio.
He thinks of the many signals
flying in the air around him,
the syllables fluttering,
saying please love me,
from continent to continent
over the curve of the earth.

From Overtime. *Reprinted with the permissions of the publisher, Eastern Washington University Press (Spokane, Washington), and the author.*

Parts of Speech	
Number of words	132 (100%)
Number of nouns	33 (25%)
Number of verbs	25 (18.9%) [helping = 4 (3%); main = 6 (4.5%); -*ing* form = 7 (5.3%); *to* + form = 2 (1.5%)]
Number of adjectives	6 (4.5%) [determiners = 22 (16.7%)]
Number of adverbs	7 (5.3%)
Number of pronouns	10 (7.6%)
Number of prepositions	26 (19.7%)
Number of conjunctions	3 (2.3%) [coordinating = 2 (1.5%); subordinating = 1 (.76%)]
Number of content words (nouns, main verbs, adjectives, adverbs)	67 (50.1%)
Number of function words (including pronouns, helping verbs, and determiners)	65 (49.2%)

Word and Syllable Count	
Number of different words used in poem	94 (out of 132)
Number of monosyllabic words	54 (used 89 times)
Number of two-syllable words	28 (used 29 times)
Number of three-syllable words	9 (used 10 times)
Number of four+-syllable words	3 (used 4 times)
Fifteen words used 53 times in the poem; 79 words used only once	
Most frequently used word	*the* (17 times)

Line Analysis	
Number of lines	26 (100%)
Number of lines ending with nouns	17 (65.4%)
Number of lines ending with verbs	2 (7.7%) [finite = 1 (3.8%); nonfinite = 1 (3.8%)]
Number of lines ending with adverbs	2 (7.7%)
Number of lines ending with adjectives	1 (3.8%)
Number of lines ending with pronouns	4 (15.4%)

Phrase and Clause Analysis	
Independent clauses	7
Dependent clauses	2 (adverbial clause = 1; relative clause = 1)
Prepositional phrases	25 (modifying a noun = 8; modifying a verb/verbal = 16; modifying an adjective = 1)
Verbal phrases	9 (-ing participle form = 7; to+ infinitive form = 2)
Appositives	5
Absolutes	1

The book *Style and Statement*, by Edward P. J. Corbett and Robert J. Connors, provided the basis for this analysis. If you want to see other methods of style analysis, this book includes six different types. The analysis here uses only a fraction of the options available in the book.

You will note after going through this analysis that Millar's poem illustrates several of the principles that have been discussed so far. Millar uses concrete nouns and verbs, many of which he places at the ends of lines. He uses adjectives and adverbs sparingly. He uses a lot of function words, such as prepositions and determiners—especially the word *the*—but that is to be expected with the number of nouns here. He also uses several of the grammar tricks—participles, appositives, and absolutes—discussed in Chapter 3.

These findings will help you if you do an analysis of your own poems. You can easily see if you are using the right number of nouns and verbs, a good selection of grammar tricks, or too many adjectives, adverbs, and pronouns. If you are unsure of how to categorize a word, make use of your desk dictionary, which will show its functions and give examples of its use.

A Revision Example

To give you an idea of how the drafting process works, take a look at two versions of the poem "Thinning" by Jeanie French. The first version is an earlier draft. The second version is the polished revision you read in Chapter 14.

Reluctant, I sit down between rows
faint lines of valiant green marching
between aisles of straw, the sun hot
on my head, burning the tips of my ears
and the back of my neck and I separate
the seedlings gently with my fingertips
feeling for the strongest, thickest shoot
in the clutch of tiny succulent leaves, for
that is the one which will survive my
tender care. I can't wear gloves—
I need all the delicacy of unimpeded touch,
nothing between the ridges of my fingerprints
and the pulpy-soft, new-sprung stalks.
I grasp a spindly clump of seedlings and pull
gently, sever their roots from nurturing earth,
and lay them aside to die in the strong spring sun.

I feel the murder in my cells as I do it,
and reach for the next sacrifice.

Reprinted with the permission of the author.

Reluctant, I sit down between rows
faint lines of valiant green marching
between aisles of straw, the sun hot
on my head, burning the tips of my ears
and the back of my neck. I separate
the seedlings gently with my fingertips
feeling for the strongest, thickest shoot
in the clutch of tiny succulent leaves,
for that is the one which will survive
my tender care. I can't wear gloves—
I need all the delicacy of unimpeded touch,
nothing but the ridges of my fingerprints
and the pulpy-soft, new-sprung stalks.
I grasp a spindly clump of seedlings and pull
gently, sever roots from nurturing earth,
lay them aside to die in the strong spring sun.

Murder lives in my cells
as I reach for the next sacrifice.

Reprinted with the permission of the author.

French does not change many words between drafts. However, in the second draft she splits the long sentence that appeared at the beginning of the first and alters the line breaks to fall more favorably on nouns and verbs. Furthermore, she compacts the language toward the end by dropping unnecessary words, and she tightens the final couplet.

Very subtle changes have been made here, but for the better. From this example, you should learn that even if you improve a single word, the effort is well worth the trouble. Though you should always revise your poetry, be sure to keep a collection of your old drafts and ideas. These may help you revise your poems further in the future, or they can just serve as nostalgic reminders of your writing process.

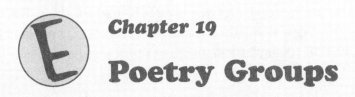

Chapter 19

Poetry Groups

For many poets, regardless of ability or publication experience, reader feedback is a valuable tool. Some poets claim that they don't need anyone to review their work, but if they plan to get it published, it will ultimately meet an editor's red pen. Poets, especially beginners, need opinions and suggestions from knowledgeable writers and readers to help them along. One of the best ways to get this kind of feedback on your work is to join (or create) a writing group.

The Perfect Mix of Members

Writing groups are comprised of individuals who share two common desires: to enhance their own writing and to help other writers improve their work. However, finding an effective mix of group members is more difficult than it may sound. If you have ever been involved in a writing workshop, you have already found that most people who write long to be told one thing: Their writing is perfect. They hope to receive a round of applause and hear the crowd cheer, "Remember us when you're on the *New York Times* bestseller list!"

ALERT!

Never walk into a writing group session on the defensive. If your group members sense that you're not in the right mood, they won't work with you. You must be prepared to receive all sorts of feedback—both compliments and criticisms. It is also imperative that the members of your writing group be willing to accept and give constructive feedback.

As mentioned in Chapter 1, there's plenty of ego involved in writing, and some people look to writing groups simply to boost their egos—not to get help or to help others. If you are only looking for a place to be praised and admired, you'd better start your own fan club. Writing groups are for people who enjoy the process of writing, appreciate the comments (and criticisms) of other writers, and are willing to give as well as receive assistance.

Finding Group Members

If you do not know anyone willing to join a writing group, visit a nearby bookstore or library. Many bookstores, libraries, and even colleges serve as hosts to writing groups. If there aren't any existing groups, you can advertise a call for members on their bulletin boards. Some educational institutions may allow you to advertise, but you will probably have to get permission first. Use caution when soliciting members; it will take time for you to get to know these people. However, regardless of the manner in which your group forms, these individuals may ultimately become some of your closest friends.

Whether you already know your group members or you're starting out fresh, these people must be dependable and honest. You will trust them with personal information in your writing, and you may feel very vulnerable at times. If the content of your writing is extremely personal, then you may prefer to work with a group of individuals whom you do not see on a regular basis. This way, your personal writing world will not interfere with your professional or family life.

QUESTION?

Does your lifestyle prevent you from forming a traditional writing group?
If you have an unusual work schedule or a lot of home responsibilities, you can try an online writing group. Do a general search for online writing groups and contact several of them to get more information.

Group Stability

A writing group becomes stable when it can maintain consistency and frequency within itself. Your group size should not exceed six members, and it should not have any fewer than four. You need an exchange of ideas and varying voices, but they cannot become so numerous that one individual's voice drowns in the conversation or so few that you don't express any ideas at all.

Time and Place

Most writing groups meet once a month. If your group is comprised of six people, you may need to meet twice a month in order to competently evaluate each person's writing. If you meet this frequently, you will have to work out a schedule for evaluating each person's writing. For example, if there are six of you, and you meet twice a month for an hour and a half each time, you should spend a half hour on each of three people's writing at each meeting.

The time of day you choose for your meetings is very important. Be careful not to schedule sessions at times when you will be too tired to fully take advantage of your group. Evening meetings are not always best because people are exhausted from the demands of work or family. Weekends are generally a good time to meet, as long as some members don't work during the weekends. The late morning or early afternoon is usually a time when people are most alert and ready to engage in conversation. During the meeting, you may want to assign one member to watch the clock. This assignment should be taken on with a certain measure of kindness. An alarm clock should not sound at the exact second the member's time is up, but you need to abide by a schedule to ensure that every member gets her turn.

As far as location is concerned, there are many options. Members can take turns hosting the meetings at their homes. Homes are great settings for group sessions because they are comfortable and give members a chance to learn a bit about each other. But for some, a home is too personal. Many writing groups choose to meet in libraries or bookstores, and others might even meet in cafés or restaurants. The location must be agreed upon by all of the group members.

Distributing Manuscripts and Criticism

Time management is best maintained when the work is distributed before the meeting. For example, if you meet on the thirtieth of each month, try to distribute your work, via e-mail or snail mail, to each member by the fifteenth or twentieth. Such a method allows each member to read the manuscripts multiple times before the meeting. No one should be reading a manuscript for the first time during the meeting itself.

When group members have time to study each other's writing in this manner, the meeting is very productive because each member is giving thoughtful input to the writer. Members can make handwritten comments on the manuscripts and refer to them as they make their suggestions during the meeting. Additionally, once the manuscripts have been returned to the writer, the same written comments give that group member something tangible to reference after the meeting.

Regardless of the form your comments take, remember that they should be both kind and meaningful to the writer. Your participation in the group means that you have a desire to enrich your own and others' writing, not to feed your ego or someone else's. So, comments such as "This is perfect" are not going to be helpful to the writer. Instead, try something like this: "The imagery in the poem is exceptional, but your reliance on passive verbs slows down the poem's rhythm." Such a comment shows that you really paid attention to the person's writing and that you want to be helpful.

Handling Chatter

Remember that the group's primary mission is to respond to its members' writing. In order to keep on task, don't allow too much time for off-topic conversation unless the entire group agrees to it. You may decide to allocate the first fifteen minutes of every session to general conversation. This will get any news or issues out of the way early so you can then focus on the writing.

Even though you want your group to be focused and effective, you also want it to be an enjoyable experience for everyone in the group. Additionally, the experience shouldn't feel like work; each member likely has enough of that to deal with on his or her own. So, in order to make things fun, your group could decide that everyone should bring a snack to share to each meeting. Or you could start the meeting with a game to break the ice and get everyone loosened up. By keeping all members comfortable and at ease, the meeting will run more smoothly and effectively.

Group Unity

Once the group has met for three or four sessions, you should begin to see noticeable improvements in your writing and your confidence. It's important to take your group members' comments seriously and work with them. Do not delay implementing their suggestions. As time goes on, your writing group will become a cohesive unit, and the advantages of such a group will become clear.

Using Feedback

Try to revise your work as quickly as possible following your meetings. Perhaps let your work and members' feedback sit for a day or two, but not any longer. If you wait too long, your energy and motivation will diminish. The suggestions you receive should still be fresh in your mind when you sit down to work them into your writing.

Group members' suggestions are much like your own ideas: If you don't consider them right away, you will lose them. As you work with the suggestions, you will find that some are useful and others are not helpful to you at the time. But even if you decide to disregard a comment or suggestion, don't put it out of your mind completely. A similar principle may apply to a future poem.

No matter whom the suggestions come from, and no matter if you use them in your revisions or not, be gracious in accepting the comments your group members have made. They have taken the time to read your work and will feel slighted if they do not feel their time has been appreciated. Likewise, be understanding if a fellow group member does not immediately employ your suggestion. Writing is a sensitive act; things can get very uncomfortable if everyone in the group does not act in a mature, constructive, and understanding fashion.

Building Chemistry

As you exchange ideas in the group, you will notice a chemistry forming between you and your group members. For instance, you may end up depending upon the insights of a particular member more than others. That's fine, but always keep an ear open to all voices. The quiet voice may be the wisest.

After a few meetings, your members will seem to assume roles—the punctuator, the line editor, the theme finder, etc. But, unlike traditional family roles, the roles within the writing group will shift depending upon the work at hand. Don't be afraid to leave your comfort zone. If you normally only offer suggestions on content, it doesn't mean you can't critique the aesthetics of a poem presented to the group. Feel free to say what comes to mind, but be sure it is constructive and intelligent feedback.

One Poet's Progress

Perhaps the best way for you to understand the benefits of a writing group is to see the changes in a couple of poems after they have received the careful attention of group members. DeAnna Beachley, a noted historian and humanities scholar, has only recently discovered her desire to write poetry. Now she writes so frequently and with such passion that she claims she cannot stop herself from writing. Her energy for poetry challenges and inspires her group to do more. One of her early submissions to the group was "Keystone Thrust Fault Trail," a poem that first appeared in the following form:

she emerges

shedding bark
leaves
as snakes shed
their skin
so that new growth
can occur

(in many ancient cultures
goddesses were depicted
with snakes wrapped
around their arms)

forces of erosion
perfect merger
of wind, rock, sun, cold, heat
strip away all that is
unnecessary

what remains is the essential self
true essence
strength
wisdom in simplicity

fault line
force of thrust
tectonic plates collide
push upward outward
exposing layers of rock
that had been hidden below
the crust
    new level
    next level

painful
noisy
thrust
drive
propel
advance with pressure
cooking far beneath the
surface

until a new being
emerges

Venus on a clamshell
    pure
    naked
    simple
cobra pose

spine elongates
tension releases
hips off the ground
arms strong
head upright looking
forward
breathing

this is just what it is

a new being
emerges
stripped of outward
burdens
engaged with the world

but detached

free
not tame
not contained
not surfaced with slick veneer
desert varnish
not covered by thick crust

what shall take root?

exposed
vulnerable
trusting absolutely
being
love
care

Initial Reactions

After reading the poem, you can probably see DeAnna's desire to capture the never-ending changes seen on a single trail. The trail is personified, and the reader embarks on a journey throughout the poem's stanzas. The earth is alive in this poem—it is vibrant, fertile, and wild. Anyone who walks on the trail is invited to explore its history, and perhaps learn more about her own.

When the poem was first workshopped, many group members were instantly impressed by DeAnna's ability to make the trail real. The poem's vitality is undeniable, due, in part, to the opening, "she emerges." The group also agreed that the poem's strength was rooted in the poem's language, which shadows the form of an actual trail, or better still, an individual's path on a trail.

Suggestions for Revision

While most members liked several parts of the poem, a few group members had comments about the poem's line lengths, line breaks, and stanza organization. The group also suggested that DeAnna draw more on her inner vision of the trail and supply the poem with more concrete details. After two or three more drafts, DeAnna presented this revision:

she emerges

shedding bark and leaves
as snakes shed their skin
leaving behind the old
for the new

(in many ancient cultures
goddesses were depicted
with snakes wrapped
around their arms)

forces of erosion
strip away all that is
unnecessary
spare language of nature

fault line
force of thrust
tectonic plates collide
painful and noisy
push upward outward
advancing with pressure

exposing layers of rock
that had been cooking far beneath
taking things to a new level
the next level

cobra pose
spine elongates
tension releases
hips off the ground
arms strong
head upright looking
forward
breathing

this is just what it is

a new being
comes forth
stripped of outward
burdens
engaged with the world

but detached

free
not tame
not contained
not surfaced with slick veneer

no desert varnish
not covered by thick crust

exposed vulnerable
trusting absolutely

what shall take root?

Results

As you read the revised poem, you can probably see the thought DeAnna took in reshaping her line lengths and reordering some of the poem's later stanzas. She maintained all the poem's many strengths. For example, stanza three was left untouched, and the poem's lack of punctuation and capitalization, which mimics nature's freedom, persists.

To get another sense of how the revisions have changed DeAnna's poem, do a style analysis of both versions. Go back to the categories used in Chapter 18, write them out on a pair of blank pages, determine what falls under them in both drafts, and compare the results.

However, the abstract language of the first draft is gone. DeAnna is relying on more sensory details to capture the pressure of the earth's surface. She also seems to be trusting her reader much more by not answering the poem's most compelling question: "What shall take root?" In this draft, DeAnna forces the reader to respond.

Another Poet's Progress

Another group member, Jeanie French—a gardener, English professor, environmental enthusiast, and fiction writer—likes to experiment with her writing through poetry. Jeanie was inspired by a classroom experience and by Langston Hughes's poem "Theme for English B" when she wrote the following draft of "Theme":

Write a page, *I said.* Let it come out
of you. Then it will be true.

What do they think when they
hear that, this kaleidoscope of young
faces before me? They look

at me—middle-aged white woman—
and wonder if I'll understand
their truths. Their truths
are hard—the inner city, gangs,
drugs, poverty, shootings, and
killings on street corners
all the fears, hopes, dreams
of families resting on their shoulders.

I've seen their truths on the news
but I haven't lived them. I'm no
stranger to poverty, but I'm white,
white bread, white wine—new grapes of wrath vintage.
Poor and white is not poor and black,
poor and Asian, poor and Mexican.
They think I won't know their truths
and they'll be right. They don't
know mine either. I tell them
we can meet on the page but
I don't know if I believe myself.

Initial Reactions

When the group first read Jeanie's poem, many members were struck by Jeanie's ability to pay tribute to the original. Hughes's poem speaks to the student's sense of isolation or distance from his instructor—an instructor who has asked him to write an essay about his identity. The Hughes poem captures the student's fear that his teacher may never understand him because of their differences in race and life experiences.

But Hughes's poem ends with the narrator's hope that despite individual differences, honesty can bridge the gap between them. Jeanie's poem takes on the other side of Hughes's poem. Her narrator, a teacher, speaks to the same issue as she anticipates the world of her students and their perceptions of her world.

Suggestions for Revision

In this early draft of the poem, the writing group was not able to visualize the faces of the students. Nor were they able to sense the narrator's fear for these students. The group encouraged Jeanie to give the students more identity and to name her narrator's fears. What follows is Jeanie's fourth and possibly final draft of the poem:

Write a page, *I said.* Let it come out
of you. Then it will be true.

What do they think when they
hear that, this kaleidoscope of young
faces before me? They look
at me—middle-aged white woman—
and wonder if I'll understand
their truths. Their truths
are hard—inner city, gangs,
drugs, poverty, shootings and
killings on street corners,
escape the champagne wish,
the diamond dream of their families.

I've seen their stories on the news
but I haven't lived them. I'm no
stranger to poverty, but I'm white,
white bread, white wine—new grapes of wrath vintage.
Poor and white is not poor and black,
poor and Asian, poor and Mexican.
They're right: I won't know their truths.
They don't know mine either.
I could tell them that escape is possible—
but they won't want to hear the rest of that truth:
you can get out but you can't leave behind who you are;
poverty is a bomb in the brain you'll never defuse.

Diamond studs wink at me from their ears;
their faces remain carefully blank
and our lives tick away.
I tell them we can meet on the page
but I don't know if I believe it myself.

Results

Jeanie's revision shows the attention she spent on developing the faces of the students who inspired her to write the poem. The addition of the fourth stanza gives them identities. Their faces are blank and their earrings "wink" at the narrator, alluding to the students' personalities and appearances.

As you did with DeAnna's poems, do a style analysis of both versions of Jeanie's poem. Use the same categories that you used for DeAnna's poems. Compare your results from both drafts, and then compare what you see in DeAnna's and Jeanie's poems to find what similarities and differences the writers display.

More poignantly, the narrator worries that her life and the students' lives will "tick" away because of their inability to connect. The teacher implores them to meet her "on the page," but even she doubts this is possible. Her fear of this lack of connection is heightened by her sense of the harm that can come to all of them. There are multiple allusions to a bomb—the danger that occurs when people cannot or choose not to understand one another. As a result of these additions, Jeanie has created a multilayered dialogue between her poem, her students, and the work of a master.

Keep It Interesting

While your regularly scheduled meetings will have the same basic format, you may want to mix things up every once in a while to add some fun to your group. For instance, you may want to expand your group activities to include attending local poetry readings and lectures together. Or perhaps you could have small parties every couple of months at members' homes. These are opportunities to get to know each other outside of the writing mindset.

Colleges and Bookstores

If you live in an area that is home to an established writer, editor, or publisher, you may want to invite the expert to speak to your group or you and your group members may choose to attend any readings or lectures given by this individual. Also, any college with an English department will likely host a number of literary events throughout the academic year.

FACT

If you broaden the activities of your writing group to include local events, you will not only learn new ways to improve your writing, but you will also receive recommendations of great books to read for fun. By visiting bookstores and attending readings, you will be among the first to discover the new literature hitting the shelves.

You may also find it helpful to visit local bookstores with your group members. Not only will the environment be fitting for a conversation about writing, but you might also hear about upcoming book events in the area. One fun activity to do at a bookstore is to have all the members of your group take ten or fifteen minutes to choose a book of poetry from the shelves. Then, once you reconvene, you can take turns reading poetry from the books you have selected. This is a nice, relaxing way to enjoy each other without the common constraints of your scheduled meetings.

Other Sources of Inspiration

All artists have the potential to inspire each other. No doubt you are familiar with Vincent van Gogh's *Starry Night* (1889). This painting inspired Don McLean's classic song "Vincent (Starry Starry Night)." The swirling white, blue, and yellow hues of the painting are captured in the soft sounds of McLean's voice. The tragedy of van Gogh's life is captured in the song's lyrics. Poets affect one another and other artists in this manner quite frequently. In Chapter 7, you read Zachary Chartkoff's contemplation of Milton's *Paradise Lost*. Earlier in this chapter you read Jeanie French's poem based on a piece by Langston Hughes.

Often, a creative-writing instructor will ask students to write a work based upon their reading of another established piece of literature or fine art. The intent of such an exercise is not necessarily to mimic the writer; rather, the purpose is to elevate the meaning of the original work or to apply the meaning of the original to the present day. You and your group members should spend some time reading poems that have been inspired by the works of others. Likewise, your group members may want to pay tribute to their favorite artists by writing a poem inspired by those other works. By gaining inspiration from the great artists who came before you, you will pass on timeless knowledge and experience and perhaps inspire some poets of the future.

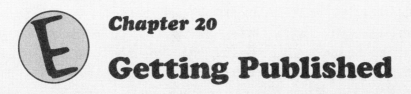

Chapter 20

Getting Published

Once you have mastered all of the material in the previous chapters of this book, you are ready to submit your poems for publication. This stage is possibly the scariest and most exciting of the writing process. Rejection happens to everyone, and it stings. But the thrill of seeing your work in print will make up for all the rejection you endured. Following a few simple procedures will give your poems their best chance for acceptance.

Literary Magazines

Literary magazines are a great way to get your poetry published for the first time. One reason for this is that there are numerous publications to choose from. No matter the style, theme, or length of your work, there is likely a magazine out there that will accept it. Also, these magazines tend to have an editorial vision that ensures a standard of quality that will serve you well. If your work is accepted, it will likely be edited well and placed in an issue where it fits with the surrounding material. Finally, the more your work appears in print, the more prestige you will build for yourself as a writer. Most literary magazines will not pay much (if anything) for your submissions, but you will establish an impressive resume that will help you build your career.

But perhaps you are wondering: What is a literary magazine? Basically, it is a publication dedicated to the fine arts. Most literary magazines publish poetry, short fiction, short literary nonfiction, reviews, interviews, and even some artwork and photography. As such, a literary magazine might not have a wide audience, but it will have an intelligent readership that appreciates fine work.

FACT

There are a handful of popular magazines, such as the *New Yorker* and the *Atlantic Monthly*, which will also take poems. These magazines are sometimes called *slicks* due to their glossy paper. However, be careful: These magazines will rarely, if ever, take any work not submitted by an agent or by a well-established author.

While literary magazines are a great option, other venues for publishing your work do exist. Some poetry groups have newsletters, either in print or online. Some Web sites invite poets to post their work. You may even live in an area with a daily newspaper that will print poems. However, these venues may not be as reliable, either because the editorial standard is questionable or their availability is scarce.

Editorial Vision

Literary magazines will often accept the best work that is submitted to them, regardless of the content. However, some literary magazines are governed by an editorial vision that limits what you may send. In other words, they are looking for poems written about certain topics and nothing else. For example, one magazine, *Witness*, has an issue each year dedicated to a specific theme, like aging or animals. You should inquire about such themes or other editorial requirements in a query letter, which will be explained later.

To give you an idea about what is meant by editorial vision, consider the following comments by Richard Logsdon, the senior editor of *Red Rock Review*, a literary magazine in Las Vegas, Nevada. Here are his responses to two questions posed by many writers in search of a literary magazine. His answers should offer you a glimpse into the mind of a magazine editor.

> *Q: What is the role of a contemporary literary journal?*
>
> *A: In a nutshell, I think the role of the contemporary literary journal is to publish the very best in fiction and poetry. To do so, of course, requires an understanding of what distinguishes a great piece of writing from something that is good or mediocre—and there's the rub. While this call to judgment may seem subjective, I do not think it ultimately so if we consider that, among the top journals, there does seem to be an agreement about what constitutes a truly great short story or a truly great poem. Thus, in a way, the aesthetic standards have already been set for the contemporary journal. It is, therefore, incumbent upon the editors to respond intelligently and creatively to these implied criteria.*
>
> *Beyond its duty to publish the very best literature, thereby reinforcing the highest of standards, I think it is the role of the contemporary journal to publish works that are timely but not trendy. That is, while avoiding works whose popularity has more to do with faddishness than aesthetic merit, the contemporary literary journal has an obligation to present those works of prose and poetry that attempt to address the question of how to live, that offer insight into some aspect of the human condition, that make some kind of an assertion. In doing so, the journal also has an obligation to rise above trendy and soon-to-be-trite themes and offer the reader something that will aesthetically, morally, emotionally, even spiritually shape his or her thoughts and perceptions.*

Q: What do you look for in poetry? What is your selection process?

A: The poems that I select for publication must be more than a string of words arranged in a pleasing fashion and containing pleasing sounds— although pleasing sounds are nice. Good poetry startles or surprises—and not merely for the sake of effect but to invoke upon the part of the reader a response both emotional and intellectual—and maybe even somewhat transcendent. In short, a good poem must make me think, and it must make me feel.

Query and Cover Letters

Your initial contact with an editor will take one of two forms, the *query letter* or the *cover letter*. A writer sends a query letter to an editor to discover submission policies concerning manuscripts. And a writer sends a cover letter to accompany the submission, explaining its contents and (hopefully) attracting the attention of the editor. While these forms of contact will usually help you get published, some publications explicitly ask that writers not include letters with their submissions. The first guideline you must follow is to abide by the instructions of the publication.

Formatting Tips

Both the query and the cover letter should follow the format of a business letter. Include a heading, an inside address, a salutation, and a complimentary close. The heading, which includes your name, address, phone number (you may also add fax or e-mail), and date of correspondence, should be located in the top left-hand corner of the page.

The inside address, which includes the editor or publisher's name, title, and address, should appear below the heading. The salutation, which includes the abbreviation Mr. or Ms. before the recipient's last name, should go two lines below the inside address. The text of your letter should begin two lines below your salutation. The complimentary close should appear two lines below the text of your letter. Below the close, you will need your handwritten signature and your typed name.

If you don't know the name of the editor when you write the query letter, use a general title such as Poetry Editor, and a general salutation such as Dear Poetry Editor. But then ask for the name and the title of the recipient in your letter so that you can address that person correctly in future correspondence.

The letter should be single-spaced, with two spaces between paragraphs in the text. Do not indent paragraphs. The number of lines between the heading and the inside address will vary according to need; make sure that your letter seems to fill the page even if it really doesn't. Spell out all streets, states, dates, and other words you may usually abbreviate.

Content Tips

Whichever letter is your first contact with the editor, use it to mention what you know about the editor's magazine. Did you first come across it in a bookstore? In a library? Have you read more than one issue? A good way to show that you're truly interested in the magazine is by naming the poems and the poets that it has already published.

In the query letter, ask for the magazine's submission standards for the appearance of the manuscript, for submission deadlines (since many magazines do not take manuscripts year-round), and for any themes or topics the magazine may require or prefer. In the cover letter, give a brief description of the central themes of your poetry to show the editor how it meets that magazine's vision. For both letters, name what enclosures you've included, if any, and be sure to thank the editor for her time.

Take a look at the following two sample pages to see how a query letter and a cover letter should look. The query letter comes first, followed by the cover letter.

Jane Rogers
123 Street
City, State 12345
(555) 555-1234

January 1, 2000

Joanne Smith
Managing Editor
ABC Magazine
123 Street
City, State 12345

Dear Ms. Smith,

I have read several issues of your wonderful magazine, including a special theme issue on the Southwestern lifestyle. In that issue, I particularly enjoyed the poems "Big Plain Living" by Zeb Jones and "Cattle Fiddle Faddle" by Jennie Barker.

I believe my own poetry would work well in your magazine and I am interested to learn how to send my manuscript to you. Would you be so kind as to send me your submission guidelines in the self-addressed, stamped envelope I have provided?

Thank you for your time and consideration, and I look forward to working with you in the future.

Sincerely,

Jane Rogers

Enc.

Jane Rogers
123 Street
City, State 12345
(555) 555-1234

January 1, 2000

John Smith
Submissions Editor
XYZ Magazine
123 Street
City, State, 12345

Dear Mr. Smith,

I recently read Eve Jones's wonderful poem "Icing" in your latest issue and it inspired me to send you three of my own poems, "The Ring," "A Question," and "Two by Two," for your consideration. I feel that these poems have all the elements desired by your editorial vision: lucid writing, strong imagery, and attention to sensory detail.

I thank you for your time, and I hope that you will enjoy reading these poems.

Sincerely,

Jane Rogers

Enc.

Formatting Your Manuscript

The word *manuscript* is used to distinguish a group of poems that have been made ready for publication. The poems are no longer simply drafts. Furthermore, the poems are no longer separate entities but part of a single submission.

The following are general manuscript format guidelines commonly demanded by magazine publishers for snail mail submissions. Some magazines, particularly online "Webzines," accept e-mail submissions. Most traditional magazines, however, accept only hard-copy manuscripts. You should learn the magazine's unique requirements before sending in a submission.

- Manuscripts should be mailed flat (with no folds) in a manila (9" x 12" or larger) envelope.
- All manuscripts must be legibly typed or computer-generated on 8½" x 11" white bonded paper.
- Avoid dot matrix printouts.
- Do not use erasable bond paper.
- Do not use colored paper in an attempt to make the manuscript stand out.
- Use standard fonts or typefaces (Courier, Helvetica, or Times New Roman) and standard font sizes (10 point on typewriters, 12 point on computers).
- Manuscripts should not show any signs of wear; send freshly typed or printed manuscripts.
- Above all, do not send the only copies of your poems. Print extra copies to keep for your records.

Specific Manuscript Guidelines for Poems

In addition to these general guidelines, you should follow a few more that pertain just to poems. These extra guidelines will give editors contact information, layout requirements, and estimations of length that will make their job easier. And making an editor's job easier can only help your purpose.

- Set the top and bottom margins at 1 inch; you can set the left and right margins and line breaks at your discretion.
- Center the title and byline at the top of the poem.
- Do not center your poems on the page; it is the editor's first sign that the submission comes from an amateur.
- Include your name, address, and phone number (single-spaced) at the top left-hand corner of every page. Your real name appears at the top of the page and your pen name—if one is used—appears in the byline.
- Include page numbers and a keyword from the title at the top right-hand corner of subsequent pages if a poem goes over one page.
- Lines of text may be single- or double-spaced.

QUESTION?

What is a byline?

A byline includes the name that you want to see in print if the poem is published. If you write under a pen name or if you have reasons to keep your real name hidden, then the byline will indicate that information to the editor.

One thing you should remember is that if your submission runs onto a second page, you should include your heading on the second page as well. This way, if the pages get separated somehow, the editor will still know that this page contains your work.

Final Submission Tips

As you engage in the process of contacting editors, there are four rules you should keep in mind. First, don't make the editor angry. If this person says that the deadline for submissions is June 1, get your manuscript there before June 1. If this person wants poems about rainwater and squash, then go to your garden and get inspiration from your vegetables. Missing deadlines or giving an editor poems on a topic not in line with the magazine's vision will guarantee that your poems never see print.

Second, always follow manuscript submission guidelines. The guidelines listed earlier should satisfy most editors, but some magazines may have other requirements. Learn these guidelines before you send your work. Editors have manuscript guidelines to make things easier for you both.

ALERT!

One submission guideline that you will have to be very careful to obey concerns simultaneous submissions. Many editors do not want you to submit your work to two or more places at once. While multiple acceptances are exciting, the situation will cause you quite a headache. To avoid this, keep it simple from the start.

Third, always include a self-addressed, stamped envelope for return correspondence. A major pet peeve among editors is not to have a way to send notifications or to return manuscripts. It is also not the editor's job to pay for your postage. Put the proper postage on the return envelope, and put your mailing address in both the return and the addressee spaces.

Fourth, don't send your entire body of work in one submission. Send only three poems per submission, and make sure they are your best samples. An editor will not take the time to read through forty of your poems to find the ones he likes. So, even though it may be hard to choose, only select a few poems to send at a time.

Don't Pay to Publish!

You may get a mailer telling you that you have been selected to feature your poetry in a beautiful hardbound book. The wording of the letter may even make it sound as if you have won some sort of contest. You may feel flattered at having been contacted and eager to see your work in print. As a result, you may not even notice the $25, $50, or $75 you will be asked to spend on the purchase of this book.

When this happens to you, you need only follow one general rule: Do not spend your money. There are several reasons to follow this rule, ranging from mild to severe. First, and most mild, is that you will gain no prestige from going this route. Unlike literary magazines, these anthologies are not edited. No criteria are set for what is included and what isn't. Whoever is publishing this book will include poems from anyone willing to pay the money. You must understand that publishing itself is not what gives prestige to your work; it is being selected for publication by an editor who can judge literary merit that gives your work the standing it deserves.

Second, the money you pay to see your work in print may or may not be used for its intended purpose. In some cases you could go through this process, pay the fee, and never see the book or your money again. In other words, you don't have any way of defending yourself against scams.

Third, and most importantly, even if your money does get you a nice, big book with your poem in it, you may be giving away your rights to your work. Whenever you publish a poem in a magazine, a book, a newspaper, an online Webzine, or any other venue, you have to give the publisher certain rights to see your work in print. A magazine, newspaper, or Webzine will generally ask you for *first serial rights*, meaning that they want the right to print it first in their publication. The rights to the work will revert to you upon that printing, and you will still own the poem.

There are some good pay-to-publish organizations available if you want to publish a book of your own poems. The cost of self-publishing can range anywhere from the low hundreds to thousands of dollars, so you will have to shop around—and make sure you have found a legitimate service.

Book publishers generally require more comprehensive rights. If, for example, you were to publish a collection of your poems with a legitimate publisher, that publisher would very likely control the rights to your poems. Anyone who wanted to publish one of your poems again would ask your publisher, not you, for permission. Ultimately, all money made is controlled by whoever owns those rights. Publishing your poem in one of these collections, therefore, may give someone else the rights to your work—and the right to make money off your work.

In the long run, your poems—and your writing career—will be better served if you stick to legitimate publishing outlets. The process of publication is frustrating and disheartening at times. However, the rewards are well worth the trouble in the end.

Contests

Many literary magazines offer contests throughout the year. These contests will allow you to compete for prize money that will not only earn you prestige but also pay for an evening out or a new purchase. Prizes can range from $10 to $10,000; however, just as with submissions, you want to be sure that there are no strings attached and that you will not lose the rights to your work by entering.

The Contest Process

You can find information about entering a contest in Appendix A of this book, but you can read a bit about the process here. The first thing you will have to do is pay close attention to the submission policies. Keep in mind what you read earlier about following submission guidelines. This rule stands (and is perhaps more important) when entering a contest.

The editorial staff, to ensure smooth processing of manuscripts and fair judgment of them, will ask you to follow many rules that may seem strange. For example, many contests will ask you to submit your work without your name appearing anywhere on the pages. Instead, you may be asked to include a cover page with your name and contact information. This rule is enforced so that the entrants go through a blind judging process that ensures a fair read.

You may also be limited in terms of how many poems you may send, and how long those poems may be. The usual limit is three to five poems per entry, each poem capped at twenty to forty lines. These limits are also imposed for the sake of fairness, and so that the staff can plan the layout of the magazine in which winning entries will appear.

You may also be limited in terms of the content or themes of your poems. The contest may be for poems about aging, poems about food, or poems about children. If a contest stipulates a theme, you must abide by it in order for your work to be considered. Another important item to keep track of is the deadline for submissions. If the rules say that no entries will be accepted if postmarked after June 1, make sure your envelope has a date no later than June 1 stamped on it. And if the rules say no simultaneous submissions, do not send the poems to another magazine or contest at the same time.

Finally, you should expect to pay an entry fee for many of these contests. Anything from $5 to $25 may be required. Many magazines use the entry fees to pay for printing costs and to raise the prize money, so if the journal itself is legitimate, the entry fee is not a scam.

Rejection: Accept It and Move On

Like all human endeavors, the act of writing for publication does have a negative side. For instance, what if a magazine doesn't accept your poems? What if you spend days, weeks, or even months preparing a submission and the publication rejects it at the drop of a hat? What's worse, you may begin to see any rejection of your writing as personal criticism, and this can wear on your self-esteem.

As discussed throughout the book, you are bound to feel a strong emotional bond with the words you have carefully crafted into poems. But experienced writers know that a rejection of their work is not a personal attack. The writing does not define the writer, and the two must be kept separate in your mind as you prepare to submit your work. Once you encounter rejection—and rejection will inevitably occur at some point in your writing career—you will be able to take that rejection for what it is worth.

As you send out your manuscripts, keep a log of which poems you have sent out, which poems have been rejected, and which magazines have rejected which poems. This way, you will not send the same poems to a magazine by mistake, and you can keep track of your progress.

If you get a rejection from a literary magazine for some of your poems, that doesn't mean you can't try again with another publication. Many factors go into the decision to choose poems, and they don't all have to do with quality. The timing could be wrong for your submission, for example. So, if you get rejected once, try again. And if you get rejected a second time, try once more. Try again and again until you get it.

Acceptance: Enjoy It and Move On

One day, you may come home from a long day at work, open your mailbox, and find a letter from an editor saying that your poems have been accepted. If this is your first acceptance among several rejections you may want to weep with joy. Go ahead—you earned it. Call friends and family to let them know about your success. This is very exciting, indeed. However, you will have a few more responsibilities before you see your poems in print.

First of all, the editor may need you to confirm that you want your work published. While it seems unnecessary, you should always confirm with the editor that you are still interested in having your work published. You may have to sign a form that says you will allow the magazine first American serial rights, or something similar. Again, granting these rights allows the magazine to print your work, and all other rights should revert to you once the poems appear in print.

QUESTION?

What is meant by *layout* and *galleys*?
Layout is the process by which a magazine takes the writers' works and prepares them for printing. Galleys are an early printing of the magazine, made so that the design and the content of the magazine can be double-checked before the final printing is completed.

At this stage, you may be asked to help with the layout in the magazine. The editor may ask you to send the latest version of the accepted poems as hard or electronic copy. You may also be given pages of the magazine galleys, with your poems included, to make sure they look right. Once you have confirmed that the poems appear as you wish them to, the editor will move forward with the printing process. Your poems may appear anywhere from two months to a year after the proofing stage, depending upon the publication's process.

If you work hard to improve your writing and get it published, success will eventually come to you. It may take more time than you'd like, but it will happen. So, don't give up until you get what you've been working for. However, don't become complacent after your first publication. Surely your goal is to build a career or hobby as a writer, not just to get published once. If this is the case, then don't ride on the coattails of your success for too long. Take some time to celebrate your achievement and then move on to the next challenge. There is more success to be had!

Appendix A

Additional Resources for Poets

Magazines

580 Split
Jessea Perry, Poetry Editor
P.O. Box 9982, Mills College, Oakland, CA 94613
✍ *www.mills.edu/580Split*

AgNI
Ellen Wehle and Rachel DeWoskin,
Associate Poetry Editors
Boston University Writing Program,
236 Bay State Rd., Boston, MA 02215
✍ *www.bu.edu/agni*

Black Warrior Review
Aaron Welborn, Editor
P.O. Box 862936, Tuscaloosa, AL 35486
✍ *www.webdelsol.com/bwr*

Bomb Magazine
Betsy Sussler, Publisher/Editor in Chief
594 Broadway, Suite 905, New York, NY 10012
✍ *www.bombsite.com*

The Briar Cliff Review
Tricia Currans-Sheehan, Editor
Briar Cliff University, 3303 Rebecca St.,
P.O. Box 2100, Sioux City, IA 51104
✍ *www.briarcliff.edu/bcreview*

Clackamas Literary Review
Brad Stiles and Kate Gray, Editors
19600 S. Molalla Ave., Oregon City, OR 97045
✍ *www.clackamas.cc.or.us/clr*

Colorado Review
Stephanie G'Schwind, Editor
Department of English, Colorado State
University, Fort Collins, CO 80523
✍ *www.coloradoreview.com*

Crab Creek Review
P.O. Box 840, Vashon Island, WA 98070
✍ *www.crabcreekreview.org*

Fence
Caroline Crumpacker, Poetry Editor
303 East Eighth Street, #B1, New York, NY 10009
✍ *www.fencemag.com*

Five Points
David Bottoms, Editor
MSC 8R0318, Georgia State University,
33 Gilmer St. S.E., Unit 8, Atlanta, GA 30303
✍ *www.webdelsol.com/Five_Points/home.htm*

Hayden's Ferry Review
Salima Keegan, Managing Editor
Box 871502, Arizona State
University, Tempe, AZ 85287
✍ *www.haydensferryreview.org*

The Idaho Review
Mitch Wieland, Editor
Boise State University, Department of Eng-
lish, 1910 University Dr., Boise, ID 83725
✍ *http://english.boisestate.edu/idahoreview*

Kalliope
Mary Sue Koeppel, Editor
Florida Community College at Jacksonville,
11901 Beach Blvd., Jacksonville, FL 32246
✍ *www.fccj.org/kalliope/kalliope.htm*

Literal Latté
Jenine Gordon Bockman, Publisher and Editor
200 East 10th St., Suite 240, New York, NY 10003
✍ *www.literal-Latte.com*

The MacGuffin
Carol Was, Poetry Editor
Schoolcraft College, 18600 Hag-
gerty Rd., Livonia, MI 48152
✍ *www.schoolcraft.cc.mi.us/
macguffin/default.htm*

Many Mountains Moving
Debra Bokur, Poetry Editor
420 22nd St., Boulder, CO 80302
✍ *www.mmminc.org*

Poetry Flash
Joyce Jenkins, Editor/Publisher
1450 Fourth Street #4, Berkeley, CA 94710
✍ *www.poetryflash.org*

Prairie Schooner
Hilda Raz, Editor; Erin Flanagan, Managing Editor
201 Andrews Hall, University of
Nebraska, Lincoln, NE 68588
✍ *www.unl.edu/schooner/psmain.htm*

Red Rock Review
Richard Logsdon, Senior Editor
English Department, J2A, Community Col-
lege of Southern Nevada, 3200 E. Chey-
enne Avenue, North Las Vegas, NV 89030
✍ *www.ccsn.edu/english/redrock-
review/index.html*

Web del Sol/Del Sol Review
Michael Neff, Founder and Editor in Chief
Poetry and prose poetry submissions
should be addressed to Aylin An and e-
mailed to *poetry-dsr@webdelsol.com*
✍ *webdelsol.com/f-subs.htm*

Witness
Peter Stine, Editor
Oakland Community College, 27055 Orchard
Lake Road, Farmington Hills, MI 48334
✍ *www.occ.cc.mi.us/witness*

Zyzzyva *(for West Coast writers)*
Howard Junker, Editor
P.O. Box 590069, San Francisco, CA 94159
✍ *www.zyzzyva.org*

Web Sites

The Academy of American Poets
www.poets.org

Council of Literary Magazines and Presses
www.clmp.org

e-poets.network
www.e-poets.net

Poets & Writers
www.pw.org

Web del Sol
webdelsol.com

Contests

American Literary Review Poetry Contest
www.engl.unt.edu/alr

Clackamas Literary Review: Willamette Award
www.clackamas.cc.or.us/clr/contests.htm

Five Points James Dickey Prize for Poetry
*www.webdelsol.com/Five_Points/guidelines/
contest.htm*

St. Louis Poetry Center's National Poetry Contest
*www.stlouipoetrycenter.org/Contest/
contest.html*

Workshops

Association of Writers & Writing Programs
www.awpwriter.org

Bread Loaf Writers' Conference
www.middlebury.edu/blwc

Community of Writers at Squaw Valley
www.squawvalleywriters.org

Nimrod/Hardman Awards Celebration and Writing Workshop
www.utulsa.edu/nimrod

Pacific Northwest Writers Association Summer Conference
www.pnwa.org

Poetry Presses

The Bitter Oleander Press
Paul B. Roth, Editor
4983 Tall Oaks Drive, Fayetteville, NY 13066
www.bitteroleander.com

BOA Editions
Thom Ward, Editor
260 East Ave., Rochester, NY 14604
www.boaeditions.org

Copper Canyon Press
Thatcher Bailey, Publisher
P. O. Box 271 Port Townsend, WA 98368
www.coppercanyonpress.org

Sarabande Books
Sarah Gorham, President and Editor in Chief
2234 Dundee Rd., Suite 200, Louisville, KY 40205
www.SarabandeBooks.org

Reading List

The Poet's Companion: A Guide to the Pleasures of Writing Poetry, by Kim Addonizio and Dorianne Laux, W. W. Norton & Company, New York, NY, 1997.

Spring Essence: The Poetry of Ho Xuan Huong, translated by John Balaban, Copper Canyon Press, Port Townsend, WA, 2000.

Blue Earth, by Aliki Barnstone, Iris Press, Oak Ridge, TN, 2004.

Algebra of Night: New & Selected Poems, 1948–1998, by Willis Barnstone, Sheep Meadow Press, Riverdale-on-Hudson, NY, 1999.

Life Watch, by Willis Barnstone, BOA Editions, Rochester, NY 2003.

Eros, Eros, Eros: Odysseas Elytis, Selected and Last Poems, translated by Olga Broumas, Copper Canyon Press, Port Townsend, WA, 1998.

Lovers in the Used World, by Gillian Conoley, Carnegie Mellon University Press, Pittsburgh, PA, 2001.

Creating Poetry, by John Drury, Writer's Digest Books, Cincinnati, OH, 1991.

Domestic Weather, by Christine Boyka Kluge, Uccelli Press, Seattle, WA 2004.

Teaching Bones to Fly, by Christine Boyka Kluge, The Bitter Oleander Press, Fayetteville, NY, 2003.

Keeper, by Jeff Knorr, Mammoth Books, DuBois, PA 2004.

Mooring Against the Tide: Writing Poetry and Fiction, by Jeff Knorr and Tim Schell, Prentice Hall, Upper Saddle River, NJ, 2000.

The River Sings: An Introduction to Poetry, by Jeff Knorr, Prentice Hall, Upper Saddle River, NJ, 2003.

Standing Up to the Day, by Jeff Knorr, Pecan Grove Press, San Antonio, TX, 1999.

A Writer's Country: A Collection of Fiction and Poetry, by Jeff Knorr and Tim Schell, Prentice Hall, Upper Saddle River, NJ, 2001.

Smoke, by Dorianne Laux, BOA Editions, Rochester, NY, 2000.

My Town, by David Lee, Copper Canyon Press, Port Townsend, WA, 1995.

My Father's Martial Art, by Stephen S. N. Liu, University of Nevada Press, Reno, NV, 2000.

Bat Ode, by Jeredith Merrin, University of Chicago Press, Chicago, IL, 2001.

In Far Corners, by Neide Messer, Confluence Press, Lewiston, ID, 1990.

Overtime, by Joseph Millar, Eastern Washington University Press, Spokane, WA, 2001.

Image Grammar: Using Grammatical Structures to Teach Writing, by Harry R. Noden, Boynton/Cook Publishers, Portsmouth, NH, 1999.

Teodoro Luna's Two Kisses, by Alberto Ríos, W. W. Norton & Company, New York, NY, 1990.

This Time: New and Selected Poems, by Gerald Stern, W. W. Norton & Company, New York, NY, 1998.

In the Next Galaxy, by Ruth Stone, Copper Canyon Press, Port Townsend, WA, 2002.

Dr. Invisible & Mr. Hide, by Charles Harper Webb, Pearl Editions, Long Beach, CA, 1998.

Liver, by Charles Harper Webb, University of Wisconsin Press, Madison, WI, 1999.

Reading the Water, by Charles Harper Webb, Northeastern University Press, Boston, MA, 1997.

Stand Up Poetry: An Expanded Anthology, edited by Charles Harper Webb, University of Iowa Press, Iowa City, IA, 2002.

Tulip Farms and Leper Colonies, by Charles Harper Webb, BOA Editions, Rochester, NY, 2001.

Reign of Snakes, by Robert Wrigley, Penguin Books, New York, NY, 1999.

Appendix B

Glossary of Terms

alliteration:
This is the repetition of sounds at the beginning of words. The *b* sounds in "big bad bear" create alliteration.

assonance:
Similar vowel sounds (like the *a* sound in "sad ant tragedy") create *assonance*.

ballad:
A narrative poem written in an iambic foot pattern, quatrains, a syllable count of 8-6-8-6, and a rhyme scheme of XAXA or ABAB.

bouts-rimés:
A poetic form created from a list of words. All of the words on the list appear at the ends of the lines in the poem.

closed form:
Any poetic form governed by rules for rhyming, meter, foot pattern, syllable count, or alliteration.

consonance:
Similar consonant sounds (like the *d* sound in "bad dog saddle") create *consonance*.

couplet:
Two consecutive lines of poetry. Also a stanza of two lines.

dramatic poetry:
A poem that relies on the exchange of dialogue between two or more characters.

enjambment:
A line break that occurs in the middle of a sentence or phrase, as opposed to *end-stopped lines*, which break where a sentence or phrase breaks.

epic:
An ancient narrative form that depends on the devices of storytelling (plot, character, setting, and point of view).

feminine rhyme:
Also called *falling rhyme*. A rhyme that falls on unstressed syllables. An example is *singing/ringing*.

figures of speech:
Any of a number of language tools that can add polish to the language of a poem. Some of the figures of speech include *metaphor*, *simile*, *synecdoche*, *metonomy*, *puns*, *onomatopoeia*, and *paradox*.

foot:
A pattern of stressed and unstressed syllables. A foot has either two or three syllables. The eight most used foot patterns in English poetics are the *iamb*, the *trochee*, the *spondee*, the *pyrrhic*, the *anapest*, the *dactyl*, the *amphibrach*, and the *tribrach*.

free verse:

The most common open-form poem. It does not depend on any patterns of rhyme, meter, foot pattern, syllable count, line length, or stanza shape.

ghazal:

A Middle Eastern poem. Originally a closed form, many of its rules have been relaxed. Currently it is a poem of five to twelve couplets.

haiku:

A Japanese form of poetry governed by a strict line and syllable count (three lines, 5-7-5 syllables). Its central image may be governed by a *sentinel word*, an image recalling a season and giving the poem its emotional charge.

lyric poetry:

Poetry that concentrates on an image, an emotion, or an argument. It is usually short, and it can be either closed or open in form.

masculine rhyme:

Also called *rising rhyme*. A rhyme that falls on a stressed syllable. An example is *before/ restore*.

meter:

In closed-form verse, the measure of feet in a line. If a line has three feet, then it is called *trimeter*. The metric measures are *monometer, dimeter, trimeter, tetrameter, pentameter, hexameter, heptameter*, and *octometer*.

monologue:

A poem in which a speaker addresses a listener or speaks within his or her own mind. No one responds to this speaker.

narrative poetry:

Poetry that has a narrative—a narrator and a story. The narrative can be quite long and can come in traditional forms, such as the epic or the ballad.

occasional verse:

A poem written about or for a special occasion, such as a birthday, a wedding, an anniversary, a death, or a historical event.

octave:

An eight-line stanza or the first eight lines of an Italian sonnet.

ode:

Originally an element of Greek drama or a song of praise, the ode later became a meditation. It is also traditionally a closed form, though it no longer follows a strict rhyme or meter.

open form:

Any poetic form that does not follow the restrictions placed upon closed-form verse. The poet may ignore the needs of rhyme, meter, and such and alter the shapes of the lines and stanzas to create a pleasing effect.

pantoum:

A Malayan form that repeats the second and fourth lines of each stanza in a pattern throughout the poem. The pantoum is written in quatrains.

quatrain:

A stanza of four lines.

rhyme:

A pattern of repeated sounds at the ends of words. You can create true rhymes *(rise/prize)*, slant rhymes *(sing/tang)*, or eye rhymes *(love/prove)*. Rhymes are usually placed at the ends of lines, though you may also work with *internal rhymes*. The pattern of rhymes in a poem is called a *rhyme scheme*.

scansion:

The process of analyzing the foot pattern, meter, and rhyme scheme of a poem.

schemes of repetition:

Methods of repeating words that create a pleasing effect. Some of the schemes include *anaphora, epistrophe, epanalepsis, anadiplosis, antimetabole, chiasmus,* and *polyptoton.*

sestet:

A six-line stanza or the last six lines of an Italian sonnet.

sestina:

A poetic form that repeats six words in a set pattern at the ends of the lines. The poem has six stanzas of six lines and a final stanza (the *envoi*) of three lines.

sonnet:

A popular poetic form of fourteen lines, usually written in iambic pentameter. Two traditional forms are the *Italian sonnet* and the *English sonnet.*

speaker:

A persona created by the poet to be the voice through which a reader experiences a poem.

stanza:

A grouping of lines within a poem into a unit, similar to the paragraph in prose.

stressed syllable:

A syllable that is voiced with more emphasis. The second syllable in the word *reTURN* is stressed.

symbol:

An image, object, person, or action that has meaning beyond itself. A white flag, for example, may symbolize surrender.

tercet:

A three-line stanza.

unstressed syllable:

A syllable that is spoken with less emphasis. The first syllable in the word *reTURN* is unstressed.

verse:

Another word for poetry. A spoken or written form composed with the tools and the forms of poetry.

villanelle:

A form that repeats its first and third lines (refrains) throughout the poem. It is composed of five tercets and a quatrain, and it follows a rhyme scheme. The *terzanelle* and the *triolet* are variations of this form.

Appendix C

Acknowledgments and Bibliography

Acknowledgments

Beachley, DeAnna, "Keystone Thrust Fault Trail." Printed with the permission of the author.

Chartkoff, Zachary, "Syn." Printed with the permission of the author.

Figler, Dayvid, "The Infinite Wisdom of the Father." Reprinted with the permission of the author.

French, Jeanie, "Theme" and "Thinning." Both reprinted with the permission of the author.

Kiraly, Andrew, "Superworld High, 1987." Printed with the permission of the author.

Kluge, Christine Boyka, "Dancing on Ice" from *Teaching Bones to Fly*, Bitter Oleander Press, 2003. Reprinted with the permission of the author.

Knorr, Jeff, "What Would My Father Have Done?" "Taking Notes on Storytelling," "Winter Turkeys," "Not an Ordinary Wednesday," and "Keep Your Dog Quiet." All reprinted with the permission of the author.

Lietz, Chad, "Camping, Northern California." Printed with the permission of the author.

Merrin, Jeredith, lecture notes on love poetry. Reprinted with the permission of the author.

Messer, Neide, "Flying Home Late," (from *In Far Corners*, Confluence Press, 1990), "A Fixed Celestial," and "Hold On." All reprinted with the permission of the author.

Millar, Joseph, "Dark Harvest" and "Telephone Repairman" from *Overtime*. Reprinted with the permissions of the publisher, Eastern Washington University Press (Spokane, Washington), and the author.

Moffett, Todd Scott, "*Tarzan* Episode 716: Jane Walks to the Watering Hole" and "The Last Man to Know Adam" reprinted by permission of the author.

Webb, Charles Harper, "Dejection: Not Even an Ode," and "Political Poem" from *Red Rock Review*. Reprinted with the permission of the author.

Bibliography

Addonizio, Kim, and Dorianne Laux. *The Poet's Companion: A Guide to the Pleasures of Writing Poetry*. New York: W. W. Norton & Company, 1997.

Benét, William Rose. *The Reader's Encyclopedia*, 2nd ed. Vol. 1. Cambridge: Thomas Y. Crowell, 1965.

Campbell, Joseph. *The Hero with a Thousand Faces*, 2nd ed. Princeton: Princeton University Press, 1973.

Carryl, Guy Wetmore. *Fables for the Frivolous*. New York: Harper & Brothers, 1899.

Corbett, Edward P. J., and Robert J. Connors. *Style and Statement*. New York: Oxford University Press, 1999.

Drury, John. *Creating Poetry*. Cincinnati: Writer's Digest Books, 1991.

Eliade, Mircea. *The Myth of the Eternal Return: Or, Cosmos and History*. Princeton: Princeton University Press, 1991.

Frye, Northrop. *Anatomy of Criticism: Four Essays*. Princeton: Princeton University Press, 1973.

Fujikawa, Gyo. *A Child's Book of Poems*. New York: Backpack Books, 2002.

Jespersen, Otto. *Essentials of English Grammar*. Tuscaloosa: University of Alabama Press, 1964.

Jung, C. G. *Psyche and Symbol*. Translated by R. F. C. Hull. Edited by Violet S. De Lazlo. Princeton: Princeton University Press, 1991.

Kennedy, X. J., and Dana Gioia, ed. *Literature: An Introduction to Fiction, Poetry, and Drama*, 9th ed. New York: Pearson Longman, 2005.

Kolln, Martha, and Robert Funk. *Understanding English Grammar*, 5th ed. Boston: Allyn and Bacon, 1998.

Noden, Harry R. *Image Grammar: Using Grammatical Structures to Teach Writing*. Portsmouth: Boynton/Cook Publishers, 1999.

Index

THE EVERYTHING SERIES!

BUSINESS & PERSONAL FINANCE

Everything® Budgeting Book
Everything® Business Planning Book
Everything® Coaching and Mentoring Book
Everything® Fundraising Book
Everything® Get Out of Debt Book
Everything® Grant Writing Book
Everything® Homebuying Book, 2nd Ed.
Everything® Homeselling Book
Everything® Home-Based Business Book
Everything® Investing Book
Everything® Landlording Book
Everything® Leadership Book
Everything® Managing People Book
Everything® Negotiating Book
Everything® Online Business Book
Everything® Personal Finance Book
Everything® Personal Finance in Your 20s
     and 30s Book
Everything® Project Management Book
Everything® Real Estate Investing Book
Everything® Robert's Rules Book, $7.95
Everything® Selling Book
Everything® Start Your Own Business Book
Everything® Wills & Estate Planning Book

COOKING

Everything® Barbecue Cookbook
Everything® Bartender's Book, $9.95
Everything® Chinese Cookbook
Everything® College Cookbook
Everything® Cookbook
Everything® Diabetes Cookbook
Everything® Easy Gourmet Cookbook
Everything® Fondue Cookbook
Everything® Grilling Cookbook
Everything® Healthy Meals in Minutes
     Cookbook
Everything® Holiday Cookbook

Everything® Indian Cookbook
Everything® Low-Carb Cookbook
Everything® Low-Fat High-Flavor Cookbook
Everything® Low-Salt Cookbook
Everything® Meals for a Month Cookbook
Everything® Mediterranean Cookbook
Everything® Mexican Cookbook
Everything® One-Pot Cookbook
Everything® Pasta Cookbook
Everything® Quick Meals Cookbook
Everything® Slow Cooker Cookbook
Everything® Soup Cookbook
Everything® Thai Cookbook
Everything® Vegetarian Cookbook
Everything® Wine Book

HEALTH

Everything® Alzheimer's Book
Everything® Diabetes Book
Everything® Hypnosis Book
Everything® Low Cholesterol Book
Everything® Massage Book
Everything® Menopause Book
Everything® Nutrition Book
Everything® Reflexology Book
Everything® Stress Management Book

HISTORY

Everything® American Government Book
Everything® American History Book
Everything® Civil War Book
Everything® Irish History & Heritage Book
Everything® Middle East Book

HOBBIES & GAMES

Everything® Blackjack Strategy Book
Everything® Brain Strain Book, $9.95
Everything® Bridge Book
Everything® Candlemaking Book

Everything® Card Games Book
Everything® Cartooning Book
Everything® Casino Gambling Book, 2nd Ed.
Everything® Chess Basics Book
Everything® Crossword and Puzzle Book
Everything® Crossword Challenge Book
Everything® Cryptograms Book, $9.95
Everything® Digital Photography Book
Everything® Drawing Book
Everything® Easy Crosswords Book
Everything® Family Tree Book
Everything® Games Book, 2nd Ed.
Everything® Knitting Book
Everything® Knots Book
Everything® Motorcycle Book
Everything® Online Genealogy Book
Everything® Photography Book
Everything® Poker Strategy Book
Everything® Pool & Billiards Book
Everything® Quilting Book
Everything® Scrapbooking Book
Everything® Sewing Book
Everything® Woodworking Book
Everything® Word Games Challenge Book

HOME IMPROVEMENT

Everything® Feng Shui Book
Everything® Feng Shui Decluttering Book,
     $9.95
Everything® Fix-It Book
Everything® Homebuilding Book
Everything® Lawn Care Book
Everything® Organize Your Home Book

EVERYTHING® KIDS' BOOKS

All titles are $6.95
Everything® Kids' Animal Puzzle & Activity
     Book
Everything® Kids' Baseball Book, 3rd Ed.

All Everything® books are priced at $12.95 or $14.95, unless otherwise stated. Prices subject to change without notice.

Everything® Kids' Bible Trivia Book
Everything® Kids' Bugs Book
Everything® Kids' Christmas Puzzle
    & Activity Book
Everything® Kids' Cookbook
Everything® Kids' Halloween Puzzle
    & Activity Book
Everything® Kids' Hidden Pictures Book
Everything® Kids' Joke Book
Everything® Kids' Knock Knock Book
Everything® Kids' Math Puzzles Book
Everything® Kids' Mazes Book
Everything® Kids' Money Book
Everything® Kids' Monsters Book
Everything® Kids' Nature Book
Everything® Kids' Puzzle Book
Everything® Kids' Riddles & Brain Teasers Book
Everything® Kids' Science Experiments Book
Everything® Kids' Sharks Book
Everything® Kids' Soccer Book
Everything® Kids' Travel Activity Book

KIDS' STORY BOOKS

Everything® Bedtime Story Book
Everything® Fairy Tales Book

LANGUAGE

Everything® Conversational Japanese Book
    (with CD), $19.95
Everything® French Phrase Book, $9.95
Everything® French Verb Book, $9.95
Everything® Inglés Book
Everything® Learning French Book
Everything® Learning German Book
Everything® Learning Italian Book
Everything® Learning Latin Book
Everything® Learning Spanish Book
Everything® Sign Language Book
Everything® Spanish Grammar Book
Everything® Spanish Phrase Book, $9.95
Everything® Spanish Verb Book, $9.95

MUSIC

Everything® Drums Book (with CD), $19.95
Everything® Guitar Book
Everything® Home Recording Book
Everything® Playing Piano and Keyboards
    Book

Everything® Reading Music Book (with CD),
    $19.95
Everything® Rock & Blues Guitar Book
    (with CD), $19.95
Everything® Songwriting Book

NEW AGE

Everything® Astrology Book
Everything® Dreams Book, 2nd Ed.
Everything® Ghost Book
Everything® Love Signs Book, $9.95
Everything® Numerology Book
Everything® Paganism Book
Everything® Palmistry Book
Everything® Psychic Book
Everything® Reiki Book
Everything® Spells & Charms Book
Everything® Tarot Book
Everything® Wicca and Witchcraft Book

PARENTING

Everything® Baby Names Book
Everything® Baby Shower Book
Everything® Baby's First Food Book
Everything® Baby's First Year Book
Everything® Birthing Book
Everything® Breastfeeding Book
Everything® Father-to-Be Book
Everything® Father's First Year Book
Everything® Get Ready for Baby Book
Everything® Getting Pregnant Book
Everything® Homeschooling Book
Everything® Parent's Guide to Children
    with ADD/ADHD
Everything® Parent's Guide to Children
    with Asperger's Syndrome
Everything® Parent's Guide to Children
    with Autism
Everything® Parent's Guide to Children
    with Dyslexia
Everything® Parent's Guide to Positive
    Discipline
Everything® Parent's Guide to Raising a
    Successful Child
Everything® Parent's Guide to Tantrums
Everything® Parent's Guide to the Overweight
    Child
Everything® Parenting a Teenager Book
Everything® Potty Training Book, $9.95

Everything® Pregnancy Book, 2nd Ed.
Everything® Pregnancy Fitness Book
Everything® Pregnancy Nutrition Book
Everything® Pregnancy Organizer, $15.00
Everything® Toddler Book
Everything® Tween Book
Everything® Twins, Triplets, and More Book

PETS

Everything® Cat Book
Everything® Dachshund Book, $12.95
Everything® Dog Book
Everything® Dog Health Book
Everything® Dog Training and Tricks Book
Everything® Golden Retriever Book, $12.95
Everything® Horse Book
Everything® Labrador Retriever Book, $12.95
Everything® Poodle Book, $12.95
Everything® Pug Book, $12.95
Everything® Puppy Book
Everything® Rottweiler Book, $12.95
Everything® Tropical Fish Book

REFERENCE

Everything® Car Care Book
Everything® Classical Mythology Book
Everything® Computer Book
Everything® Divorce Book
Everything® Einstein Book
Everything® Etiquette Book
Everything® Mafia Book
Everything® Philosophy Book
Everything® Psychology Book
Everything® Shakespeare Book

RELIGION

Everything® Angels Book
Everything® Bible Book
Everything® Buddhism Book
Everything® Catholicism Book
Everything® Christianity Book
Everything® Jewish History & Heritage Book
Everything® Judaism Book
Everything® Koran Book
Everything® Prayer Book
Everything® Saints Book
Everything® Torah Book
Everything® Understanding Islam Book

All Everything® books are priced at $12.95 or $14.95, unless otherwise stated. Prices subject to change without notice.

Everything® World's Religions Book
Everything® Zen Book

SCHOOL & CAREERS

Everything® Alternative Careers Book
Everything® College Survival Book, 2nd Ed.
Everything® Cover Letter Book, 2nd Ed.
Everything® Get-a-Job Book
Everything® Job Interview Book
Everything® New Teacher Book
Everything® Online Job Search Book
Everything® Paying for College Book
Everything® Practice Interview Book
Everything® Resume Book, 2nd Ed.
Everything® Study Book

SELF-HELP

Everything® Great Sex Book
Everything® Kama Sutra Book
Everything® Self-Esteem Book

SPORTS & FITNESS

Everything® Fishing Book
Everything® Fly-Fishing Book
Everything® Golf Instruction Book

Everything® Pilates Book
Everything® Running Book
Everything® Total Fitness Book
Everything® Weight Training Book
Everything® Yoga Book

TRAVEL

Everything® Family Guide to Hawaii
Everything® Family Guide to New York City, 2nd Ed.
Everything® Family Guide to RV Travel & Campgrounds
Everything® Family Guide to the Walt Disney World Resort®, Universal Studios®, and Greater Orlando, 4th Ed.
Everything® Family Guide to Washington D.C., 2nd Ed.
Everything® Guide to Las Vegas
Everything® Guide to New England
Everything® Travel Guide to the Disneyland Resort®, California Adventure®, Universal Studios®, and the Anaheim Area

WEDDINGS

Everything® Bachelorette Party Book, $9.95
Everything® Bridesmaid Book, $9.95

Everything® Elopement Book, $9.95
Everything® Father of the Bride Book, $9.95
Everything® Groom Book, $9.95
Everything® Mother of the Bride Book, $9.95
Everything® Wedding Book, 3rd Ed.
Everything® Wedding Checklist, $9.95
Everything® Wedding Etiquette Book, $7.95
Everything® Wedding Organizer, $15.00
Everything® Wedding Shower Book, $7.95
Everything® Wedding Vows Book, $7.95
Everything® Weddings on a Budget Book, $9.95

WRITING

Everything® Creative Writing Book
Everything® Get Published Book
Everything® Grammar and Style Book
Everything® Guide to Writing a Book Proposal
Everything® Guide to Writing a Novel
Everything® Guide to Writing Children's Books
Everything® Screenwriting Book
Everything® Writing Poetry Book
Everything® Writing Well Book

. . . .

We have Everything® for the beginner crafter!
All titles are $14.95

Everything® Crafts—Baby Scrapbooking
1-59337-225-6

Everything® Crafts—Bead Your Own Jewelry
1-59337-142-X

Everything® Crafts—Create Your Own Greeting Cards
1-59337-226-4

Everything® Crafts—Easy Projects
1-59337-298-1

Everything® Crafts—Polymer Clay for Beginners
1-59337-230-2

Everything® Crafts—Rubber Stamping Made Easy
1-59337-229-9

Everything® Crafts—Wedding Decorations and Keepsakes
1-59337-227-2

Available wherever books are sold!
To order, call 800-872-5627, or visit us at *www.everything.com*
Everything® and everything.com® are registered trademarks of F+W Publications, Inc.